Perspectives on West Asia

The Evolving Geopolitical Discourses

Editors

Priya Singh
Susmita Bhattacharya

Maulana Abul Kalam Azad Institute of Asian Studies, Kolkata

SHIPRA

ISBN: 978-81-7541-637-6

First Published in India in 2012

Perspectives on West Asia: The Evolving Geopolitical Discourses

Published by:
SHIPRA PUBLICATIONS
H.O.: LG 18-19, Pankaj Central Market, Patparganj,
I.P. Ext., Delhi-110092, Tel: 91-11-2223 5152, 2223 6152
Br.Off.: 4617/18, Ansari Road, Darya Ganj,
New Delhi-110002, Tel: 6594 6453, 9810522367
E-mail: info@shiprapublications.com
www.shiprapublications.com

Contents

India and West Asia

Preface

West Asia (Southwest Asia) is an expression that refers to the western most part of Asia. The term is partly coterminous with the *Middle East*, which describes the geographical position in relation to Western Europe rather than the location within Asia. Due to the perceived Euro centrism, international organizations such as the United Nations, have replaced *Middle East* with *West Asia*. In the Western academia, the term *Middle East*, which replaced the term *Near East* continues to be the favoured expression, although it reflects spatial perspectives firmly anchored in a Eurocentric world.

West Asia broadly refers to those countries that are members of the League of Arab States, Israel (with its Jewish and Arab population), and the non-Arab countries of Turkey and Iran (which have small Arab populations). These countries are clustered into three sub regions:

1. North Africa, which includes the countries of Algeria, Egypt, Libya, Morocco and Tunisia.
2. The area along the eastern part of the Mediterranean is the Fertile Crescent (Levant of the colonial times) that includes Syria, Lebanon, Jordan, Israel, the West Bank and Gaza Strip, as well as non-Arab Turkey to the north.
3. The oil-producing countries of the Gulf and Arabian Peninsula, namely, Iraq, Saudi Arabia, Bahrain, Kuwait, Qatar, the United Arab Emirates, Oman, Yemen and the non-Arab, Persian state of Iran. The UN also includes Armenia and Azerbaijan (parts of Caucasus) in its extensive

categorization of West Asia. Afghanistan is also sometimes incorporated into a broad definition of "Western Asia."

The debates questioning the logic behind the clustering of countries, which are as varied historically and culturally, as Iran, Turkey, Israel, Somalia, Yemen and Tunisia under a single category (Middle East/West Asia) arose from time to time. Yet, the grouping (West Asia/Middle East) does have an underlying principle, as the category of nations do share historical experiences in the spread of Islam, the reach of the Ottoman Empire and the experiences of European colonialism. The point, here, is not to settle on a better or more accurate category but, as Schwedler and Gerner[1] have pointed out, to recognize the myriad ways in which the region coheres as a whole around some issues, less so around others.

Contemporary West Asia is typically portrayed as a region of intrigue and war, the cradle of terrorism and religious extremism. The impression conveyed is that the region is unique. However, authors like Cammock, Pool and Tordoff[2] and Bromley[3] reiterate that there are no myths to explode, that West Asia is just like any other developing region. From their perspective, this region, like any other region, suffers from the effects of modernization, lack of political participation, slow economic growth and foreign indebtedness to the West, competition for arms and increasing urbanization.

In recent times the growing interest in the region has been accompanied by an increasing number of academic journals, texts and books devoted to the study of the area. From the mid 1990s, a vast array of subject areas covering West Asia, from political discussion groups, government and official websites, research centers, libraries and cultural developments could be accessed through the World Wide Web (www.)

The two major centres of West Asian (Middle Eastern) studies globally are the United Kingdom and the United States of America. The current debates over West Asia (Middle East) involve questions of national interest and security for the United Sates and the United Kingdom, particularly since the events of September 11, 2001 and July 7, 2005. As a result, arguments for further development of West Asian (Middle Eastern) studies with a strong academic base are linked with questions of national security and international stability.

In Asia, among others, India and Singapore now have specialized academic centres on West Asian and Middle East studies, besides such academic programmes in the countries of the region itself. Such programmes seek to cultivate interest in these areas as also reflect on the common problem zones afflicting the different parts of Asia, especially issues of conflict resolution and peace processes.

In continuance with the growing interest in the region, an International Seminar on West Asia was convened on 17-18 January 2011, in Kolkata. The aim of the seminar, which was pertinently dealt with in the inaugural session was to contend with three crucial issues: (i) how West Asia is currently constructed?, (ii) the "securitization" of West Asia where it is intermittently viewed in terms of security roles and problems, and (iii) alternative perceptions of West Asia.

This volume encompasses an array of perspectives on West Asia offered by the participants of the seminar. The idea behind this endeavour is to raise a few relevant issues and address a few significant questions with regard to the region with the aim of supplementing this effort in future compilations.

Mustapha Kamel Al Sayyid traces the phases of the Arab-Israeli conflict, outlines the major issues of the dispute, identifies the causes of the failure of the attempts to resolve it and explains its links with other major conflicts in the region. Ghanem As'ad analyzes the alternative options to the current discourse on the Israeli-Palestinian conflict, and investigates the old/new idea of one state/bi-national solution as an instrument to initiate new dynamics and fresh thinking to the existing impasse. Mohanad Mustapha's essay is in the nature of a critical assessment of the process of empowering of the *extreme right* in Israel, with particular emphasis on the rise of the *Yisrael Beiteinu* party.

Gulshan Dietl articulates the evolution and significance of *Area Studies* in the context of West Asia, calling it 'an imperative of our time.' Michael Hudson focuses on the debates contending with the labelling and conceptualization of the region with particular emphasis on the American perspective in terms of the definition of the region, its framing and conception, and the consequent American involvement in the economics and politics of region. Itzchak Weismann's essay contends that with the advent of modernity, South

Asia, in significant ways, came to fulfil the place of the Middle East as the most influential religious centre in the 'expanding and ramifying networking' of the Muslim World. Sima Baidya's essay analyzes the complex process of the formation of resistance politics/ movements in the region and delves into the nature, direction and course of actions of these movements in the GCC states. Kingshuk Chatterjee's essay interrogates the prevailing discourse on Tehran as a factor of instability in the politics of West Asia, and advances instead a contention that there are elements in Tehran's policy that could actually serve to stabilise the region.

Sujata Ashwarya Cheema interprets the multiple layers in the complicated issue of the emerging 'US factor' in India-Iran relations. Navras Jaat Aafreedi voices concern over the apathetic nature of India's policy towards Israel and the Jews, which, in his opinion is the outcome of domestic compulsions. Dr. A.K. Pasha's essay delves deep into the historical, maritime, commercial and cultural links between India and West Asia and also examines the nature and significance of these connections in modern times.

The collection of essays thus, explores a plethora of themes encompassing the perceptions of the region (West Asia) in geopolitical, cultural as well as economic terms and offers insights into the complex web of relationships of influence and control/ interstices and continuities that characterize the region. Keeping in mind the central role played by the United States in the region, the compilation also focuses on an inquiry into the post World War II American initiatives and policies – economic, political, diplomatic and military in/towards the region, as well as the attitude of the region towards the United States. In addition, it investigates the aspect of intra-regional politics/the issue of intra-regionalism along with an inquiry into the politics of resistance, which in turn, implies dissecting the political realities of the region. Moreover, at the level of formulation itself, one of the two core issues for deliberation was to be the question of the centrality of the Israel-Palestine conflict in the regional context, the other being an exploration of India's historical links with the region, her interests in the region, the contours and dilemmas of her policy towards West Asia and the changing perspectives in an era of globalization. Both these issues have in fact been accorded primacy in this collection.

Notes

1. Jillian Schwedler and Deborah Gerner, *Understanding the Contemporary Middle East* (Boulder: Lynne Rienner, 2008).
2. Paul Cammock, David Pool and William Tordoff, *Third World Politics: A Comparative Introduction* (Basingstoke: Macmillan Publishers, 1993).
3. Simon Bromley, *Rethinking Middle East Politics* (Austin: University of Texas Press, 1994).

ISRAEL-PALESTINE

1

The Transformation of the Arab-Israeli Conflict

Mustapha Kamel Al Sayyid

Few decades ago, some commentators on the Arab-Israeli conflict argued that its centrality in Middle East politics had become a thing of the past. They pointed to the Iraq-Iran war which was in their view costing much more lives than all the Arab Israeli wars. It divided the region between countries that supported Iraq and others like Syria who sided with Iran. The Iraqi invasion of Kuwait in1990-1991 led to large scale suffering by people in Iraq, Kuwait and forced hundreds of thousands of Arab and foreign workers to escape war in the two countries and to sacrifice their savings and properties to rescue their own lives. On the other hand, almost all was quiet on the Israeli borders as peace treaties were signed between Israel, on the one hand and Egypt, Palestine Liberation Organization and Jordan, on the other. Apart from some clashes with Israeli soldiers in Southern Lebanon, Israel enjoyed quiet along all its borders including those with Syria. Besides Lebanon was the scene of a civil war from 1975-1991, and the Palestinian people were mounting peaceful resistance to Israeli occupation of the West Bank and Gaza. Thus, it was easy to see that the Middle East was home to many unrelated conflicts, and that the Arab-Israeli conflict was only one of these conflicts but not necessarily the bloodiest nor was it related to other conflicts in the region. Abraham Sela, an Israeli professor at the Hebrew University in Jerusalem could thus claim that the Arab-Israeli conflict was on the decline.[1] Other Israeli scholars and politicians would add that it is impossible to resolve this conflict.[2]

While the first argument does not seem credible at present, the second argument about the intractability of the conflict is often articulated by supporters of the Likud-led government in Israel as well as some other commentators. They hold that the conflict could not be resolved because the most widely held scheme for its resolution, namely the two state solution, is impossible to realize. Israel has already confiscated large areas of the Occupied Territories used as settlements and ring roads linking settlements, with no contiguous territory left to the Palestinian people to build their own state. The settlers have become a formidable electoral force in Israel, with their party becoming the third largest party in the country. If the establishment of a Palestinian state means abandoning the settlements, this would amount to a political suicide to any Israeli government endorsing it. The only reasonable prospect left to the Palestinians is to accept remaining under the authority of a Jewish state. They should not aspire to an independent statehood. The best that Israel could offer them is the so-called "economic peace". They could presumably go about indulging in economic activities, may be prosper, but should not even dream of becoming full citizens in any state, unless they migrate and seek citizenship in any other country, preferably Jordan, as the alternative Palestinian state.[3]

This paper argues that neither argument is valid. The Arab-Israeli conflict has been transformed over the years. It is no longer exclusively an Arab-Israeli conflict. The rise of the Islamist movement has made it a Middle Eastern conflict bringing to the Arab side non-Arab countries in the Middle East and drawing the sympathy of Muslims all over the world. Moreover, the two states solution remains the only realistic proposal not only for resolving the Palestinian problem but also of laying the foundations for a real comprehensive peace in the region.

From an Arab-Israeli to an Intra-regional Conflict

The Arab-Israeli conflict has gone through several phases. Respective positions of the parties have shifted over the years, the scope of the conflict has widened and the military capabilities of its parties have escalated. While demands of the Arab side have tended to moderate over the years, positions of domestic and regional actors have hardened. With Arab countries possessing only conventional weapons at the start of the conflict in 1948, nuclear proliferation in the region has become a real possibility with other weapons of mass destruction abundantly at the disposal of several countries of the region, Arab and non-Arabs alike. The conflict went through three important phases. The first phase covered the period between the first and the third Arab-Israeli wars, from 1948-1967. The second was initiated by Arab defeat in the June 1967 war and ended with two events of contradictory implications for the conflict. The two took place in the same year, 1979 with only one month separating them. The first was the conclusion of an Arab-Israeli peace treaty in Washington and the second was the victory of an Islamist revolution in Iran. The victory of the 'Islamist revolution in Iran was only one of many manifestations of the mounting influence of an Islamist movement that swept almost all countries of the region with far reaching consequences for political stability of governments that opted for peace with Israel and for the regional balance of power.'[4]

The First Phase: From the First to the Third Arab-Israeli War

The Arabs felt that the establishment of a Jewish state in Palestine at the expense of the original Palestinian people was an act of injustice. Jews were persecuted in Europe and not in the Middle East. Moreover the call for a land without people for a people without land, as the Zionist slogan went, was not applicable to Palestine. It was inhabited for well over a millennium and half by Palestinians with little remaining of the Jews who had lived in it, as well as in other parts of the Middle East thousands of years ago. Arab countries that were independent in 1948 rejected the UN Partition resolution and five of them sent troops to resist the establishment of a Jewish state in May 1948. The entry of Arab troops in Palestine was preceded by the presence of volunteers of Arab countries as irregular forces fighting side by side with the Palestinians. The outcome of the first Arab-Israeli war in 1948-1949 is well-known. Jewish troops, composed of soldiers of

European descent triumphed over scattered and ill-equipped military forces of several Arab countries. The war situation and the deliberate attempts by Jewish military organizations to evict Arab inhabitants of Palestine from their own homes led to the influx of large numbers of Palestinian refugees in neighbouring Arab countries, namely Jordan, Syria, Lebanon and Egypt.[5]

During this phase, Arab countries refused to recognize the consequences of that war. Their position on the question of Palestine was guided by three slogans, formulated later in 1967 in an Arab summit in the Sudanese capital Khartoum: no recognition, no negotiations and no peace with Israel. The governments and the masses continued to dream of the day when the whole of Palestine would be completely liberated. The West Bank of the river Jordan was annexed to Jordan and Gaza Strip fell under Egyptian administration. These territories were presumably kept under the authority of the two states pending the time when the rest of Palestine would be restored to its original inhabitants. Then the whole of Palestine would be reunited again under an Arab government. Governments which called for less than this maximalist goal were treated as betraying the Arab cause. That charge was levelled against Al-Habib Bourguiba, the Tunisian head of State, when he suggested in 1965 that Arab governments should accept the UN Partition Resolution No. 181 of 1947 that divided Palestine into three parts: Jewish and Arab with an international status for Jerusalem.

That vision was not shared by the Non-Arab Muslim governments of the Middle East. Both Iran and Turkey who were members of a military alliance supported by the US and UK known as the Baghdad Pact maintained close relations with Israel. Each exchanged ambassadors with the Jewish state and intensified military and intelligence cooperation with it.[6]

The Second Phase: From the 1967 Defeat to the Conclusion of the First Arab-Israeli Peace Treaty

This aspiration to liberate the whole of Palestine was shattered by the defeat of three Arab armies by Israel in June 1967. There are two narratives of this war. According to the Arab narrative, Israel was preparing to initiate war on Syria in retaliation for the raids carried out by Palestinian commandos launched from Syrian territory. Tension was mounting further between the two countries since April 1967, when Israeli air force battled Syrian planes over Damascus shooting down some of these planes. Egypt was committed to Syria's defence by virtue of a mutual defence agreement signed between the two countries a year earlier. Yielding to popular pressures, King Hussein of Jordan decided to join Syria and Egypt in late May 1967. The Israeli narrative described the June 1967 war as a pre-emptive attack by Israel against Arab armies who were about to launch military operations against it.[7]

Given the Israeli pattern of massive retaliation in response to any Arab military action, well-established in preceding years, it is difficult to escape the conclusion that Israel took advantage of Arab war rhetoric to strike decisive blows against the armies of its two arch-enemies in the region, namely the radical regimes of Egypt and Syria. The war ended with Israel occupying the whole of Palestine as the West Bank of the River Jordan including Jerusalem fell into Israeli hands. Both Golan Heights and Sinai Peninsula were occupied by Israeli troops.

Although the three famous "No's" were launched in the Khartoum Arab Summit in October 1967, the aftermath of the war saw gradual abandonment by Arab countries of each of these three No's. The beginning of this gradual erosion of Arab hard-line positions was signalled two months after the Khartoum Summit. The goal of the liberation of the whole of Palestine gave way to the more modest goal of "liquidating the consequences of Israeli aggression" which meant restoring territories occupied by Israel in June 1967. That was signalled by the acceptance of both Egypt and Jordan of the UN Security Council Resolution 242, which called simply for the evacuation by Israel of "The territories occupied in the war" or in the French version "Des territoires occupes pendant la guerre". The two countries were to engage in negotiations with Israel, first indirectly through UN envoys, and later on directly in Camp David and Washington for Egypt. It became known later that King Hussein of Jordan had direct meetings with Israeli top government officials in both Jordan and Israel, prior to the signing by the two countries of a peace agreement in Wadi Al-Araba in 1994. It was reported that the King had met the Israelis seventeen times over the years before the signing of this agreement.[8] On the other hand, the two non-Arab Muslim countries of the Middle East maintained their privileged relations with Israel, particularly in military and intelligence fields. The two shared with Israel hostility to radical regimes in the Arab world and close relations with the United States.[9]

The Third Phase: 1979-Peace with Israel and the Rise of Islamist Movements

This third phase of the Arab-Israeli conflict started with two contradictory developments. On the one hand, Egypt, the largest Arab country concluded a separate peace agreement with Israel in March1979, a radical shift in Arab positions followed later by both the Palestine Liberation Organization in 1993 and Jordan in 1994. Some other Arab countries echoed this development by exchanging consular and commercial offices with Israel. Meetings took place also between Israeli officials and those of Arab countries. Even Lebanon had signed a short-lived peace treaty with Israel in May 1983, which was scrapped following the assasination of Bashir Al-Jumail, the Lebanese President who had signed it. On the other hand, the Islamist movement came to the fore as a potent challenge to all Muslim Middle East governments, particularly those that had established close relations with Israel. An Islamic-led revolution took place in Iran in 1979, overthrowing the Shah, who was definitely Israel's best friend from the region. President Anwar El-Sadat, the first head of an Arab state to sign a peace treaty with Israel was assassinated by Islamist commandoes on October 6 1981. Other leaders who joined Sadat in signing peace treaties with Israel found their authority challenged by the Islamist movement. The Islamist movement made large strides in Jordan winning almost 40 per cent of parliamentary seats in 1991. HAMAS or the Islamic Resistance Movement mounted a serious challenge to the influence of FATAH in both Gaza and the West Bank until it won legislative elections in 2006. Following a brief period of a coalition government the two movements clashed with each other in July 2007 splitting Palestinian territories under two administrations, with Gaza remaining under the authority of HAMAS while the West Bank fell under a FATAH government. In other Middle East countries, the Islamist movement expanded its following, becoming the major force of the opposition and in some countries took part in or even exclusively formed the government. The Shi'ite Hizb'allah mounted its influence in Lebanon following the end of the Lebanese civil war in 1991 and since 2005 became the pace setter in Lebanese politics. Parties of Islamic background formed the government in Turkey, in the beginning as coalition partners in 1998 and won sufficient majority since 2003 to become the sole party in the government.

These two developments have changed the regional scene of the Arab-Israeli conflict in four important respects, the character of the conflict, its parties, its intensity, as well as the terms for its resolution.

The rise of the Islamist movement in all countries of the Middle East and beyond a dimension has amplified one aspect of the conflict, namely the religious one. This dimension had been earlier overshadowed by the presence of nationalist regimes in a good number of Arab countries, particularly the two front line states of Egypt and Syria. This dimension was also paralleled in Israel herself as religious parties such as Shas started to attract large numbers of voters and soon rivalled the secular Labour Party that had dominated Israeli cabinets since the establishment of Israel until 1977.

This development has changed also the pattern of alliances in the Middle East. The two non-Arab Muslim countries of the region which had recognized Israel as early as 1949 and 1950 came at different moments to distance themselves from the Jewish state. One of them, i.e. Iran, moved from close cooperation with Israeli intelligence services to become the arch enemy of Israel in the region. Following its Islamists-led revolution in 1979, the Islamic Republic of Iran not only broke diplomatic relations with Israel, but declared its total support for the Palestinian struggle, offered diplomatic, economic and military assistance to Palestinian organizations, particularly the Islamic Resistance Movement, and proclaimed its rejection of any kind of peaceful settlement that does not put an end to the existence of Israel herself.[10]

The secularist principles of Kemalist Turkey did not shield the second Non-Arab Muslim country in the Middle East from Islamic resurgence. An increasing section of Turkish public opinion became disappointed with the performance of Turkish secularist parties and was attracted by Islamist parties who had offered a model of honest and efficient administration at the local level. Thus the Refah Party was the principal partner in a short-lived coalition government in 1996-1997 with the Right Path Party of Tansu Schiller. That government was forced down by the military but a new scion of the Refah Party won elections in 2003 with a comfortable majority. In power, the Justice and Development Party declared its support for the Palestinian cause and initiated a new phase in Turkish foreign policy, bringing Turkey closer to the Arab and Muslim world. Although it did not break diplomatic relations with Israel, unfavourably perceived by a large section of Turkish public opinion, it did not spare an opportunity to criticize Israel's administration of Palestinian territories, and particularly its siege of Gaza. It demanded openly an apology from Israel for its commando's assault on a Turkish ship that was carrying humanitarian assistance to besieged Gaza in 2010.[11]

A major feature of this new pattern of alliances in the Middle East is that it set a number of Arab countries against others. One group was made up of those who were usually favourable to a negotiated settlement of the Arab-Israeli dispute orchestrated by Washington and based on the principle of exchange of territory for peace. The other group included Arab and Middle Eastern countries as well as non-state actors opposed to this type of a negotiated settlement. This counter alliance was made up of Syria, Iran, HAMAS and Hizb'allah of Lebanon.

The conflict became more alarming for the region's security for two other reasons. One reason being the military capability of the regional actors. It was widely believed that Israel possessed a superior military capacity due to its monopoly of nuclear weapons in the region. Several reports suggested that Israel had an arsenal of no less than two hundred nuclear weapons besides long range aircrafts and ballistic missiles.[12] The government of the Islamic Republic of Iran re-activated the nuclear programme initiated by the Shah and became capable of enriching uranium to high levels, suspected by major Western powers and Israel to eventually enable her to develop nuclear weapons. Israel, determined to remain the only nuclear power in the region, had destroyed in July 1981 Iraq's nuclear reactor before it was completely built. Together with the five permanent members of the UN Security Council besides Germany, it strove to dissuade Iran from continuing with its nuclear programme, declared by Iranian authorities to be conducted only for peaceful purposes. Till the time of the writing of these lines, it has failed to do so, but several reports suggest that neither Israel nor the US is willing to allow Iran to continue this programme and exclude no option in their attempt to realize this objective. The impressive conventional weapons capability of Iran, which could be used in retaliating against any assault by the US or Israel is definitely one of the reasons that compel the two countries to weigh their options carefully before they proceed to any military action.[13]

Other countries in the region have contemplated developing peaceful nuclear capacity. This is the case with Egypt which has already two nuclear reactors and has adopted a programme of establishing a number of nuclear power stations. Saudi Arabia is considering a similar option. Israel has raided a site in Syria claimed by Israeli authorities to have been a secret building site of a nuclear reactor. Syria and Iran are known also to possess considerable amounts of weapons of mass destruction but probably no match to Israeli military capacity.[14]

Finally, these shifts in patterns of alliances in the Middle East affected proposed terms of settlement as well as modalities of this settlement. Arab countries in general stood for the principle of exchange of territory for peace as exemplified by the Egyptian-Israeli peace treaty signed in Washington on March 27, 1979. Thanks to this treaty, Egypt regained the totality of its territory occupied by Israel in June 1967. In return, Egyptian government accepted full diplomatic, economic and cultural normalization of relations with Israel. It established full diplomatic relations with Israel, engaged in trade with its former enemy and allowed Israeli tourists to come to Egypt and toned down hostile language in media reporting on Israel. This normalization was greeted enthusiastically by Egyptian public opinion immediately after the signing of the peace treaty. Public opinion in the country was disappointed later because fruits of peace or the so-called "peace dividend" did not materialize and the hoped for comprehensive peace proved to be rather illusory. Normalization of relations between Israel and Egypt amounted to no more than "cold peace" according to Dr. Boutros Boutros Ghali, former Minister of State for Foreign Affairs in Egypt before his election as Secretary General of the United Nations in 1991. However, the Egyptian-Israeli peace treaty served as a model which other Arab governments and peoples of the so-called frontline states aspired to. The Oslo Agreement between the Palestine Liberation Organization and Israel signed in 1993 was based on this model. It also inspired the conclusion of a peace treaty with Jordan in 1994 although no exchange of territory resulted from this agreement. The Syrian government claimed that the Israeli government led by Itzak Rabin pledged to accept this principle in a confidential deal witnessed by Bill Clinton, the US President at the time. More generally Arab peace plans proposed first by Prince Abdallah in 1982 while he was the Crown Prince of Saudi Arabia and later on in an Arab Summit in Beirut in 2002 did not deviate from this principle. Briefly stated, the Arab position evolved over the years to accept total peace for total Israeli withdrawal from all occupied Arab territories.[15]

The rhetoric that came from Islamists, particularly HAMAS, Iran and most Islamist movements in the Arab world was different. For them, the conflict with Israel was not about territory, but it was about the existence of Israel herself, seen as an act of extreme injustice done to the Arab people of Palestine. They would accept no negotiations with Israel, no recognition of its government and no peace with its people. While most Arab governments favoured a negotiated settlement sponsored by the US, the Iranian-Syrian camp supported by Hamas and Hizb'allah called for armed struggle against Israel as the only way to regain all occupied territories including the whole of historical Palestine.[16]

There are many indications that for some of these parties at least, rhetoric was one thing, real politics was another. Having come to the government in 'Occupied Palestinian Territories' and later only in Gaza, HAMAS softened its position. According to its chief Khaled Mesh'al, if Israel accepts the two states solution, HAMAS could commit herself to a long term truce extending perhaps to one hundred years.[17] The Syrian government accepted also indirect negotiations with Israel, mediated by the Turkish government in 2009. There could have been no other conceivable basis for these negotiations except the principle of exchange of territory for peace.[18]

This period also witnessed two military setbacks for Israel. It had to withdraw its troops from Southern Lebanon in 2000 as a result of the high number of casualties caused by the Lebanese resistance led by Hizb'allah. It also experienced the bitter taste of no decisive victory following a devastating six weeks war with the same Lebanese resistance group in the summer of 2006. Hizb'allah's successful confrontations with Israel inspired the belief among many Arabs and Muslims that after all, the Israeli armed forces are not invincible.[19]

In all these ways the Arab-Israeli conflict has been transformed. It has evolved from an Arab-Israeli conflict to an overall intra-regional one with all countries of the region, Arab and non-Arab, taking a stand on it. It has also implications that go beyond the boundaries of the Middle East to affect far away places ranging from New York and Washington, Madrid and London, to Nairobi, Dar es Salam, and cities in Pakistan and Indonesia all targeted by militant groups declaring their sympathy with the Palestinian cause. These groups were just one manifestation of a broader movement that swept almost all Muslim countries driven by the double hostility to incumbent regimes as well as Western governments who continued to support Israel. The Arab-Israeli conflict cast its shadow also on other conflicts in the region, with Israel providing support to opposition and separatist movements that took up arms against governments that backed the Palestinian cause. It is well-known that Israel offered military assistance to the Maronite Christians in the early years of the Lebanese civil war,[20] to Kurdish groups in Iraq,[21] the Sudanese People's Liberation Army and the Sudan Liberation Front based in Darfur which fought the Khartoum government.[22] It weighed heavily on decisions of major powers regarding the position to be adopted towards certain regimes in the region, particularly those of Iraq under Saddam Hussein, the Islamic Republic of Iran and most recently the fate of Gaddafi's regime in Libya.[23]

Regional and International Implications of the Arab-Israeli Conflict

With the end of the Iran-Iraq war and the forced evacuation of Iraqi troops from Kuwait in 1991, the Arab-Israeli conflict came back to dominate the politics of the Middle East and at times, indirectly international politics. The prominence of this conflict could be explained in four different ways:

First, of all other conflicts in the region, this is the conflict that no country could afford to ignore. Most governments of the region do not recognize Israel out of solidarity with the Palestinian people and in protest against Israel's determination not to acknowledge the national rights of the Palestinian people in the territories it continues to occupy. Even the countries that did establish diplomatic relations with Israel, or allowed Israel to open commercial and consular missions in their capitals, soon had to reduce these relations to the strict minimum required by their legal commitments under the normalization treaties they signed with its government, or were forced under pressure of their public opinion to close these missions. Egypt and Jordan belong to the first category and Morocco, Tunisia, Oman and Qatar belong to the second. The Islamic Republic of Iran broke diplomatic relations with Israel following the revolution in 1979. Turkish relations with Israel soared following the election of the Justice and Development Party government in 2003. It is true that Israeli leaders had the opportunity to meet Arab officials, whether those of governments which signed peace treaties with Israel, as Egypt and Jordan or those that accepted partial normalization with it as Morocco and Qatar. Israel remained on the whole diplomatically isolated in the region as these relations were reduced to the minimum in almost all these countries particularly following the election of the Netanyahu led government in February 2009.Hostility towards Israel was also one of the driving forces behind the resurgence of Islamic movements since the 1970's. There is no doubt that the so-called Islamic awakening had its roots also in the domestic conditions prevailing in Arab and Muslim countries, such as the deteriorating position of the educated middle class in many of these countries, the failure of development models which were inspired by either the experience of Socialist or Capitalist countries and the loss of legitimacy of nearly all governments in the region. The repeated defeats of Arab countries by the armed forces of Israel fed a feeling of humiliation experienced by young Arabs and Muslims that found an outlet in the involvement in activities of the Islamist movement, whether these activities were peaceful or violent. Not being capable of directing their anger at Israel herself, they targeted Western interests and peoples or governments seen as collaborating with Israel and Western countries.[24] The two towers of the World Trade Centre, the Pentagon and presumably the White House, were targeted on September 11, 2001 because the US was seen by young Saudis, Kuwaitis, Emiratis and Egyptians to be siding unjustly with Israel. The Al Qaeda organization, led by the late Osama Bin Laden, was initially called the Worldwide Front to Combat Imperialism, Christianity and Zionism.[25]

Moreover, development of nuclear power in the region would stir no problem if it took place in countries ruled by governments friendly to Israel. The Iranian nuclear programme had been initiated under the Shah. At that time, the Iranian government was assisted by both France and the US with Israel raising no objection. But running a nuclear programme, even for peaceful purposes by Saddam Hussein or under the Islamic Republic was a different matter. Israel raided the site of the Iraqi nuclear reactor in July 1981 and getting rid of what was believed to be an active nuclear programme was publicly one of the reasons cited as a justification for the occupation of Iraq by the US, UK and other countries in 2003. The hostile statements made by Mahmoud Ahmadinejad, the Iranian president led all five permanent members of the UN Security Council, besides Germany to impose sanctions on Iran in the hope of persuading its government to give up its nuclear programme. Several reports suggested that Israel was preparing to launch a military assault on Iranian nuclear research facilities to slow down Iranian progress in uranium enrichment, before the country reaches the capability of making a nuclear weapon. Israel would like to maintain her monopoly of nuclear power in the region.[26]

Finally, several domestic conflicts in countries of the region seemed to be an extension of the Arab-Israeli conflict. Even before the creation of a Jewish state in Palestine, Jewish organizations did lend support to Maronite Christian factions in Lebanon. Such factions continued to get military support and training during the early phase of the Lebanese civil war that lasted between 1975-1989. Those factions were fighting the Lebanese nationalist movement that was backed by the Palestinian 'Liberation Organization. Both

Israeli troops and Maronite forces launched military action against this nationalist movement that ended in the occupation of large parts of Lebanon and the driving out of Palestinian guerrillas from the country in the summer of 1982. The forced departure of Palestinian guerrillas from Lebanon did not put an end to Israel's interest in Lebanese politics. The alliance between Hizb'allah on the one hand, Syria and Iran on the other led Israel to continue to eye the military power of Hizb'allah. Its leaders did not forgive that party for its successful resistance of Israeli troops in Southern Lebanon and the heavy casualties inflicted on them by its fighters that forced Israel to evacuate Southern Lebanon in 2000. Since then it has tried several times to remove the weapons of Hizb'allah from areas close to its borders and to prepare for decisive battle against it to obliterate the memory of its unsuccessful war against it in the summer of 2006. No longer an active participant in Lebanese domestic politics, it still favours Lebanese parties which are not on good terms with Hizb'allah.[27]

Hoping to weaken its adversaries in Arab countries, Israel also lent its support to all those who took up arms against Arab governments. That was definitely the case with the different groups in Southern Sudan who fought the central government in Khartoum, dominated by Muslim Arabs. When the conflict in Darfur province broke out, one of the local factions that led the fight and rejected any attempt at a peaceful deal with the government was the Sudan Liberation Front which maintained offices in Jerusalem.[28] The Kurdistan Democratic Party which launched a civil war against the Iraqi government in Baghdad was known to have received military support from Israel. It was reported that following the US invasion of Iraq in 2003, Israeli companies became active in Iraq's Northern region governed by two Kurdish parties who had de facto autonomy vs. the central government in Baghdad.[29] In all these cases, Israeli policy was guided by the well-known strategic principle which says that "the enemy of my enemy is my friend".

Is There Any End in Sight?

The preceding sections of this paper have made it abundantly clear that the policies of the state of Israel continue to provoke tensions on many fronts, between Israelis and Palestinians in Occupied territories, Israelis and Arab countries whether they are frontline states or states far away from Israel's borders, Israel and non-Arab Muslim states and even between Israel and the Islamist movements that swept most Muslim countries.

The Israeli rightist government led by the Likud Party and which includes the 'Yisrael Beiteinu' ('Israel is Our Home') party led by Avigdor Lieberman seems to be hoping that such tensions would simply go away with time. It is almost certain that Israel's military and technological superiority would get the Arabs to finally resign themselves to its existence. Its leaders like to believe that Palestinians would eventually be content with their life under Israeli occupation once they taste the fruit of what the Israelis call "economic peace," namely improvement in their work and living conditions. But even this outcome is quite problematic as it could lead to the presence of an Arab majority within the borders of what is called "Eretz Israel" or "Greater Israel" a prospect which is not acceptable to sections of the Israeli public who insist on keeping the "Jewish character of Israel".

Some of the Israeli politicians even toyed with the notion of "transfer" meaning expelling the Palestinians to an alternative home in Jordan. The "transfer" does not seem to be morally acceptable or practically feasible. It would be resisted by the Palestinians, Jordan, world public opinion and would worsen Israel's relations with almost all countries.[30]

The two states solution is the only proposal that would be satisfactory to all parties. Most of the Palestinians would welcome it. The recent reconciliation agreement between FATAH and HAMAS signed in Cairo on Wednesday, May 4, 2011 could pave the way for the election of a Palestinian government that would accept to negotiate with Israel on the basis of this proposal. The elements of a Palestinian-Israeli agreement are almost known, given the many rounds of negotiations that the two parties had in Camp David in 2000 and elsewhere. It is also acceptable to Arab governments and to the famous Quartet which includes US, the European Union, the Russian Federation and the United Nations. HAMAS leaders' declaration that they are willing to accept a long term truce with Israel is predicated on the understanding that Israel would relinquish its control over Palestinian territories. A settlement inspired by the principle of exchange of land for peace is a good model for resolving dispute with the other Arab country which has a territorial dispute with Israel, namely Syria. It is true that there are other issues of the Arab-Israeli conflict which are difficult to resolve such as those of refugees, Israeli settlements in the Occupied territories and the status of Jerusalem. However, once the principle of land for peace is accepted, it would be possible to come to grips with other complex issues. This would defuse tensions in Israel's relations with Arab and Muslim countries and would open many gates of hope for a prosperous and peaceful Middle East.

Notes

1. Avraham Sela, *The Decline of the Arab-Israeli Conflict: Middle East Politics and the Quest for Regional Order* (Albany: State University of New York Press, 1998).
2. Yossi Alpher, *The Future of the Israeli-Palestinian Conflict: Critical Attitudes Affecting Israel* (United States Institute of Peace, 2005), Special Report 149.
3. Ibid.
4. Michael Dumper (ed.), *Arab-Israeli Conflict: Major Writings in Middle Eastern Studies* (4 volumes). (London and New York: Routledge, 2009).
5. Ian J Bickerton and Carla L. Klausner, *The History of the Arab-Israeli Conflict* (Boston, New York: Prentice Hall, 2010), 96-111. For the different narratives of the conflict, Dumper, Vol.1, Part 2, 217-355.
6. Ibid, 96-130.
7. Theodore Draper, *Israel and World Powers, Roots of the 'Third Arab-Israeli War* (London: Secker &Warburg, 1968), 3-135; Mohammed Hassanein Heykal, *Sanawat Al-Ghalayan (Years of Upheaval),* (*Cairo*: Markaz al-Ahram lil-Tarjamah wa-al-Nashr, 1988) & *Al-Infijar (The Explosion)* (Cairo: Markaz al-Ahram lil-Tarjamah wa-al-Nashr, 1990).
8. Heykal, *Secret Channels: The Inside Story of the Arab-Israeli Peace Negotiations* (London: Harper Collins, 1997).
9. David Menashri and Trita Parsi, "Israeli Relations with Iran," (Encyclopaedia Iranica, 2007).
10. Ibid.
11. Turgut Pelin, "Friends No More? Why Turkey and Israel Have Fallen Out," October 14, 2009. Time.CNN World. See www.time.com/time/world/article/0,8599,1930203,00.html
12. FAS (Federation of American Scientists), 2007, "Israel Nuclear Weapons." www.fas.org/nuke/guide/israel/nuke on May 11, 2011.

13. Greg Bruno, "Iran's Nuclear Program: Backgrounder," Council on Foreign Relations, www.cfr.org/Iran/Irans-nuclear-program/p16811. Accessed on May 11, 2011.
14. James A. Russell, *Proliferation of Weapons of Mass Destruction in the Middle East* (London & New York: Palgrave Macmillan, 2006).
15. Ian J. Bickerton and Carla L.Klausner, *The History of the Arab-Israeli Conflict* (Boston, New York: Prentice Hall, 2010, chapters, 8, 10, 12).
16. Ibid, 369-388
17. *Dar Alkaleej,* "Hamas with truce and no recognition of Israel," 2010, www.alkhaleej.ae/portal/4b2b6a20-0168-447b-953c-7a7dc1c1f59c.aspx
18. *New York Times*, May 22, 2008.
19. Efraim Inbar, "How Israel Bungled the Second Lebanon War," *Middle East Quarterly*, Summer 2007, 57-65. Seymour Hersch, "Watching Lebanon: Washington's Interest in Israel's War," *The New Yorker*, August 21, 2006, 1-3.
20. H. Khashan, "The Evolution of Israeli-Lebanese Relations: From Implicit Peace to Explicit Conflict," *Israel Affairs*, October 2009, Vol. 15, No. 4, 319-334.
21. M. Kibaroglu, "Clash of interest Over Northern Iraq Drives Turkish-Israeli Alliance to a Crossroads," *Middle East Journal*, Spring 2005, Vol. 59.No.2, 246-264.
22. J. Abadi, "Israel and Sudan: The saga of an enigmatic relationship," *Middle East Studies*, 1999, Vol. 35, No. 3, 19-41.
23. John Mearsheimer and Stephen M.Walt, *The Israeli Lobby and US Foreign Policy* (London and New York: Penguin Books, 2007).
24. Mark Tessler, "The origins of Popular Support for Islamist Movements: A Political Economy Approach," in John Pierre Entelis, (ed.), *Islam, Democracy and the State in North Africa* (Bloomington: Indiana University Press, 1997), 107-113.
25. Ron Geaves and Others, *Islam and the West Post 9/11* (Aldershot and Burlington: Ashgate Publishing Company, 2004).
26. Greg Bruno, "Iran's Nuclear Program: Backgrounder," Council on Foreign Relations, www.cfr.org/Iran/Irans-nuclear-program/p16811. Accessed on May 11, 2011.
27. Nubar Hovsepian, (ed.), *The War on Lebanon: A Reader* (New York: Olive Branch Press, 2008).
28. J. Abadi, "Israel and Sudan: The saga of an enigmatic relationship," *Middle East Studies*, 1999, Vol. 35, No. 3, 19-41.
29. M. Kibaroglu, "Clash of interest Over Northern Iraq Drives Turkish-Israeli Alliance to a Crossroads," *Middle East Journal*, Spring 2005, Vol. 59. No. 2, 246-264.
30. Will Youmans, "Israel may transfer Palestinians during the War on Iraq," *Counter Punch*, October 9, 2002. Available at http://www.counterpunch.org/youmans1009.html.

2

Bi-Nationalism: Towards Alternative Model for the Future Solution of the Palestinian-Israeli Conflict

As'ad Ghanem

Introduction

The continuing hostility and the growing enmity between the Israelis and the Palestinians and their leadership, has cast doubts over their ability to resolve the conflict. The aftermath of the 1993 Oslo "peace accord" actually produced more violence than before. Rather than launch progress towards a peace agreement, the past two decades in the century-long conflict have been associated with hostile confrontation. As the conflict becomes more desperate, the need to end it becomes even greater. Yet, any suggestions to resume the "peace process" seem to be based on the same premises and frameworks as in previous failed attempts, disregarding any lessons gained from the Oslo process.

Due to a variety of reasons, the last two decades have seen various peace plans fail. The basic assumption underlying most proposed plans was that the preferable solution would be a partition of the territory of Mandatory Palestine into two separate states. In examining this, it becomes clear that due to sizeable demographic changes and the number of newly established settlements in the past generation, this presumption has many flaws which, in turn ensures stalemate and despair for both the parties.

More than seventeen years after the Oslo agreements and a decade after the Al-Aqsa *intifada* erupted, it seems like the idea of separation between Israel and Palestine and the partition of the country into two independent states is no longer possible or attainable.

Such a partition would leave over one million Palestinians under Israeli sovereignty and citizenship, and hundreds of thousands of Israeli settlers living in Palestinian territory. As a consequence, security restrictions, Israeli settlements, and widespread opposition from both sides, would prevent the establishment of a Palestinian state with territorial continuity and integrity. It would create an unworkable state, divided into gerrymandered districts with no sufficient geographical link between them. Accordingly, there is no apparent way that this track might lead towards an operable, just, and comprehensive end to the conflict. Any border drawn to divide the country would be artificial, leaving dissatisfied militant elements on both sides to continue the struggle and counter the implementation of any signed agreement.

Ironically, the Oslo initiative and its inbuilt shortcomings led us to the inevitable conclusion that its architects never anticipated; that the Palestinian-Israeli conflict was unwittingly moving away from the concept of separation that would lead to "two states for two nations." Instead, rather than exclusive, it was leading all involved towards an ultimately integrated and pluralistic state, an existence that would ultimately lead towards full equality, parity, mutuality, common humanity, and the establishment of a common destiny for all.

In practice, this has become the new and important verity that the Oslo process generated. From our own point of view, this reality might lay the foundations for a joint Palestinian-Israeli struggle, emanating from a realization that the lives of Palestinians and Israelis are inextricably intertwined. There was and remains a common interest in the economy, employment, water distribution, ecology, human rights, and foreign relations, and the great challenge is how to make this vision acceptable to all.

Further to the existing demographic mix of both nations,

common sense would suggest that issues like the above mentioned, as well as others such as the environment, economy, transportation, and communication, will in the coming years be dealt with centrally and with utmost coordination. Two separate states and administrations would be unable to man these essential matters in an effective way.

On the emotional level, it is important to note that the vast majority of both sides, Palestinians and Israelis, regard the whole country as their sole respective homeland. Both believe in their natural right to enjoy the sovereignty over the entire territory of Eretz Yisrael/Filastin. A just and lasting solution to the conflict would have to alleviate the violence, deep alienation, and mistrust between the two nations. To establish a tolerable way of living together, such a solution would have to satisfy the great majority of both populations and bring stability and prosperity to all the inhabitants of the land. It is therefore reasonable to assume that there is a great need to seek new directions and ideas for the resolution of the conflict. In the long quest for an acceptable answer that would do justice to all, few have noticed that since the British Army occupied Palestine 93 years ago, the area has most of the time (75 years) been ruled as one territory.

Bi-Nationalism as a Preferred Tool for Conflict Management in Deeply Divided Societies

For an understanding of the future of the Palestinian/Israeli problem it should be studied in the context of the diverse options found in the literature on ethnic relations in comparable situations. To begin, I note that the conflict management options I describe below share many common characteristics, while in practical terms they display minor variations in technique.

The preliminary question in coping with the resolution of conflict in general and with internal disputes within the same political or social framework in particular is the following: are the conflicts between groups living in proximity amenable to solution at all? The answer to this question is contentious. Some scholars of ethnic and national conflicts believe there is no solution. Such conflicts derive from the most basic level of emotions and psychological needs, and are unrelated to material needs which can be dealt with in the economic, social, cultural or political spheres. Instead of striving unsuccessfully towards an unreachable solution, efforts should be invested to contain the conflict and to diminish its intensity.[1] Other scholars have gone further and claimed that there is a rising negative relationship between the level of group pluralism and the level of political stability. Pluralistic societies are aware that protracted conflicts constantly threaten political stability and public order.[2]

I will argue here that ethnic and national conflicts are amenable to solution and that they can be located in the appropriate and reasonable acceptance of the needs of the various groups. The application of specific techniques can guarantee stability and the preservation of social order in pluralistic societies. Guidelines to the settlement and eventual solution of ethnic and national problems can be found in a combination of the demands and needs of the groups, and the attitudes of the majority and the state towards these needs.

The theoretical literature dealing with conflict solutions in ethnic, religious, national and other group clashes reveals a range of measures aimed at either eliminating the crucial divisions or by putting them in acceptable order. I can find arrangements demanded by the groups or imposed by the state, or agreements based on negotiations between the groups, in an effort to seek an agreed upon solution.[3] Among these solutions I can find the following: Irridenta and Separation[4]; Autonomy and Bi-nationalism[5]; Integration and Pluralism;[6] and Territorial Partition.[7]

As part of the democratic options, the alternative to territorial partition with the aim of achieving possible equality is to enable the groups to live in proximity within a united equitable political framework. This alternative would eliminate the dominance of one specific group with whom the state has been identified, and grant full equality to all groups, with the state adopting a neutral stance in inter-group dialogue. The state would then identify in equal measure with all the population groups. This could be achieved in one of two possible ways:

The first would be the establishment of a federation or confederation of population groups, whose representatives would agree to divide the centres of power, symbols, wealth, economic, cultural and social benefits. This division could be formulated using a group measure, either proportional or equalitarian, according to the numbers and strength of the various groups. This form of agreement existed in Lebanon until the mid 1970s, and is being implemented today in Belgium and Switzerland.[8]

The second technique advocates total abandonment of one-group-dominance and of state identification and its political system allied to one specific group. It includes formal rejection of the communal organization of the population in distributing centres of power, deciding on symbols, or allotting economic, social and cultural resources. This would bring about the establishment of a liberal democratic order relating to all individuals as citizens and not as a member of one of the groups comprising the population. Some of the freedoms within this system would include the right to organize communally, though without state aid and without the state being a partner to such organization. The most notable example of a state choosing this track is France and the United States of America.

To summarize, the two alternatives presented above need not be implemented as a whole. In reality, the most successful enactment would be to adopt principles from both options concurrently. Thus, in certain areas, as in participation in the centres of power and government, the method of group competition (consociationalism, power sharing that contains an agreement between the representatives of the group or their elites) could be employed, while in others the liberal competition between individuals would prevail.

In the age of nationalism, the dynamic essence of local, regional and international politics, the foundation of democratic inter-group conflict management is based on the efficient handling of ethnic problems, and the vying of national groups for control, autonomy and self management. Struggles between groups are an existing feature in practically all modern states. Apart from a few cases such as North and South Korea, the Irish Republic, and instances of states with one national-ethnic group, other states are deeply divided into various ethnic and national groups as majorities or minorities.

Legitimate and healthy competition exists between groups and their representatives in democratic, liberal and consociational arrangements, whose democratic regime is the source for political stability, and in turn is a condition for economic, social and cultural development. In contrast, most non-democratic states fail to provide equality in the eyes of the law, freedom, and genuinely inclusive citizenship, although some have a formal democracy consisting of rotating regimes, external separation of powers, etc. The lack of a real democracy in these states creates struggles between the groups, which may deteriorate into violence and massive use of force in order to preserve political stability. These states' moment of truth lies in a deeper process of democratization in the context of group relations, which may preserve their political systems and assure development in the protection of rights. This process aims to bring about equality both between the citizens as individuals and between the groups as collectives. As such, their right for group self-determination is a basic condition for reconciling them with the system and ensuring their wish to belong, rather than aiming for separation and the establishment of new entities, or joining existing neighbouring states.

I claim that liberal arrangements based on the detailing of group attributions and creation of civil societies whose members are equal as individuals but not as members of wider groups, are unattainable when ethnic and national identities are a solid reality. The processes of group crystallization undergone by ethnic and national groups since the end of the second world war, that have strengthened with the help of modernization, increased levels of education, development of mass media, and a considerable rise in the awareness of individual and group rights, have led to a situation where group members will be unwilling to give up the group factor, seeing it as significant and essential to the resolution of their status as both individuals and part of a group. Therefore, I believe the only remaining option for democratic settlements is the possibility of establishing communal (consociational) democracies. These arrangements can and should be based on the following main tenets:

1. A wide coalition of political elites. The stability of a bi-national state is dependent upon a strong coalition between the elites of both nations and the presence of political leadership representing the majority in each nation. Such a

coalition will be responsible for leading and peace keeping, managing internal and external affairs, and striving to reach consensus and compromise on problematic issues.

2. Mutual right of veto. Efficient and effective management of a bi-national state must be accompanied by the possibility of using a right of veto by members of one group in extreme cases, even in relation to the internal affairs of the other groups. Such an arrangement will require the representatives of one group to consider the interests of the other.
3. Fair representation for both groups. The political and public common institutions of the bi-national system must include fair and proportionate representation for each group. Each group would have a "quota" reserved for its representatives. Certain offices such as President, Prime Minister and Ministers will require representatives of both groups to agree to rotation of positions or doubling of offices, in which each office is filled by two people; one from each group.
4. Internal autonomy for each group. The internal affairs of each group, such as education, culture, municipal government etc., will be administered separately. Such autonomy may be territorial, personal, or mixed, according to the arrangement reached between the representatives of the two groups. In dealing with overlapping issues or with regions of mixed populations, representatives will need to cooperate for fair management even of areas perceived as theoretically separate.

The Future of the Palestinian-Israeli Conflict: Four Political Options

During the last decade, since the outbreak of the second *intifada* and Ariel Sharon's rise to power (in 2001), the fundamental conditions in which the conflict has been conducted changed completely from those that prevailed until the end of Ehud Barak's tenure as prime minister in 1999.

When the Oslo accords were signed in 1993, they marked the start of a historic process of reconciliation between the two national movements, the Palestinian and the Zionist, and in practice the beginning of the implementation of the option of territorial separation between the two states of Israel and Palestine. At this stage of the conflict, Yasser Arafat controlled the Palestinian national movement and the pragmatic and conciliatory Labour Party, led by Itzhak Rabin, held power in Israel. The agreement between Arafat and Rabin was made possible with significant support from the United States and major assistance from the Europeans, Russians, and Chinese, as well as, the active agreement of Egypt and Jordan and the tacit consent of most Arab countries, with the Gulf States and Saudi Arabia expressing a willingness to extend major financial support.

Since February 2001, and in light of the results of the Israeli elections and Sharon's subsequent ascent to power, the option of territorial separation for two complete sovereign states has ceased to be relevant, along with all of the participating players. Israel has 'reoccupied' the Palestinian territories, strengthened and enlarged the settlements, and reinforced the protection of the settlers. In parallel, Israel closed down Palestinian public institutions in Jerusalem and tightened its grip on East Jerusalem. Prime Minister Sharon repeated his willingness to establish a Palestinian state on about 40 per cent of the West Bank, and the Gaza Strip, knowing that no Palestinian leader could accept such an offer. As a result of these policies of the past few years, the parties that supported separation for two viable states did not realize that this has lost its relevance as a possible solution to the Palestinian-Israeli conflict.

The US administration under President George Bush (2000-2008) automatically supported the policy sketched out by Sharon and the Israeli government. Even after the Bush era, the US administration has not come up with an independent line and in practice is not relevant to any practical process of separation. The Europeans, whom the Israeli government distrust, suspecting them of harbouring pro-Palestinian sympathies, are excluded from exerting any influence and therefore are irrelevant to the conflict—their influence is limited to regular and ineffectual meetings with the parties. The Arab states provide window dressing for an imaginary process, but the positions they take from time to time, such as that put forward at the Arab League summit meeting in Beirut in 2003, are irrelevant for what is taking place in the region;

not to mention the fact that they are toothless and have no serious capacity to influence or counteract the Israeli position. Apparent also in Israel and among the Palestinians, the promoters of Oslo and the idea of separation are no longer applicable for what is going on the ground. The Labour Party is no longer a relevant political force; at best it can merely provide an attractive wrapper for the right-wing government and its crimes against the Palestinians. The PLO and its followers are in a difficult position; on the one hand, official Israel abuses and accuses them of responsibility for terrorism over which they have only partial control, and on the other hand, most Palestinians are disillusioned and view them as responsible for the stark situation into which they have been forced, accusing them of negligence, corruption, and a lack of concern for the well-being of the general public.

This continuing conflict of the past 10 years has been waged between two antithetical and belligerent options; Israeli apartheid practices and a Palestinian Islamic state. The Israeli government appears to be in an attempt to lead the Palestinians to despair of ever establishing a sovereign Palestinian state. It is as if it is striving to achieve a comprehensive victory in this conflict-ridden land with unilateral domination of the entire country, possibly tempered by a willingness to permit the Palestinians to live in some sort of autonomy (Quasi-state- or Canton) under overall Israeli supervision and control. In practice, construction has begun to establish a regime similar to the apartheid regime with the systematic infringement of Palestinian basic rights by Jewish rule. In order to realize this option, Israel employs tough and at times cruel means of repression of the sort not seen since the end of the 1948 war and the establishment of Israel. On the Palestinian side, the radical Islamic movements, Hamas and the Islamic Jihad, are pushing for the establishment of an Islamic Palestinian state, where Jews could live as a vanquished minority. To advance this realization, the Islamic movements employ harsh methods against the Jews, of which the roughest manifestation are attacks on citizens in the heart of Israeli cities.

None of these options are realistic or endurable. Separation is no longer relevant because Israel will no longer even consider a willingness to withdraw to the 1967 borders and implement the meaning of United Nations Resolution 242. Even if the Israeli left were to return to power in the foreseeable future (a totally unrealistic possibility) it would not risk a civil war that would ensue in any attempt to uproot all or most of the settlements. The continuing unilateral Israeli governance (In fact already exists on the ground) might be possible, but it cannot endure for long. Palestinians constitute 50 per cent of the total population of the country and they resolutely resist Israeli control. Hence, the Israeli despotic regime will never be stable and its citizens will be endangered as are the Palestinians. An Islamic state has no prospect in the current balance of power and will be rejected by the Jews and large segments of the Palestinian population and would most definitely encounter vigorous opposition from parts of the surrounding Arab countries.

What this means is that Palestinians and Israelis will inevitably have to examine the possibility of the fourth alternative, that of a bi-national state. Only by working together to outline a possible escape from the cycle of conflict, confrontation and bloodshed, can they continue the strive for a single political entity, while making maximum use of techniques of partnership and compromise on fundamental questions, issues, and key positions.

The bi-national option attracted considerable attention in the Zionist leadership before the birth of Israel and was nurtured by Jewish leftists as a solution for the individual and collective existence of the Jews in the country. Currently, some Jewish intellectuals are gradually coming to believe that this may prove to be the more practical solution for resolving the century long violent conflict with the Palestinians. Among the Palestinians too, there has been an increasing body of opinion that views this option as the only outlet for their future collective existence in the country. Those on both sides who consider this option are willing to accept the other, the Jew or the Palestinian, as a partner in a shared state in which the rights of individuals to a life of equality and dignity are recognized, as are the collective rights of both the Palestinians and the Jews to express their national aspirations and desires in a shared state. Only in this way can there be true concord between the two national movements. In our opinion, international and Arab parties wishing to be involved in the resolution of this conflict must examine this option too, and adapt their positions towards its realization. Without moving towards such a track and compromise, they will continue to be irrelevant and the conflict will continue to take its toll of human lives and material and other resources, with no realistic solution on the horizon.

Post-Oslo: The Crisis between Israel and the Palestinians and the Future Solution

The working premise calling for the separation is supported by the UN Security Council Resolution 242, that is, the Israeli withdrawal from the West Bank and Gaza Strip. Since implementation would require a physical, territorial and national separation, listed below are factors that will detail why such a separation is untenable, making it impossible as a political act. These factors will demand an entirely different strategy, namely joint rule throughout the country by representatives of both groups. This would be the one practical way to make progress towards solving the continuing conflict between Israelis and Palestinians over the control of the land: Different expectations of separation among the two sides; common issues such as water resources, environment, employment, a product market, routes of passage, ports, etc., these elements cannot be separated; Israeli settlements in the West Bank and Jerusalem; the future of Jerusalem as one city; the refugees and their right to return to their homeland; and finally the image of the 'homeland' for Jews and Palestinians. Both Jews and Palestinians view the whole land, from River to Sea, as their ancestral homeland.

In September 2000, Ariel Sharon, accompanied by various right-wing politicians, Israeli security personnel, and journalists, provocatively entered the plaza of the Al-Aqsa Mosque (Haram al-Sharif) in East Jerusalem. This action sparked a wave of demonstrations and protests among Palestinians and throughout the Arab world. This also brought about the termination of the Barak government's attempt to reach an accord with the Palestinians, and subsequently led to Barak's defeat in the February 2001 elections to Ariel Sharon. The confrontations and bloodshed that followed between the Palestinians and Israeli security forces and settlers, reached a scale unknown since the signing of the Oslo Accords and the establishment of the Palestinian Authority (PA). Hundreds of Palestinians and Israelis were killed during hostile operations initiated by each side in the other's territory. Inside Israel proper, members of the Islamic Jihad, Hamas, and the Popular Front for the Liberation of Palestine, conducted operations against Israeli citizens; Israeli security forces and settlers carried out offensive operations in the territory under the control of the PA. These operations in the West Bank and Gaza destroyed the foundations of the PA and its institutions. Sharon's aim was to weaken the emerging Palestinian self rule and to initiate an Israeli unilateral withdrawal from the Gaza Strip and parts of the 'occupied territories,' thereby constructing the post-Oslo reality.

Despite attempts to revive the Oslo Accords, which involved the mutual recognition of Israel and the PLO and formed the foundation for the establishment of the PNA (Palestine National Authority), they have ceased to be the basis of the negotiating process since Sharon's assumption of office. Sharon gave his vision a political context by advancing the unilateral withdrawal project as the only possible means for Israel to deal with the Palestinian issue in the short term.

The Alternative: As mentioned earlier, the post-Oslo vision created by Ariel Sharon, essentially shifted policy from 'conflict solution' to 'conflict management'. The terminology fails to conceal that this project of annexing large swathes of the West Bank along the Green Line and in the Jordan Valley for Israeli settlement, leaves the Palestinians concentrated in segregated enclaves—the first such enclave to be established was Gaza. The substantive modification in Sharon's stance or vision was not in accepting the need for the division of the "Land of Israel", but rather in the attempt to term the Palestinian enclaves a "state".

One of the most important components of the post-Oslo Israeli mode of governance has been its evasion of responsibility for the daily needs of Palestinians living under occupation, and its expectation of the PNA to shoulder this burden. Since the outset, Israel has been facilitating the establishment of the PNA by dictating its concept of form and content, as well as the introduction of legislative and institutional changes in order for it to meet Israeli interests and to enable the delegation of Israeli responsibilities.

During the second (Al-Aqsa) *Intifada* in 2002, Israel adopted several measures to restrain the PNA; the most brutal being a full-scale military offensive waged on PNA ruled territory. The Israeli army systematically destroyed Palestinian infrastructure, crushed the Palestinian security forces, terminated communications between the presidency in Ramallah and the remainder of the territories under PNA rule, obstructed the delivery of social services, and greatly constricted Palestinian diplomatic relations, particularly with Europe and North America. However, in spite of these heavily restrictive measures, Israel stopped short of totally destroying the PNA. Its existence was intentionally preserved to allow the claim that a Palestinian body exists which is responsible for providing basic services to the Palestinians, and accordingly to spare Israel these responsibilities under international law. It also provided Israel with a convenient scapegoat and a tangible enemy to be held accountable for actions against Israel and for Palestinian domestic problems.

Under Sharon's rule and following the death of Yasser Arafat, Israel continued to pursue the same policy. It shut down the channels of negotiation and obstructed President Abu Mazen's (Mahmoud Abbas) efforts to reopen them, yet refrained from taking steps that could have led to the demise of the PNA.

After assuming a 'caretaker' office following Sharon's illness, Ehud Olmert continued in the same vein; with plans for the unilateral dismantling of a number of West Bank settlements and implementation of similar withdrawals over the coming years. The 2006 Israeli election saw the rise of a new party, Kadima, with Ehud Olmert as its leader and newly elected prime minister. He initiated peace talks with the PA President, Mahmoud Abbas, but these failed to make any substantive progress before Olmert was forced to leave office following accusations of corruption by the Israeli attorney general.

Parallel to the 'peace negotiations' with Abbas, the Olmert government's most powerful impact was directed at Gaza. In the last week of 2008, and as a reaction to the firing of rockets into Israel from Gaza by Hamas and other Palestinian armed factions, Israel launched a new war on the Gaza Strip. Supported by the air-force and artillery, Israeli forces attacked civilians, governmental buildings, and military armed forces. In response to this offensive, Hamas intensified its rocket attacks on the major southern Israeli cities. An Israeli ground invasion followed the initial wave of airstrikes, demolishing houses and properties in its wake. The war ended in January 2009 and the Israeli forces withdrew from Gaza. The outcome of the war resulted with close to 1400 Palestinian and 13 Israeli deaths, more than 400,000 Gazans left without running water, approximately 4000 homes destroyed, and hundreds of thousands of Gazans left homeless. A UN investigation mission, established and headed by the South African judge, Richard Goldstone, produced a report that accused both Israel and Hamas of conducting crimes against humanity.

The Israeli-Hamas war on Gaza carries far-reaching and historic implications for Palestinian politics, marking this event as possibly the most important since the June 1967 war. While the 1967 war represented a new phase and laid the groundwork for factors that played a role in the years that followed, transforming and consolidating the PLO's position as the "sole" representative of the Palestinian people, the war on Gaza marked the official beginning of the post-PLO period in modern Palestinian history. The most striking development was the absence of any role for the PLO and the limits imposed on its participation by the Palestinian Authority (PA) on the one hand, and Hamas on the other. The Gaza war was the first Israeli-Palestinian conflict since the re-emergence of the Palestinian national movement in the 1950s and 1960s in which the PLO did not officially take part in the fighting. Mahmoud Abbas, president of the PA and leader of the PLO, implicitly justified the Israeli attack on Gaza and held Hamas responsible—this was preceded with a campaign of incitement against Hamas. On the other hand, at the end of the war, Khaled Mash'al as head of the political bureau of Hamas declared that Hamas will establish an alternative political organization to represent the Palestinians instead of the PLO.

Conclusion

In conclusion, I may refer to the following summary of the "Palestinian-Israel situation":

1. The Palestinian side is split into factions. On one side, there

is the official position of both the Fatah organization and the PA which advocates presenting the 'Palestinian struggle' as a popular struggle of national liberation from the Israeli occupation of the West Bank and Gaza Strip, and has reservations about actions directed against Israeli civilians within the Green Line. On the other side, the main opposition groups (Hamas, Islamic Jihad, and the Popular Front) advocate the radical line of a total struggle against Israel and Israelis, permitting their members to act both in the territories of the PA and in Israel proper, presenting the confrontation as part of a comprehensive war against Israel and Zionism.

2. The Israeli majority supports the right wing government headed by Benjamin Netanyahu. This government asserts that it remains committed to the peace process, but has failed to advance any political programme that would make it possible to begin negotiations to end the occupation.
3. Both officially and implicitly, Israel continues to encourage Jews to settle in the West Bank and Gaza Strip, commending the establishment of 'new outposts' populated by a few extreme settlers, with the object of asserting control over as much land as possible. In practice, there is an ongoing debate between the main coalition partners, Likud, Israel Beitenu, and Labour, on the continuation of this situation.
4. Negotiations have halted between Israel and the Palestinians since Netanyahu became Prime Minister in March 2009. The main contact has been through foreign brokers and the media, replete with mutual insults, and accusations alleging the other's responsibility for the situation. Palestinians continue to advocate an end to the conflict based on international resolutions, including Israeli withdrawal from the entire West Bank, dismantling of the settlements, the partition of Jerusalem, and the return of Palestinian refugees or payment of compensation in accordance with UN General Assembly Resolution 194. On the Israeli side, public opinion has hardened in its rejection of all Palestinian demands as part of a comprehensive solution to the conflict.

Several options are available to the parties. The most extreme involves unilateral Israeli action aimed at producing another wave of Palestinian refugees fleeing to areas adjacent to Israel proper for the heart of the West Bank, or even the East Bank of the Jordan. Of course this option would produce a wave of Palestinian and pan-Arab resistance, and wall-to-wall condemnation in Europe and even North America. It would cost Israel dearly, thus making its implementation unlikely. However, it remains possible, and is relevant to the current situation. Another option would be prolongation of the current situation for the foreseeable future, with a concomitant willingness by both sides, and especially Israel, to pay a limited price. Such a long-term continuation of the current situation will involve more Jewish settlement activity in the West Bank and perpetuation of Israel's iron-fist policy vis-a-vis the Palestinians.

As time passes, isolating the West Bank from Israel will become increasingly impractical and even irrelevant, eventually paving the way for the possibility of establishing a joint political entity with broad internal autonomy for each group. The continuing situation is liable to augment mutual hostility, but also the mutual dependence of the two groups. Especially on the Palestinian side, the call for consideration of a shared bi-national Israeli-Palestinian state is becoming louder. It is difficult to envision today, but a change in leadership, and fatigue with the present situation, could lead to changes in the scope, nature, and form of the 'longing for peace' between the two peoples.

Notes

1. W. Connor, *Ethnonationalism: the Quest for Understanding* (New Jersey: Princeton University Press, 1994) John McGarry and Brendan O'Leary, "The Macro-Political regulation of ethnic conflict," in John McGarry and Brendan O'Leary, (eds.), *The Politics of Ethnic Conflict Regulation* (London and New York: Routledge, 1993), 1-40.
2. G. Almond, "Comparative Political Systems," *Journal of Politics* XVIII (August) 1956, 391-409, M. R Haug, "Social and Cultural Pluralism as a Concept in Social System Analysis," *The American Journal of Sociology*, 1967, Vol. 73, 294-304, A. Rabushka and K Shepsle, "Political Entrepreneurship and Patterns of Democratic Instability in Plural Societes," 1971, *Race and Class* 7, 461-476.

3. T. R. Gurr and Harff, *Ethnic Conflict in World Politics* (Boulder & San Francisco: Westview Press, 1994); T. R Gurr, *Minorities at Risk: A Global View of Ethnopolitical Conflict* (Washington: U.S. Institute of Peace Press, 1993); I Lustick, "Stability in Deeply Divided Societies: Consocialism versus Control," *World Politics* 1979, 31: 325-344; D. Horowitz, *Ethnic Groups in Conflict* (Berkeley: University of California Press, 1985)
4. Horowitz, *Ethnic Groups in Conflict,* 229-288.
5. Horowitz, *Ethnic Groups in Conflict,* 601-652.
6. A. Lijphart, *Democracy in Plural Societes* (New Haven CT: Yale University Press, 1977).
7. S. Smooha and Hanf, "The Diverse Modes of Conflict-Regulation in Deeply Divided Societies," *International Journal of Comparative Sociology* XXXIII, 1992, 1-2: 26-47.
8. Lijphart, *Democracy in Plural Societes.*

3

The Empowering of the Israeli Extreme Right: The Rise-Up of the 'Yisrael Beiteinu' Party

Mohanad Mustafa

Introduction

The Israeli right was victorious for the first time in the elections for the 9th Knesset, held in 1977. Since then, the balance between the 'right' and 'left' camps has been maintained, with small shifts in each direction. The narrow victory of the left in the 1992 elections gave rise to a leftist government led by Yitzhak Rabin, a government that signed the Oslo Accords and recognized the PLO (Palestine Liberation Organization) as the representative of the Palestinian people. The rise of the leftist government to power is partially attributable to the first Palestinian Intifada and Israel's inability to quash the popular uprising of the Palestinians.

The latest change entails the rise of the 'extreme right' in the recent elections (February 10, 2009).[1] The extreme right became a dominant power, controlling about a third of Israel's Knesset (38 seats: 15 Yisrael Beiteinu, 11 Shas, 5 United Torah Judaism, 4 National Union and 3 Habayit Hayehudi). When added to the Likud, which also grew from 12 seats in the outgoing Knesset to 27 seats in the current Knesset, it created a broad basis for a rightist coalition of 65 Knesset members, a situation the right had not enjoyed since 1977.

In this article, we will try to analyze the rise of the extreme right in the recent elections, and will seek to answer the question: Is the ascent of the extreme right temporary, or does it reflect an Israeli situation that has developed over the years, a situation that will change Israel's political map and its internal and external political conduct?. The article is divided into three parts; first, we will present the social and political background for the rise of the extreme right in Israel; second, we will analyze the results of the last Knesset elections in Israel, including the rise-up of the extreme right in these elections; and third, we will present the empowerment of the Yisrael Beiteinu party and Lieberman as a leader of the extreme right in Israel.

Background for the Ascent of the Extreme Right in Israel: Social Change, Ethno Nationalism and a 'Nation under Siege"

The rise of the right in Israel in general and the rise of the extreme right in particular is not a sudden phenomenon[2]. This rise began in the 1980s and grew stronger in the last decade, in light of the escalation of the sense of 'nation under siege' in Israeli society that was expressed through a public feeling that the state and the Israeli society are facing protracted and complicated problems. It was perceived that those problems became very difficult to overcome while using the "traditional democratic" methods that are already in use and parts of the Israeli society started searching for new approaches in order to overcome the challenges. The feeling of the 'nation under siege' was developed and deepened in light of the failure of the peace process and the intensification of the conflict with the Palestinians and neighbouring Arab societies, on the one hand, and the growth of internal problems, on the other hand.

The efforts to understand the rise-up of the Israeli extreme right were developed in the last decade, following Mudde,[3] concerning the 'extreme right' political parties in Europe, Pedahzur[4] and Pedahzur and Perliger[5] presented a comprehensive analysis about the rise of the extreme right in Israel. They claim that the empowerment of the extreme right refers to a 'combined approach' and a cluster of variables, including the ideological, economic, social and political ones. According to Pedahzur,[6] the rise-up of the 'extreme-right' parties in Israel can be better explained by using what he called "the pyramid shaped explanatory model" where the factors introduced in the model start with the very basic foundations of the political culture, proceeding to the social level with discussion on the foundations of social cleavages, towards the top of the pyramid, where he addresses narrower factors (structural and political) and at the top of the pyramid are variables such as the party scene and party organization.

These studies refer mainly to historical developments that occurred until the beginning of the current century, while our aim in this article is to analyze the latest developments and the rise of the 'Yisrael Beiteinu' party in the last Israeli general election.

I argue that the explanation for the rise of the extreme right may be found in the political sphere that mainly addresses the changes in the structure of power, the character of ethnic nationalism in Israel and its cultural and political expressions in situations of pressure that approximate a reality of "a nation under siege," as it occurred in Italy, Germany, Spain and Turkey following World War I. As in these countries, in situations of pressure stemming from external crises vis-à-vis neighbouring countries or internal situations of social or economic crisis, ethnic nationalism based on blood ties and an imagined forefather tends to converge inwardly and seek salvation by strengthening the internal solidarity of the ethnic nation. This includes searching for a strong and unifying leadership that promises to suitably contend with the challenges facing the nation.[7] The extreme right parties and leaders in these cases made big efforts in order to combine the 'external dangers' with the internal weaknesses and fragmentation and present them as one complex entity that abuts the future of the nation in a concrete danger. Below, we will present the different variables behind the latest development that refers to the rise of the extreme right, in general and 'Yisrael Beiteinu,' in particular.

Demographic and Social Changes: Changes in the social composition of Israeli society, resulting from demographic processes and developments, led to the rise of the right in Israel. In general, the Ashkenazi Jews—that is, Jews originating from Europe or America (before they were joined by the Jews from the former Soviet Union who immigrated to Israel in the 1990s), tended to vote for the left, and for the Labour Party, in particular, while the Mizrahim, the Jews originating from Asia or Africa, tended to vote for the right and the Likud.[8] The growing percentage of Mizrahim in Israeli society in the 1960s and 1970s, and their shift toward the right, led to the political turnabout in Israel in 1977 and the ascent of the right. The decline of the left since the 1990s is also related to the changes in the demographic composition of Israeli society.

The changes in the Israeli political culture are related to the demographic changes in the composition of the population. Between the years 1990-2001, more than 900,000 people immigrated to Israel from the former Soviet Union. At the end of 2001, some 805,000 immigrants from the Soviet Union were living in Israel, comprising about 12 per cent of Israel's population and 16 per cent of its Jewish population.[9]

About a third of the Jews in Israel in 2005 were Israeli-born (at least second generation in Israel). Some 40 per cent were of European or American origin (including the immigration from the 1990s); about 64 per cent of this group was born in Israel. About 12.4 per cent were from Asian origin; 30 per cent of this group were Israeli-born, and about 15.4 per cent were of African descent; some 37 per cent of this group was born outside Israel.[10] The population of ultra-Orthodox Jews, who voted en masse for the right-wing parties (religious parties), is estimated at 700,000, comprising 15.8 per cent of the Jewish population. The fertility rate of ultra-Orthodox women is 7.7 children, but the fertility rate of Jewish women who are non-ultra-Orthodox is only 2.6 children. According to a simple calculation, the ultra-Orthodox population will grow to 2.9 million by 2025.[11]

The population of Jewish settlers who tend to vote for the extreme right in Israel has also grown. The number of settlers in the occupied Palestinian territories has doubled, despite the peace process between the Palestinians and the Israelis. During the past 12 years, the population of settlers in the West Bank grew by 107 per cent, from about 130,000 in 1995 to about 270,000 in 2007. This compares to a growth of about 29 per cent of the overall population of Israel during this period. This trend also continued during the last three years of this period (2005-2007), when the Jewish population in the West Bank grew at a rate that was three times higher (about 5% annually) than the average growth rate in the overall population of Israel (1.7% annually). None of the other regions in Israel experienced such dramatic growth during the same period. Consequently, the West Bank settlers' share of Israel's overall population grew to 3.8 per cent at the end of 2007 and about 4.9 per cent of the Jewish population in the country.[12]

Ethnocentric Political Culture: The results of the elections for the 18th Knesset in Israel, the public's rightward shift and the collapse of the Israeli left are not coincidental. They are the product of a political culture that is non-democratic and even anti-democratic. The political culture that is coalescing in Israeli society reflects a trend of growing extremism among the Jewish majority and a tendency to justify the use of aggressive methods vis-à-vis the other, the Arab and the Palestinian, including the Palestinian citizens of Israel.[13] Studies that examined the positions of the Israeli public and the youth expose the essence of the political culture, which advocates encouraging the emigration of the Arab citizens in Israel and revoking their rights, and a longing for strong leadership as an alternative to a liberal, democratic regime.

The annual survey conducted by the Jaffee Centre for Strategic Studies at Tel Aviv University in 2002 found that 46 per cent of the Jews in the State of Israel support the transfer of the Palestinian residents of the occupied territories, and 31 per cent support the transfer of the Arabs citizens of Israel. About 60 per cent of the respondents said that they currently support encouraging the emigration of the Arab citizenry from the state, and 61 per cent believe that they constitute a security threat to the state.[14]

In the Israeli Democracy Index conducted in 2003, some 53 per cent of the Jews opposed full equality of rights for the Arabs, and 77 per cent believed that there must be a Jewish majority when making crucial decisions. The majority (57%) were in favour of encouraging emigration of Arabs.[15]

In the Democracy Index conducted in 2004 among teenagers, 60 per cent of the Israeli youth expressed a longing for a strong leader as a substitute for a legal framework. Support among adults for this was nearly as strong, reaching 58 per cent. Some 43 per cent of the youth and 51 per cent of the adults supported prohibiting speeches that included criticism of the State of Israel.[16] In the Democracy Index conducted in 2006, most of the respondents (61%) said that strong leaders could benefit the state more than discussions and laws.[17]

The Index of Arab-Jewish Relations in Israel conducted in 2006 shows that a Jewish majority (80%) believes that decisions about the character of the state and its borders must be backed by a Jewish majority and not only by a majority of the citizens.[18] In the Index of Arab-Jewish Relations conducted in 2007, a third of the Jews supported stripping the Arabs of Israel of their right to vote, and 37 per cent supported adopting a policy of encouraging the emigration of Arabs citizens from Israel.[19]

In an extensive study on political extremism, conducted by the Centre for National Security Studies at the University of Haifa, about 63 per cent of the Jewish respondents said that the government of Israel should encourage Arab citizens to emigrate, and 55.3 per cent thought that the Arabs of Israel pose a danger to the state. Some 45.3 per cent supported revoking the right of Arabs in Israel to vote and to be elected, and 25 per cent said they would consider voting for a party like Kach.[20]

The growth of the extreme right in Israel led to several legislative attempts that were invalidated by the Knesset presidium, such as the "Soul for a Soul" bill submitted by the National Union Party in 2004. Article 3 of the bill stipulates: "If a decision is made to evacuate a Jewish settlement, an Arab settlement located within the domain of the State of Israel, with a similar number of residents, will be evacuated in parallel, as specified in an order, and its residents will be transferred to the area [of the occupied territories]".[21] This bill is one of dozens of legislative proposals that have attempted to restrict the rights of the Arabs in Israel. A well-known example of such legislation that was approved by the Knesset is the amendment to the Citizenship and Entry to Israel Law, which prevents family reunification of Arabs citizens of Israel with their Palestinian spouses from the occupied territories.[22]

Ethnic Nationalism and "A Nation under Siege": The main reason explaining why a high percentage of Israelis look to the right for answers, derives from a cumulative sense of "a nation under siege." Several events occurred during the 1990s that intensified the feeling of a "nation under siege" on the part of the Jews in Israel—for example, the failure of the Oslo Accords and the beginning of a new stage in the armed struggle of the Palestinians; the massive influx of immigrants from the former Soviet Union who came with right-wing and nationalistic ideas and views; the erosion of the standing of the Israeli left because of the failure of the peace process and also because of its inability to provide a socio-economic alternative to the liberal approach and market economy of the right.

The 18th Knesset Election Results: The Rise of the 'Extreme Right' and the Decline of the 'Historical Left'

The elections for the 18th Knesset in Israel were held on February 10, 2009. Of a total electorate of about 4.8 million, some 71 per cent participated in the voting: 3,416,587 votes were cast, and the total count was 3,373,490 after subtracting invalid ballots. Competing in the elections were 34 party lists, only 12 of which surpassed the threshold of 2 per cent of the valid votes. (See Table 1)[23]

According to the political system in Israel, the number of Knesset seats each party receives is important—but much more important is the strength of each bloc in competing to form a government coalition supported by at least 61 members of Knesset (of a total of 120 MKs). From the establishment of the state until 1977, a centre-left coalition led by Mapai (the Land of Israel Workers' Party) governed Israel. In 1977, the rightist bloc led by the Likud Party was victorious and a balance between the two camps has been maintained ever since. This became more acute during the past decade and, in fact, led to early elections every three years rather than every four years as the law stipulates.

The victory of the right is the most significant aspect of the elections for the 18th Knesset. From a historical perspective, the rise of the right—and particularly the extreme right—became a political trend after the political turnabout in Israel in 1977. However, the balance of power between the two blocs, right and

Table 1: Party lists that Surpassed the Threshold Percentage, and their Number of Knesset Seats

Party	*No. of Voters*	*No. of Seats (of 120)*
Labour, led by Ehud Barak	334,900	13
Habayit Hayehudi—the New Mafdal	96,765	3
United Torah Judaism—Agudath Yisrael—Degel Hatorah	147,954	5
Balad—al-Tajamu' al-Watani al-Dimuqrati	83,736	3
Hadash—The Democratic Front for Peace and Equality	112,130	4
National Union—Tekuma, Hatikva, Eretz Yisrael Shelanu, Moledet	112,570	4
Kadima—with Tzipi Livni for prime minister	758,032	28
Yisrael Beiteinu, led by Avigdor Lieberman	394,577	15
Likud—Achi, led by Benjamin Netanyahu for prime minister	729,054	27
The New Movement—Meretz	99,611	3
The United Arab List—The Arab Movement for Renewal	113,954	4

left, was almost equal—until the last elections. The results of the elections for the 18th Knesset led to the rise of the rightist bloc (with 65 seats), but especially to the collapse of the Zionist Israeli left. The two parties of the Zionist left, Labour and Meretz, together won only 16 of the 120 Knesset seats, the lowest number since the establishment of the state in 1948.

Arian and Shamir[24] believe that the rise of the right is the salient characteristic of Israeli politics since the 1970s. They argue that in the ten election campaigns held between 1969 and 2003, the rightist bloc consolidated its control, while support for the leftist bloc declined. The leftist bloc succeeded in attaining a majority of the Knesset seats three times (1969, 1973 and 1992), but the rightist bloc won a small majority in all of the election campaigns since 1977, except for the elections held in 1992.

The main change in the latest elections was the rise of the extreme right in Israel. Contrary to many projections about the waning of the extreme right in Israel, the extreme right continues to flourish in Israeli society, and this is despite the banning of the

Kach movement in the mid-1990s[25]. The peace process and the failure of the Oslo accords led to a new wave of political violence by the right in Israel.[26]

In the elections for the 17th Knesset, held in 2006, the rightist bloc won 50 seats (including the ultra-Orthodox religious parties such as Shas and United Torah Judaism). The ultra-nationalist parties of the extreme right won 20 seats, while the Zionist leftist bloc, Labour and Meretz, won 24 seats. In the most recent election, the extreme right received an additional 15 seats at the expense of the centre-left bloc.

The extreme right-wing parties won 13 seats in the 15th Knesset elections (in 1999), maintained the same level of representation in the Knesset elections held in 2003, and increased its strength to 20 seats in 2006. It reached its peak in 2009, when it won a total of 38 seats. The ascent of the Yisrael Beiteinu party is an important indicator in the rise of the extreme right in Israel and in winning over a considerable part of Israeli society to the right's vision and outlook.

Table 2: Balance of Power between the Blocs in the Israeli Political System, 1992-2009

Year	*Leftist Bloc*	*Centrist Bloc*	*Rightist Bloc*	*Arabs*
2009	16	28	65	11
2006	24	36	50	10
2003	28	15	69	8
1999	38	12	60	10
1996	43	4	64	9
1992	56	—	61	5
1988	47	2	65	6

Notes on the Table:

1. The rightist bloc also includes the ultra-Orthodox parties such as Shas and United Torah Judaism.
2. In two election campaigns (1996, 1999), Knesset elections were held parallel to elections for the prime minister. In the 1996 elections, the candidate of the right, Benjamin Netanyahu, was victorious; and in the 1999 elections, the candidate of the left, Ehud Barak, won.
3. The Arabs appear in a separate category because they comprise a constant opposition to all Israeli governments, left and right, and have never been invited to join a coalition.

The Rise of the 'Extreme Right' Parties: The Case of 'Yisrael Beiteinu'

Although the right wing parties in Israel compile a group of parties and various (religious and secular) political movements, it is clear that the most powerful phenomena in the last decade, is the rise up of 'Yisrael Beiteinu' party, headed by the current Israeli foreign minister, Avigdor Lieberman. Lieberman was born in 1958 in the former Soviet Union and immigrated to Israel in 1978. Upon his arrival in Israel, he joined the extreme rightist Kach movement in 1979,[27] which was subsequently banned. The former secretary-general of the Kach movement notes that he was responsible for issuing a membership card to Avigdor Lieberman, then, still a new immigrant from Moldova. "I don't recall to what extent he was active in the movement, but if he denies it, I am ready to testify in any forum that Lieberman was indeed a member for a short time"[28]. Another activist in the Kach party says that he met Lieberman for the first time in the offices of Kahane, the leader of Kach, on Ussishkin Street in Jerusalem: "I remember this very well, because I arrived there one day after I immigrated to Israel in 1979."[29]

After leaving the Kach movement, Lieberman joined Benjamin Netanyahu in 1988 and became his right-hand man until forming the Yisrael Beiteinu party. When Netanyahu was elected to be chairman of the Likud party after the election defeat of 1992, he appointed Lieberman as director-general of the party in order to rebuild it. In the 1996 elections, Benjamin Netanyahu won the election for prime minister and Lieberman played an active role in this victory. Netanyahu appointed Lieberman as director-general of the Prime Minister's Office, but Lieberman remained in this position for only one year due to a police investigation initiated against him.

Lieberman resigned from the Likud party and founded the Yisrael Beiteinu movement prior to the 1999 elections. The party initially relied on the Russian vote,[30] with the Russians constituting an important electoral power since the large influx of immigrants from the former Soviet Union in the 1990s. Today, one of every six Israeli voters is an immigrant from the former Soviet Union who arrived in Israel in the 1990s. The Russian electoral strength is one of the factors that led Lieberman to establish the Yisrael Beiteinu party. A study that examined the connection between ideology and voting in the 1999 elections indicated that about 25 per cent of the Russian voters who defined themselves as rightists voted for Yisrael Beiteinu, versus 7 per cent of the Russians who defined themselves as leftists.[31]

In the elections held in 2003, the Yisrael Beiteinu party merged with two extreme right-wing parties—Moledet, which openly advocates for the transfer of Palestinians as a solution for the conflict, and Tekuma, a party that relies on the support of the settlers. The three parties formed the National Union list, but the Russian vote remained the primary source of strength for the merged party: 24 per cent of the Russian electorate cast their vote for this party bloc.[32] Prior to the 2006 elections, Lieberman left the National Union party and Yisrael Beiteinu competed separately, winning 11 seats (out of 120 in the Knesset).

The Yisrael Beiteinu party gained strength in the elections for the 18th Knesset, garnering support from 12 per cent of all voters and winning 15 seats, thus becoming the third largest party in Israel after Kadima and the Likud. This compares to 9 per cent of the vote and 11 seats in the elections for the 17th Knesset, and 5.5 per cent of the vote and 7 seats in the elections for the 16th Knesset (when it ran as part of the National Union party).

The party's leaders and activists are already talking about the next elections, when they expect to win 30 seats and become the largest party in Israel.[33] Though such assessments are exaggerated, they reflect the ambitions of this party.

Table 3: Support for Yisrael Beiteinu in Selected Cities (%)

	2003— 16th Knesset Elections	*2006— 17th Knesset Elections*	*2009— 18th Knesset Elections*
Haifa	6	12	16
Jerusalem	6	7	6.3
Be'er Sheva	9	20	25
Tiberias	22	14	16
Ariel	22	35	31
Sderot	10	19	23
Acre	6	17	22

The Yisrael Beiteinu party won significant support in most of the regions of Israel. In the West Bank settlements, 10 per cent of the electorate voted for the party; it received 17.2 per cent of the vote in southern Israel (Be'er Sheva) and 16.2 per cent in Haifa. The party won support in nearly every locality and in all sectors of the Israeli society. For example, in Acre, the scene of confrontations between the city's Arabs and Jews in October 2008[34] Yisrael Beiteinu was the only active party in the city, from the Jewish side. According to a 26-year-old activist in the party, "There is no doubt that the disturbances that occurred in the city, and the war afterwards, generated a rightward trend toward the party, and not only among the new immigrants but also among the Israeli-born and young people."[35]

Development towns—towns located in the periphery, where most of the residents are of Mizrahi extraction and where parties such as the religious Shas party and the Likud enjoy strong electoral support—also became a centre for the activity of the Yisrael Beiteinu party. People who had voted in the past for the Shas movement in development towns shifted their support to the Yisrael Beiteinu party. The comments of one such voter illustrate this phenomenon: "As long as I can remember, I have voted for the Shas movement, but for us Lieberman speaks the truth while the others are lying."[36] Another voter explained his support by saying: "Despite Lieberman's views on religious issues, he reflects my views on the security issue."[37] The support of development towns for Yisrael Beiteinu comes despite the party's anti-religious platform. The residents of these towns (such as Netivot and Ofakim) are generally traditional people who tended to vote in the past for the religious Mizrahi party, Shas. Today, they tend to vote for the secular Yisrael Beiteinu party, which has a Russian character.

In the latest Knesset elections, the Yisrael Beiteinu party also won support in the traditional stronghold of the Israeli left—the kibbutzim and moshavim—particularly in those bordering the Gaza Strip. In Kibbutz Kerem Shalom, which was built in 1966, the Yisrael Beiteinu party received more than 21 per cent of the vote, twice as much as the Labour Party and 1.5 times that of Meretz. On average, Yisrael Beiteinu received about 4 per cent of the vote in kibbutzim.

Previously, Lieberman had received virtually no support in most of the moshavim and kibbutzim.

The Yisrael Beiteinu party and its Knesset list are no longer solely comprised of Russian speakers. The number two slot on the list is filled by a representative of the traditional rightist camp who quit the Likud, Uzi Landau. The list also includes Israel's former ambassador in the U.S., Danny Ayalon, and a representative of the Druze community in Israel, Amar Hamad, as well as other representatives from the periphery in Israel. Yisrael Beiteinu is no longer a party of Russian speakers; it is a pan-Israeli party. It also is not tied to a particular socio-economic class or educational level. Support for Lieberman is also expressed in institutions of higher education: In mock elections held at the College of Management on January 20, with 700 students participating, Lieberman's party came in third with 24 seats, trailing only the Likud (34) and Kadima (29). At Tel Aviv University (2,682 voters), Yisrael Beiteinu doubled its strength in comparison to a similar vote conducted prior to the previous elections and received 12 seats[38]. In a survey conducted at Ben-Gurion University in Be'er Sheva among 3,000 students, Yisrael Beiteinu received 20 seats, Kadima 24 seats, Labour 17 and Likud 21.[39]

A survey conducted in ten high schools in central Israel, encompassing 2,877 students, also indicated Yisrael Beiteinu's growing strength in all strata of Israeli society and the party's popularity among the Israeli youth. When the votes were tallied at these ten high schools, Yisrael Beiteinu came in first with 19.76 per cent, ahead of the Likud (19.5%), Labour (15.8%) and Kadima (14.1%).[40] One of the Jewish students (age 18), an activist in the Yisrael Beiteinu party, explained the trend among the youth to support Lieberman: "We are really fed up here with the left-wing democracy. People have labelled Lieberman a dictator because of the things he says. But the truth is that Israel cannot be a complete democracy when there are Arabs here who are opposed to it."[41]

In the elections held in 2006, two-thirds of Yisrael Beiteinu voters came from the Russian-speaking public. Today the party estimates that about half of its support comes from the general Israeli public, with the other half coming from Russian speakers.

Table 4: Election Results of the Yisrael Beiteinu Party since its Formation

Year	*%*	*Knesset Seats*
1999	2.6	4
2003*	5.5	7
2006	9	11
2009	11.7	15

* In a coalition with other right-wing parties.
Source: Central Elections Committee.

Similar to extreme rightist parties that were established and operated in the 20th century, Yisrael Beiteinu clearly defines those who belong to the ethnic nation (us) and those who are external to the national project (them). The ethno-national character of the state takes precedence over its democratic character, and the state should be an instrument for strengthening the exclusionary character vis-à-vis the minorities.

The Yisrael Beiteinu party believes that Israel should comprise of only Jewish people and only then can it be democratic. The party does not even advocate that Israel should be a state of the Jews, but rather a Jewish state, and its Jewishness is more important than its democratic value. The party's vision, as posted on its Internet site, states:

> "The State of Israel was designed to be a Jewish state—as opposed to a state of the Jews or a state of all of its citizens. It is no coincidence that Israel is defined as a Jewish and democratic state, in that order—as a state that is first of all Jewish and only then democratic. The order of the words is not just a coincidental or semantic matter. It testifies to the salient Jewish orientation and the clear hierarchy according to which the State of Israel should exist."[42]

The Yisrael Beiteinu party adopts a liberal approach to religion and an ultra-nationalist approach toward the Arabs in Israel and the Palestinian question. This is also related, among other factors, to the ideological orientation of the immigrants from the Commonwealth of Independent States (CIS). Peled and Shafir[43] state that there are two discourses of citizenship among the immigrants from the CIS: a liberal discourse vis-à-vis religion and the state, and an ethno-national discourse vis-à-vis the Arab-Israeli conflict and the peace process. It should also be noted that immigrants from the CIS do not hold liberal views on any issues except for state-religion relations and the economy, the Yisrael Beiteinu party advocates a free market economy.

At the Herzliya Conference held in February of 2009, Lieberman said that "Israel is under a combined terror attack, from within and from abroad, and the terror from within is always much more dangerous than the terror from abroad. We should understand this and should also act accordingly."[44] In an article he published, Lieberman states: "Iran, Hezbollah and Hamas are problems that are difficult to ignore, but the lack of loyalty at home is no less dangerous a threat to the existence of Israel as a Jewish and democratic state."[45]

Lieberman thinks that the debate surrounding his slogan "No citizenship without loyalty" established a new agenda in Israel. He claims that the discussion about this issue will ultimately protect the Jewish Zionist and democratic character of the state.[46] He also emphasizes the Zionist character of the state and not only its Jewish character because he wants to distinguish his approach vis-à-vis both the ultra-Orthodox Jews and the Arabs. With regard to the Jewish character of the state, the intention is to deepen its nationalistic Jewish character.

Lieberman suggests in an interview a formula for implementing his slogan of "No citizenship without loyalty." He proposes legislation that would require a citizen who goes to the Ministry of Interior to receive an identity card to sign a declaration of loyalty to the State of Israel, the flag, the anthem, the declaration of independence and to affirm that Israel is a Jewish and Zionist state. The person must also commit to military service or alternative service.[47] In the same interview, he proposes "transfer" for those refusing to sign a declaration of loyalty to the Zionist state, explaining: "First of all, there is an equation between citizenship and loyalty. The second equation is between social security benefits and national service. But there is also a third element. Just as they have the chutzpah to demand the right of return, there is also the right of expulsion—for inciters. I wouldn't hesitate to kick them the hell out of here."[48]

Lieberman wants every citizen to sign a declaration of loyalty to the state. He writes in one of his articles: "In the next Knesset, Yisrael Beiteinu will work to pass a Citizenship Law that will restore our national dignity and give content to the word loyalty. The law will require each citizen to sign a declaration of loyalty to the Jewish state, its principles and its laws. Whoever refuses to do so will forfeit his right to vote and be elected. In addition, Yisrael Beiteinu will work to define a closer connection between military service or national service and the rights offered by the National Insurance Institute—all of this in the spirit of the clear principle that those who are more loyal will receive more."[49]

In Yisrael Beiteinu's political platform, the party advocates exchanges of territory and population, such as transferring Arab citizens from Israel to the territory of the Palestinian state to be established, and annexing settlement blocs in the West Bank. The platform emphasizes that the principle guiding the party is "peace in exchange for peace" and non-withdrawal from the Golan Heights. The proposal of Yisrael Beiteinu for the Palestinian-Israeli conflict is based on a single principle: maximum separation between populations and exchanges of populations and territory.

Lieberman has been more determined than any other politician in regard to territorial exchanges. This issue has been on and off the agenda since the mid-1990s and has been debated by leaders of the right and by leaders of the left. Rightists were not the only ones to propose territorial exchanges.[50] But Lieberman was more persistent than any other Israeli leader in raising this issue. In the election campaign of 2006, his slogan was "Disengage from Umm al-Fahm"—that is, disengage from the second largest Arab city in Israel, which is located on the Green Line.

Lieberman believes that there is no reason to seek a solution that is not linked to the Arabs in Israel, and he proposes separating from them in the framework of the permanent accord. Lieberman thinks that the issue of the Arabs in Israel is the main problem facing the State of Israel: "The main problem, the obstacle, is the Arabs of Israel. The problem of the Arabs of Israel is more profound, acute and complex than the Palestinian problem. The separation in my view also includes them. When I speak about territorial exchanges, I am also talking about exchanges of population."[51]

Conclusion

In the latest elections, the extreme right in Israel won an unprecedented achievement. This change is profound, comprehensive and reflects deep processes in Israeli society and politics. Israel is undergoing profound social changes, such as the rise of the exclusive importance of the religious Jews, the Mizrahim, the Russians and the settlers as forces that opposed the model the labour movement tried to forge in Israel. These forces, for various reasons, tend to support the right and, in fact, constitute the human infrastructure for its ascent and for its potential growth in the future. The 'Israel' that established the labour movement is in deep crisis and steadily disappearing.

In addition to these social processes, a number of factors have led to the intensification of the sense of crisis in Israeli society, including the development of an overall situation of "a nation under siege." This model is known from other cases in the past, such as the experience of a number of European countries between the two world wars. In this case, Israel—on both levels, among the public and the leadership—is not managing to cope with a number of fundamental challenges such as the Iranian nuclear force, the success of Hezbollah in the Second Lebanon War, the Palestinians who comprise about half of the population that Israel controls, the Palestinians in Israel who are raising, by their elites, an explicit demand to transform Israel into a bi-national state, and the problems between different groups in the Jewish society. All this comprises the background for the Israeli search for possible solutions, including increased support for the extreme right and the longing for charismatic leadership to save Israel from its deteriorating situation, for many Israelis Yisrael Beiteinu party headed by Lieberman was the answer to their fears in the last Israeli Knesset election.

The unprecedented rise of the extreme right raises basic questions that must be addressed, including the possible nature of Israel's approach to the Palestinian problem in general and the status of Israel's Palestinian citizens in particular, the state of relations between Israel and the international community in the event that the right adopts political measures in line with its political platform, and the question of how the Jews will contend internally with the challenges posed by the extreme right. Will the deteriorating relations lead to fateful decisions or will Israel and the Israelis continue to ascribe greater importance to national unity than to an anti-democratic and even fascist situation, which is now developing in the state?

Notes

1. In principal we distinguish between the 'right' whose empowerment can be traced to the 1960s and the 'extreme right' that was empowered due to recent developments which will be presented later.
2. Ehud Sprinzak, *The Ascendance of Israel's Radical Right* (New York: Oxford University Press, 1991); Ehud Sprinzak, "Extremism and Violence in Israel: The Crisis of Messianic Politics," *Annals of the American Academy of Political and Social Science 555* (1998), 114–26.
3. C. Mudde, "Right Wing Extremism Analyzed," *European Journal of Political Research* 1995, 27(2): 203–24; C. Mudde, "The war of Words Defining the Extreme Right Party Family," *West European Politics* 1996, 19(2): 225–48; C. Mudde, "The single-issue party thesis: [European] extreme right parties and the immigration issue," *West European Politics* 1999, 22(3): 182–97; C. Mudde, *The Ideology of the Extreme Right,* (Manchester: Manchester University Press, 2000).
4. Ami Pedahzur, *The Extreme Rightist Parties in Israel, From Growth to Decline?* (Tel Aviv: Tel Aviv University; 2000); Ami Pedahzur, "Supporting Condition for the survival of the Extreme Right-Wing Parties in Israel," *Mediterranean Politics*, 2000, Vol. 5 (3): 1-30.
5. Ami Pedahzur and Arie Perliger, "An Alternative Approach for Defining the Boundaries of 'Party Families': Examples from the Israeli Extreme Right-Wing Party Scene," *Australian Journal of Political Science*, 2004. Vol. 39 (2), 285–305.
6. Ami Pedahzur, "Supporting Condition for the survival of the Extreme Right-Wing Parties in Israel," *Mediterranean Politics*, 2000, vol. 5 (3): 1-30.
7. Herbert Kitschelt, *The Radical Right in Western Europe: A Comparative Analysis,* (Michigan: University of Michigan Press, 1997).
8. Asher Arian, *Politics in Israel: The Second Republic* (Washington: CQ Press, 2005).
9. "The Population of Immigrants from the Former Soviet Union: Demographic Trends 1990-2001," *Central Bureau of Statistics* (Jerusalem, 2006), 11.
10. "The Demographic Situation in Israel 2005," *Central Bureau of Statistics* (Jerusalem, 2007), 16.

11. "Demographic, Economic and Social Characteristics of the Ultra-Orthodox Population in Israel," *Central Bureau of Statistics* (Jerusalem: 2004).
12. *Statistical Annual for Judea and Samaria, 2007 & 2008,* (Ariel: Ariel University Centre, 2008).
13. Sammy Smooha, *Index of Arab-Jewish Relations 2004* (Haifa: The Jewish-Arab Centre, University of Haifa, 2005); Asher Arian, Pazit Ben-Nun and Barnea Shlomit, *The 2004 Israeli Democracy Index*, (Jerusalem: The Israel Democracy Institute, 2004); Nimr Sultani, *Israel and the Palestinian Minority 2004* (Haifa: Mada al-Carmel, 2005).
14. Sha?ul Ari?eli, Doubi Schwartz, Hadas Tagari, *Injustice and Folly: On the Proposals to Cede Arab Localities from Israel to Palestine* (Jerusalem: Floersheimer Institute for Policy Studies, 2006).
15. Asher Arian, David Nachmias, Doron Navot and Danielle Shani, *The 2003 Israeli Democracy Index,* (Jerusalem: The Israel Democracy Institute, 2003).
16. Asher Arian, Pazit Ben-Nun and Barnea Shlomit, *The 2004 Israeli Democracy Index*, (Jerusalem: The Israel Democracy Institute, 2004).
17. Asher Arian, Nir Atmor and Yael Hadar, *The 2006 Israeli Democracy Index*, (Jerusalem: The Israel Democracy Institute, 2006).
18. Sammy Smooha, *Index of Arab-Jewish Relations 2006* (Haifa: University of Haifa, 2006).
19. Sammy Smooha, *Index of Arab-Jewish Relations 2007* (Haifa: University of Haifa, 2007).
20. *Haaretz*, June 21, 2004.
21. Nimr Sultani, *Israel and the Palestinian Minority 2004* (Haifa: Mada al-Carmel, 2005), 27.
22. For more on the legislative efforts aimed against the Arab citizenry, see Nimr Sultani, *Citizens without Citizenship* (Haifa: Mada al-Carmel, 2003); Nimr Sultani, *Israel and the Palestinian Minority 2004* (Haifa: Mada al-Carmel, 2005); Mtanes Shihadeh, *Israel and the Palestinian Minority 2005* (Haifa: Mada al-Carmel, 2006).
23. For detailed results, see: http:// www.knesset.gov.il/elections18/heb/Results/main_results.aspx
24. Asher Arian and Michal Shamir, "On Mistaking a Dominant Party in a Dealigning System," in *The Elections in Israel – 2003*, eds. Asher Arian and Michal Shamir (Jerusalem: The Israel Democracy Institute, 2004), 27-52.
25. Ami Pedahzur, *The Extreme Rightist Parties in Israel, From Growth to Decline?* (Tel Aviv: Tel Aviv University; 2000)
26. Ehud Sprinzak, *Between Extra-parliamentary Protest and Terror: Political Violence in Israel* (Jerusalem: Jerusalem Institute for Israel Studies, 1995).
27. The Kach movement was established by Rabbi Mier Kahane who was

the first political leader who did not hesitate to emphasize aspects of ethnic exclusivism and adamantly demanded that all Palestinians, regardless of citizenship, be expelled, by all methods, including using force. For details see Yoav Peled, "Ethnic Exclusionism in the periphery: The Case of Oriental Jews in Israeli development Towns," *Ethnic and Racial Studies,* 13, 345-367, 1990; also see Ehud Sprinzak, "The Emergence of the Israeli Radical Right," *Comparative Politics*, vol. 21, no. 2, 1989, 171-192.

28. *Haaretz,* February 4, 2009.
29. Ibid.
30. Zvi Gitelman and Ken Goldstein, "The 'Russian Revolution' in Israeli Politics," in *The Elections in Israel – 1999*, eds. Asher Arian and Michal Shamir (Jerusalem: The Israel Democracy Institute, 2001), 203-232.
31. Ibid, 221
32. Zvi Gitelman and Ken Goldstein, "From 'Russians' to Israelis?" in *The Elections in Israel – 2003*, eds. Asher Arian and Michal Shamir (Jerusalem: The Israel Democracy Institute 2004), 351.
33. *Haaretz*, February 10, 2009.
34. Ala Hilehel, *October 2008 in Akka (Acre) - Course of Events* (Acre: Akka Residents Coalition, 2008).
35. *Haaretz*, February 3, 2009
36. *Haaretz*, February 2, 2009.
37. Ibid.
38. *Haaretz*, February 6, 2009.
39. *Haaretz*, February 3, 2009
40. *Haaretz*, February 6, 2009.
41. *Haaretz,* February 6, 2009.
42. http://beytenu.org.il/147/2674/article.html
43. Yoav Peled and Gershon Shafir, *Being Israel: The Dynamics of Multiple Citizenship* (Tel Aviv: Tel Aviv University, 2005).
44. *Haaretz*, February 3, 2009.
45. *Yedioth Ahronoth*, February 10, 2009.
46. *Haaretz*, February 11, 2009.
47. *Haaretz,* January 20, 2009.
48. Ibid.
49. http://beytenu.org.il/147/2674/article.html
50. Sha?ul Ari?eli, Doubi Schwartz, Hadas Tagari, *Injustice and Folly: On the Proposals to Cede Arab Localities from Israel to Palestine* (Jerusalem: Floersheimer Institute for Policy Studies, 2006).
51. Nimr Sultani, *Israel and the Palestinian Minority 2004*, (Haifa: Mada al-Carmel, 2005), 66; see also Avigdor Lieberman, *My Truth* (Tel Aviv: Maariv Publishing, 2004).

References

Dani Filc and Lebel Uri, "The Post-Oslo Israeli Populist Radical Right in Comparative Perspective: Leadership, Voter Characteristics and Political Discourse," *Mediterranean Politics*, 2005 10(1), 85-97.

As'ad Ghanem, "Israel and the 'Danger of Demography," in *Where Now for Palestine?,* ed. Jamil Hilal (London: Zed books, 2006), 98-116.

As'ad Ghanem and Mustafa Mohanad," Coping with the Nakba - The Palestinians in Israel and the 'Future Vision' as a Collective Agenda," *Israeli Studies Forum*, 2009, 25 (1).

Danny Gutwein, "How the left elevated Lieberman," *Haaretz,* February 12, 2009, B2.

Amal Jamal, "The Political Ethos of Palestinian Citizens of Israel: Critical Reading in the Future Vision Documents," *Israeli Studies Forum*, 2008, 23 (2), 3-28.

Baruch Kimmerling, *Politicide: Sharon's War Against the Palestinians* (London: Verso, 2003).

Dov Waxman and Peleg Ilan, "Neither Ethnocracy nor Bi-Nationalism: In Search of the Middle Ground," *Israeli Studies Forum*, 2008, 23 (2), 55-73.

WEST ASIA

4

West Asia as an Area Study: An Imperative of Our Time

Gulshan Dietl

The paper proposes to trace a brief history of the evolution of area studies, locate West Asia within it and underscore the absolute criticality of pursuing the same—for its own sake and for a broader understanding of the world.

Area Studies: An Overview

The concept of Area Studies is as old as the political science itself. Aristotle compared the political institutions of Greek city-states, and treated them as an area of his study. The ancient world travellers like Huen Sang or Al-Biruni were the scholars and practitioners of the area studies. The area studies are driven by human curiosity about others. It is only by knowing others that one knows oneself. The self and the other are perpetually defined with reference to each other.

It was only during the World War II, however, that the area studies acquired the form and status as a distinct discipline. The United States did not join the War till the very last phase of it. The country prepared for that certain eventuality, nonetheless. Apart from military readiness, it was necessary to understand the languages, geographies, economies, politics, and cultures of the far flung areas to cope with the military demands of a constantly expanding battle-theatre. The Pentagon ran short, intensive crash courses were conducted for its officers to prepare them for black, brown and yellow worlds before sending them "out there" to fight and win. The area studies specialists—like many new rich, who shy away from acknowledging their poor, not-so-presentable parents—do not dwell upon this phase in the evolution of their discipline. The fact remains that the Pentagon is the cradle of modern area studies.

After the War, the ideological differences between the United States and the Soviet Union resulted in the scholarly specialisation on each other's military capabilities, political institutions and philosophies. The same ideological differences led both the Super Powers towards a quest for "winning the hearts and minds of the peoples" in Asia, Africa and Latin America—and with this, the area studies on both sides gradually became universal. The Post-War "cultural diplomacy" also necessitated training in foreign languages and area studies for the diplomatic and foreign administrative personnel. The Columbia and the Harvard Universities in the US, the School of Oriental and African Studies in Britain, as well as the Soviet Academy of Sciences in the Soviet Union—all of them started special area studies programmes.

Thus, the modern rebirth of area studies is a direct result of strategic needs of the governments during the World War II and after that subsequently the Cold War period. Interestingly, the terms like the Middle East or the Far East are not so much the geographical terms as they are the convenient strategic terms. They became popular after the Allies' war-time usage of the terms like the Middle East Command, the Middle East Supply Centre etc. The term Third World also owes its origin to the Cold War terminology of the East and West or the First and Second Worlds.

The basic concept of Area Studies is that the people of a definable geographic sector, acting in their society and their environment offer an appropriate unit for scholarly attention.[1] The area is a cluster of countries which because of certain policy preoccupations, geographic propinquity, or common problems and theoretic interests, can be studied as a unit. Its political and economic systems, languages, history, culture and psychology are jointly explored by representatives of various disciplines in universities and government departments.[2]

Once recognised as a distinct and independent scholarly pursuit, the Area Studies were expected to yield raw-material for comparison and theorisation on the political processes, institutions and philosophies. A four-step process was chalked out that would lead to an enriching of social sciences: first, data-collection about foreign areas through field-research; second, comparison of similar problems; third, development of new theories based on these; and four, influence of these theories on identifying fresh problems for investigation. An expansion and enrichment of social sciences was, therefore, expected as a positive outcome.

That did not happen though. Very often, the Area Studies specialists remained just that—the Area Studies specialists. An area remained a mid-level rung of analysis, that is, something between country studies and the global analyses. It was a canvass that the scholars chose themselves for their academic scrutiny. Once the area was selected, they either worked on it in all its facets or they tested a theme within the confines of their areas. A systematic analytical framework was not developed and comparative perspectives were not evolved. The end result has been culturally contextualised knowledge on the one hand and overarching macro theories on the other. A synergy between the two has occurred every now and then—not always though.

In nineteen seventies, the regional systems theories rechristened the area as a region—almost as a fresh departure point. They conceived the regions as patterns of relations or interactions within a geographic area that exhibit a particular degree of regularity and intensity to the extent that a change in one point in the system affects other points. "Regional Security Complexes", identified by Barry Buzan, focussed exclusively on the security interdependencies among the regional states. A regional security complex is a set of states continually affected by the one or more security externalities that emanate from a distinct geographic area. In such a complex, the members are so interrelated in terms of their security that actions by any member, and significant security-related developments within any member, have a major impact on the others. The existing regional security complexes often have one or more significant great powers able to project force over distance that are not physically located in the geographic area that is the locus of the complex.

Geography defines the physical area from which security externalities radiate, not the set of states that may be members of a regional security complex.[3] The security complexes, if they move in the positive direction, evolve into security communities.

The change in the ground realities, no doubt, provided the necessary impetus toward the development in regional studies. The Cold War had internationalised many otherwise local conflicts. As local combatants appealed for assistance from outside powers and as one Super Power, fearing the other may provide decisive aid and thereby gain political advantage was driven to assist him, and as a consequence the local conflicts were inexorably pulled into and lost within the Cold War. At the same time, each Super Power sought to restrain the conflict in its own sphere of influence, out of the concern that an open dispute would create an opportunity for the other to intervene. In an area of competition, it circled the other in a dangerous dance of mutual restraint. By whatever means, the Super Powers did exercise a degree of management to counteract the increased regional tensions, keep conflicts within bounds, and occasionally even impose settlements.[4]

There has been less scrutiny of the region as an economic unit—as compared to its scrutiny as a politico-security unit. One of the reasons for it may well be that the trend toward economic regionalism is perhaps more mixed than the trend toward security regionalism. In the international economy, globalisation and regionalisation appear to be pushing states in conflicting directions. In a rare exercise of economic regionalism, a study defines the Red Sea as a sub-region, and concludes that the smaller economies demonstrate a high degree of trade dependence on the larger economies, whereas the larger and stronger economies of Egypt, Saudi Arabia and Israel are linked more to the global economy than to the regional system. Their economic interaction with their neighbours, while useful for political and strategic reasons, does not currently make a great contribution to their development and prospects for growth.[5]

With the end of the Cold War, the mosaic of regions on the global map has undergone a qualitative change. The sole Super Power is a member of every region however are they defined and delimited. Security interdependencies, economic integration and political interactions are necessarily larger than regional in scope. The wars are fought, interventions are made and regimes changed by an external member/members of the region. Geographically distant extra-regional powers have rendered the regions weak and porous.

The emerging global architecture towards multi-polarity may yet make the regions more relevant.

West Asia as an Area

Outside of India, West Asia is known as the Middle East. Many other countries and regions are named by their conquerors and discoverers. The term "Middle East", however, is unique in two senses. One, it originated in military lexicon during the Wartime. The Middle East Command and the Middle East Supply Centre were formed in Cairo during the World War I. Two, it was London-centric.

From within the region, two alternative nomenclatures have been offered, though not widely accepted. Ali Eddin Hillal Dessouki and Jamil Matar have coined the term the "Arab regional order" to replace the term "Middle East", which according to them is a "euphemism for secure spheres of influence". The argument they advance in support of their nomenclature is that the term Middle East "tears up the Arab homeland as a distinct unit since it has always included non-Arab states" and that the term Arab regional order serves better as a key for the analysis of "interactions among Arab states with their neighbours and with the international system at large".[6] These are precisely the arguments that could be addressed from the other end, that is, the new term overemphasises the Arab character of the region whilst downplaying the presence of three non-Arab states—Iran, Turkey and Israel. It also diminishes the non-Arab people among the population of the geographic entity, even though they are numerically greater.

A second alternative term offered is the "Islamic World". In principle, it includes all land in which the Muslims live and aims at Islamic revival and unity. Used as such, it would expand the definition of the region much beyond its present confines. Additionally, it would do so in a highly selective fashion and would challenge the legitimacy of the territorial states. The "Islamic World" would take in the Arab states, Iran and Turkey, but leave out Israel. Would the states with the largest Muslim populations like Indonesia, India, and Bangladesh be in or out in this scheme of things?

For our purposes, West Asia denotes all the Arab countries in Asia plus Turkey, Iran and Israel comprising roughly twenty-five states and nearly half a billion people. It has been the birthplace of three monotheistic religions; Islam, Christianity and Judaism. It has been the location of three ancient civilisations; Pharaonic, Mesopotamian and Dilmun.

Geographically, it is at the tri-junction of Asian, African and European continents. Geologically, it contains some sixty-five percent of global oil reserves and forty percent of global gas reserves.

West Asia: Major Issues

Domestic Situation: Non-participatory politics, rentier economy, youth-bulge demography, disempowered women and ethnic/ sectarian strife characterise the processes within the political entities. The patriarchal social order and rentier economies have impacted domestic political systems. Between and among the states, territorial disputes flare up every once in a while. The state itself is fragile. The supra-state ideologies of Arabism and Islamism as also the sub-state sectarian and ethnic affiliations render it vulnerable.

Energy: The vast stocks of oil and gas have not been unmitigated blessings. Unlike other aspects of non-traditional security, energy security has been very closely linked with military security. Very often, it is the powerful state consumers seeking to preserve an uninterrupted supply of energy at an affordable price, who threaten and use military force. At times, it is individuals and groups within the energy-producing countries seeking to resist energy-driven foreign interventions, which disrupt the supplies. The energy-military nexus is at its peak in the present circumstances, mainly in Iraq but also in the energy-rich West Asia.

Nuclear: The central issues in the Non-proliferation Treaty are three: disarmament, non-proliferation and peaceful application of nuclear energy. It is a grand bargain between the nuclear haves who would assist the non-nuclear parties with their civilian nuclear programmes and move towards a nuclear disarmament among themselves. In return, the nuclear have-nots will agree not to develop nuclear weapons. That bargain has not worked. The Nuclear Five are blatantly in violation of Article One. The US and France have supplied nuclear know-how to Israel and China has done the same to Pakistan. Today, the nuclear card has whipped up the nationalist feelings in Iran. The US and Israel have been hinting at surgical strikes at the Iranian nuclear assets. The UN has imposed four sets of increasingly tighter sanctions to stop or slow down the Iranian nuclear programme.

External Intervention: The region has had an enduring fascination for the Empire Builders since the time immemorial—from Alexander, Caesar and Napoleon all the way to George Bush. Since the World War II, many of the US Presidential Doctrines have been West Asia-specific: the Truman Doctrine, the Eisenhower Doctrine, the Nixon Doctrine, the Carter Doctrine and the Bush Doctrine. The re-flagging and escorting of Kuwaiti oil tankers in the late eighties was the biggest projection of US power after its withdrawal from Vietnam. The meticulously assembled coalition during the Gulf War in 1991 and a unilateral attack on Iraq in 2003 followed. The war on terrorism is directed at, though not confined to, West Asia. Today, West Asia is the most highly penetrated region in the world. Most of its problems can be traced to this circumstance.

The Palestine Conflict: The Israeli military occupation of the Palestinian land is an abiding source of problems in the region. Israel claims a legal right to statehood on the basis of the United Nations General Assembly resolution 181 of November 1947. That resolution envisioned an independent state of Israel, an independent Arab state and an international city of Jerusalem. Only the first of its provisions has been realised to date. In fact, Israel occupied 78 percent of the Palestinian land in a war in 1948 and the rest of the 22 percent in a war in 1967.

Since 1993, a peace process has been limping along over the fate of the latter 22 percent of the land. Since the Israeli withdrawal from the Gaza strip in August 2005, the peace process is in the formaldehyde. The Israeli settlers from there are being relocated in the West Bank. The Gaza remains a crowded prison exposed to air strikes and military incursions. On the West Bank, a wall is being erected, which may take in as much as forty-three percent of the Occupied West Bank, leaving it deeply sliced and its people separated from their farms and villages.

West Asia as an Area Study

The major issues identified above are relevant within West Asia and much beyond it. The foremost among them is the issue of Palestine. As stated by Edward Said, it is not just a Palestine cause, or an Arab cause, it is a global moral cause. Apart from its normative aspects, its historical, legal and geopolitical aspects must never be lost sight of. The world must not be allowed to forget or turn a Solomon's eye to it.

Energy, terrorism, non-proliferation and democracy are critical issues to the world peace and well being. Terrorism and the War on Terror are considered priority items on the global agenda. An uninterrupted supply of oil and gas at a reasonable price is a major concern in the national capitals. The global acceptance of Israeli monopoly over the nuclear weapons in the region and the global pressure on Iran not to develop a civilian nuclear capability defies logic. And the fourth wave of democracy is finally reaching the West Asian shores—belatedly but ferociously.

There have been more wars fought in West Asia since the World War II than anywhere else. There have been state to state wars, wars between a state and a non-state actor, asymmetrical wars and proxy wars. And also the wars imposed from outside. The United States is militarily engaged in three armed conflicts at present—in Afghanistan, Iraq and Libya. In Iraq alone, it has cost the US Treasury a staggering sum of three trillion dollars.[7] What is the explanation for this inexplicable phenomenon?

Besides active military engagements at present, the US has been energetically constructing several large scale permanent bases. The US military presence in them during normal times and the US military involvement during war times would seek to shape and keep the region according to US preferences. At the United Nations, it has cast an overwhelming number of vetoes on the issues related to the region, more specifically the Arab-Israel issues. The US diplomacy and the UN weaknesses constitute an entire field of exploration in itself.

The sum total of US actions in the region can be visualised as a second coming of imperialism. The pretensions this time around are the same as at the first coming—the White Man's burden to civilise, modernise and democratise the natives. Deepak Lal, a proud defender of the American project, is emphatic in suggesting that "The primary task of a pax Americana must be to find ways to create a new order in the Middle East. ... It is accusingly said by many that any such rearrangement of the status quo would be an act of imperialism and would largely be motivated by the desire to control Middle Eastern oil. But far from being objectionable, imperialism is precisely what is needed to restore order in the Middle East".[8]

On the other hand, West Asia has witnessed a genuine revolution that resisted the US Empire and its local potentates. John Foran, one of the foremost theorists of the revolution, prefers to call the 20th century the age of the revolution. He asserts that except for the Soviet Revolution at the very beginning of the 20th century and the revolutions in East Europe towards the end of the 20th century, most of the revolutions in the 20th century happened in the Third World countries. He singles out five revolutions and calls them social revolutions in the aftermath of which the social and political changes reinforced each other in a mutually consolidating way. These are the real revolutions, according to him. Iran was one of them, Nicaragua, Mexico, Cuba and China being the other four.[9]

Conclusion

It is only though an understanding of West Asia that one could begin to scratch the surface of these intractable problems.

As mentioned earlier, it was in Pentagon that the modern discipline of Area Studies was born. It was an American exercise in "know your enemy". During the Cold War, the American scholars studying the Soviet Union and the Soviet scholars studying the United States were rated high—not just as academics but also as having policy influence. They were considered the best and the brightest. They were in the universities and—through the revolving doors—in the corridors of power and back in the academia.

Today, the highly-rated and influential scholars are located in the centres of "Middle East" studies. West Asia is the other that defines the self. "Know your enemy" all over again.

It is, therefore, an imperative that West Asia receives an objective and honest scholarly scrutiny, unencumbered by extraneous considerations or calculations.

NOTES

1. Bryce Wood, "Area Studies," in *International Encyclopaedia of Social Sciences*, ed. David Sills (New York: Macmillan and the Free Press, 1968), vol. 1, 401.
2. Roy C. Macridis, "A Survey of the Field of Comparative Government," in *Comparative Politics: A Reader*, eds. Harry Eckstein and David J. Apter (New York: The Free Press, 1963), 46.
3. David A. Lake and Patrick M. Morgan, "The New Regionalism in Security Affairs," in *Regional Orders: Building Security in a New World*, eds. David A. Lake and Patrick M. Morgan (University Park: Pennsylvania State University Press, 1997), 12.
4. Ibid, 4.
5. Emma Murphy, "Trade and Transport around the Red Sea: Prospects for Regional Tendencies" (abstract presented at the International Conference on Borders, Orders and Identities of the Muslim World, University of Durham, July 12-14, 2000).
6. A. E. H. Dessouki and G. Mattar, *The Arab Regional System: An Examination of Inter-Arab Political Relation,* Centre for Arab Unity Studies, 1979 (in Arabic), quoted in Abdel Monem Said Aly Abdel Aal, "The Super Powers and the Regional Security in the Middle East," in *Regional Security in the Third World: Case Studies from Southeast Asia and the Middle East*, ed. Mohammed Ayoob (London: Croom Helm, 1986), 197-198.
7. Joseph E. Stiglitz and Linda Bilmes, *The three trillion dollar war: the true cost of the Iraq conflict* (London: Allen Lane, 2008).
8. Deepak Lal, "In Defense of Empires," in *The Imperial Tense: Prospects and Problems of American Empire,* ed. Andrew Bacevich (Chicago: Ivan Dee, 2003).
9. John Foran, *Taking Power: On the Origins of Third World Revolutions* v(Cambridge University Press, 2005).

5

The United States and West Asia

Michael C. Hudson

For an American Middle East specialist recently transplanted to Singapore, it is dis-"orienting" (so to speak) to be looking at the Middle East from the "other" side, and to listen in on the debates in Asia over how to label and indeed conceptualize this region. On the strategic level Americans, as heirs to the Anglo-French hegemony, have thought of the region as a part of the Western security architecture designed to contain Soviet communism, secure oil resources, and protect Israel (which is widely regarded as an organic extension of "Western civilization"). On the intellectual level Americans see the Middle East as inextricably shaped by Western "modernization"—economic and social, intellectual and ideological, political and strategic. Asia, on the other hand, from an American perspective, seems disconnected. While most Americans may not be aware of certain historic trade and religious linkages between the Middle East and Asia, but even those that are probably regard them as quite tenuous compared to the ties that bind the West to the Middle East.

We are all becoming aware of long-term global strategic economic shifts that are fostering convergences between Asia and the Middle East. But it is curious that from both the Asian side and the Middle Eastern side there is some confusion and growing debate over nomenclature. Technically, the Middle East is mostly in Asia, although this ignores the fact that most of Egypt (the largest Middle Eastern country) is in Africa and that growing Arab communal awareness now requires the inclusion of the rest of North Africa in this area. One must note as well that Turkey uneasily balances its claim to be European with its renewed sense of Middle Eastern-Islamic but not necessarily "Asian" identity. But while it may be more or less in Asia it apparently is not of Asia. A small example may underline the point: at a recent major conference in Singapore called "Asian Interconnections" the organizers were disappointed that there were hardly any submissions from the "Asian" Middle East; and the Asian scholarly community seemed tacitly to assume that the real Asia goes no farther than the Indian subcontinent.

As for Middle Easterners themselves, from my unscientific observation, I have never heard an inhabitant of this nomenclaturally contested area, when asked "Who (or what) are you?" reply "Ana sharqalawsati" ("I am Middle Eastern"). More likely he or she will say "I am an Arab" or "I am Egyptian" or "I am Muslim". Middle Eastern intellectuals of my acquaintance bridle at the term "Middle East" which they correctly associate with a Western imperial point of view. But as "Asia rises" on the Middle Eastern horizon I am already hearing those same intellectuals complaining that they don't care to be defined as "West Asia". Who wants to be defined by adjectives like "middle," or "west"? The nouns are not much better: what is "the East" and what, for them, is "Asia"? World Bank acronyms like "the MENA region" are no better.

1. What's in a Name?

That said; let us turn to the subject at hand. How does the United States, and how do Americans, define, frame, and understand this region? First, for reasons mentioned above, the term "West Asia" as an alternative to the much more familiar "Middle East" is not much understood or used. But the "Middle East" itself has taken various shapes over the past century or so, both as a strategic and cultural concept.[1]

From the strategic perspective the starting point is the work of Captain Alfred Thayer Mahan, the influential theorist of sea power, who in 1902 coined the term "Middle East" and defined it roughly as a broad stretch of land and water from Suez to Singapore—an area he considered strategically vital for Great Britain and its empire.

This is definitely not the Middle East that Americans understand today; but, curiously, it may be coming back (albeit under another name) as strategic concept driven by economic globalization and the gradual rise of India and China as great powers in an increasingly multipolar world. Robert D. Kaplan, for one, argues that the Indian Ocean is becoming a new focal point of geopolitical competition.[2]

Mahan's term was congruent with, if not inspired by, Britain's strategic worldview at the end of the 19th century: the Near East was the shrinking Ottoman Empire—essentially the Balkans, Anatolia and Turkey's Arab possessions and Egypt; Mahan's Middle East was the bridge to the Far East of Southeast Asia and Australasia. Gradually the term "Near East" lost currency in Whitehall and the Middle East was used to designate post-World War I Turkey, Egypt, the eastern Arab world, Iran, and in some formulations parts of the Indian subcontinent and Central Asia. The United States, gradually emerging as a global power, followed strategically in Britain's footsteps. In the post-World War II period, while the State Department experimented with several administrative models (at one point an assistant secretary boasted that he was responsible for an area from Marrakesh to Bangladesh), a certain consensus may have been represented by the new Washington-based Middle East Institute (with its strong ties to the State and Defence Departments and the oil companies), which launched *The Middle East Journal* in 1947 with a map generously defining the region from Morocco across Arab North Africa, dipping down into the Sudan, Ethiopia and Somaliland, and leaping eastward beyond Iran to include Afghanistan, Muslim Central Asia, Pakistan, and India. By 2005, however, the Institute modified its map to exclude India and the Horn of Africa while expanding farther into the Caucasus and Central Asia. For its part the Central Intelligence Agency has established an office of Near Eastern and South Asian affairs since 1975 which includes all of the Arab world, Iran, Pakistan, Afghanistan, India and Bangladesh (yet excluding Turkey), while conceding that "the Near East" and "South Asia" are different regions.

For Americans the region has also been defined in cultural terms. During the 19th century the popular imagination was galvanized by Protestant Christian missionaries to the "Holy Land" who produced a great quantity of religious-travel books. And of course there was great interest in converting the Muslims, who were portrayed in exotic "Orientalist" terms. Mark Twain's *The Innocents Abroad*, while satirizing naïve American travellers, paints a largely negative picture of the natives of the Middle East. While Edward Said's classic *Orientalism* has largely demolished the ahistorical and pejorative depiction of the Middle Eastern "natives" for the academic community, the American public, fed by Orientalist stereotyping from Hollywood and in the mass media, still perceives the Middle Easterners as "others" who need to be approached with caution.

One might ask whether to Americans the term "Oriental" applies to Asians as well as Middle Easterners, and I think the answer is no. America's encounter with the Middle Eastern "Orient" starts from an Atlantic standpoint, mediated through Europe and the Mediterranean. The "Holy Land" is home to three monotheistic faiths, even if to many people Muslims don't quite fit into the "Judeo-Christian" civilization. And there is the widespread perception of a beleaguered Israel ("people like us") trying to survive in a world of murderous, intolerant, devious, sexually predatory, lazy adherents to a threatening religion—Islam. America's encounter with Asia is Pacific-oriented, with a history of Asian immigration to our West Coast, our imperial adventures in Hawaii and the Philippines, our war in the Pacific against Japan, later the Korean and Vietnam wars, and today the preoccupation with China, a huge trade and finance, and even cultural connection. Asians from Japan, China, South Korea, Southeast Asia and India are not stereotyped any longer in the negative way that many Americans view Middle Eastern "Orientals."

Perhaps the most authoritative culturally-inspired delineation is the area of scholarly competence spelled out in 1970 by The Middle East Studies Association (MESA), the largest scholarly organization of its kind. It includes the Arab countries from the seventh century to modern times, plus Afghanistan, Iran, Israel, Pakistan and Turkey, as well as Spain, Southeastern Europe, and the Soviet Union for periods when they were under Middle Eastern influence. However, in 2005 MESA expanded its domain to include Muslim South Asia as well as opening its journal to articles on minority Muslim or Middle Eastern communities outside the traditional geographical boundaries.

So despite a rough conception among Americans that the Middle East essentially includes the Arab world of North Africa and the Middle East, Turkey, Israel, and Iran it is interesting to note that both for strategic and cultural reasons there has been an eastward push. Modern communications, economic globalization, migration patterns and trans-national, trans-local ideological movements seem to be moving the "Middle East's" centre of gravity farther eastward—in a sense going back to Mahan's 1902 conception. It is not surprising, then, that the Middle East Institute in Singapore sponsors lectures on Afghanistan and encourages research on economic, ideological and strategic convergences between the traditional Middle East (especially the Gulf) and "heartland" Asia. So far, however, my impression is that neither Middle Easterners nor Asians are feeling that they are together part of some larger Asian community.

2. The History of US Involvement in the Region

The story of American involvement in "West Asia" begins at the very beginning of the American republic.[3] The enlightenment liberal ideology of America's founding fathers (an erudite group of gentlemen) fostered the discourse of exceptionalism: America was "a city on a hill" whose destiny was to be better than the old powers of Europe. This impulse was entirely consistent with a deep Christian religiosity that drove a missionary movement to bring Christ to the misguided people of the Middle East and, indeed, of Asia. As direct religious conversion proved very difficult (especially in the Muslim world), these missionaries turned to education as a way to uplift the natives. For around a century American missionaries, educators, and merchants comprised the link between the US and the Middle East. To be sure there were frictions, of which the most important were the skirmishes fought between the fledgling US navy and the Barbary pirates—privateers operating out of the North African ports of Tripoli and Algiers, mainly, who were preying on American and British merchant shipping. But on the whole the 19th century was, in retrospect, a "golden age" in US-

Middle East relations. Today the American University of Beirut and the American University in Cairo stand as enduring monuments to a fruitful "people-to-people" relationship.

If the 19th and early 20th centuries were a "golden age" in US-Middle Eastern relationships it was because the US was not yet an emergent Great Power and it had no vital interests in the region. All this changed after the First World War. First, the US felt that it had to have a share of the vast quantities of oil being discovered in the Gulf—Iran, Iraq, and most importantly Saudi Arabia. So it worked to insist on a share of the concession agreements hitherto dominated by European-based oil companies. Second, during the inter-war period the question of the Jews, emerging Zionism, and Palestine intruded into the American domestic political scene, so that by 1948 the Administration of President Harry Truman threw American support behind the fledgling Jewish state. Shortly thereafter America's third major vital interest in the region crystallized as the Cold War broke out between the US and the Soviet Union. While the main zone of confrontation was Eastern and Central Europe, the Middle East quickly came to figure in the equation. Washington feared both the ideological challenge of Communism and the strategic challenge of the Soviet state to Western domination of the oil fields around the Gulf. The "Middle East" most important to the US, then, was the Palestine area, the oil-rich Gulf and the "northern tier" countries (Turkey, Iran, Pakistan) which would theoretically serve as a barrier to Soviet ambitions. But because of the rise of pan-Arab nationalism, America's Middle East was actually considerably broader. The Egyptian revolution that brought down the monarchy in 1952 signalled the rise of a charismatic nationalist officer, Gamal Abdel Nasser, who was able to project influence across the Arab world, from Morocco to Yemen. Nasser naturally championed the Palestinian cause against US-supported Israel; and the Soviet Union saw an opportunity to cultivate Arab opinion by also weighing in on the Palestinian side. For Washington the entire region from the Atlantic to the Gulf, plus the "northern tier" countries constituted a zone of competition with the Soviet Union. America's growing involvement in Asia from the 1950s through the 1970s was understood as an entirely different and mostly unrelated theatre of activity. The late 1960s saw the triumph of Israel in the 1967 "Six-Day War" and the eclipse of pan-Arab nationalism. It seemed as if America's three main interests—oil, Israel, and anti-Soviet containment, were being successfully protected. In Asia, by contrast, the whole post-World War II period was marked by setbacks: first, the "loss" of China to the Communists; then Korea; then the Vietnam War—a grievous defeat with fundamental domestic ramifications. In American eyes there were no significant linkages between these two distinct regional sub-systems: the Middle East more or less ended in Iran and perhaps Pakistan and Asia more or less ended in Southeast Asia. But in the 1990s things began to change, prompting American officials to confront signs of convergence between these hitherto separate regions.

3. Contemporary Involvements

America's Middle East has been expanding eastward into Asia proper since the late 1970s. The year 1979 is a useful starting point. Five events that year profoundly changed the regional system and shifted America's priorities. The first was the peace treaty between Egypt and Israel, which it was thought (too optimistically) would open the way for resolution of the interminable Arab-Israeli conflict. American attention was drawn farther eastward by the four other upheavals of 1979.

Farther to the east, in Iran, an even greater challenge had emerged. Iran's pro-American leader, Shah Muhammad Reza Pahlavi, had been forced to leave Tehran in January 1979, and the Islamic Revolution was fully under way a month later. The coming-to-power of Ayatollah Rouhollah Khomeini undermined a 'pillar' of US security interests in the region dating back to the early 1950s. Decades of Iranian popular resentment at the American intervention erupted, symbolized by the seizure of the American embassy on 4 November 1979, and the holding of US hostages for over a year. The hostage crisis traumatized American public opinion and contributed to the defeat of President Carter in 1980. It also reignited negative perceptions of Islam among Americans and of America among Muslims. During the first phase of the Islamic Revolution from 1979 until Khomeini's death in 1989 the Iranian regime waged an ideological campaign against the traditional (and pro-American) oil monarchies on the Arab side of the Gulf. So, when Iraq's leader, Saddam Hussein, decided to attack Iran in 1980, he was able to count on financial support from the Arab gulf regimes and military intelligence support from the United States. But the Iranian challenge extended well beyond the Gulf: Tehran also helped develop and support the Islamist militant organization Hezbollah in Lebanon, elements of which were responsible for the murder and kidnapping of Americans and other Westerners, and for the disastrous bombings of the US embassy and Marine barracks in Beirut.

As if the 'fall' of Iran were not enough of a problem for Washington, the Soviet invasion of Afghanistan in December 1979 triggered fears among some American strategists that the Soviets would use Afghanistan as a springboard for extending their influence into the Persian Gulf area and perhaps beyond. Such fears revealed ignorance of geography and topography as well as of Soviet capabilities. To prevent a new Russian march towards warmer waters, the Carter administration warned that Washington regarded the Gulf (on the Arab side at least) as vital to American interests, and it also undertook an energetic effort, with the support of Pakistan and Saudi Arabia, to roll back the Soviets in Afghanistan by mobilizing Islamist militants called mujahidin. Armed with American shoulder-launched Stinger missiles, the mujahidin were able to inflict severe damage on Soviet military helicopters and entrap their ground forces in the rugged Afghan terrain. But the defeat of the Soviets, which led in part to the collapse of the Soviet Union itself, not only failed to bring security to Afghanistan and the Gulf area; it also left a chaotic 'failed state' of warring Islamist militias. Worse still, with the battle against the Soviets won many thousands of these militants, who had come from Arab and other Muslim states, left Afghanistan in a mood to promote puritanical Islamic reform by force of arms against the American presence in their home countries.

Meanwhile, an ominous event had occurred on the Arab side of the Gulf: on November 20, 1979 a well-organized group of Islamist radicals seized the Grand Mosque in Mecca—the holiest site in the Islamic world. It took three weeks for the Saudi authorities, reportedly with help from French commandos, to quell the rebellion. While the militants were executed forthwith, the incident suggested that the Saudi regime—notwithstanding its conservative Islamic credentials—was vulnerable to Islamist opposition. Around the same time there was an uprising by Shi'i militants, perhaps inspired by the Iranian revolution, in Saudi Arabia's heavily Shi'i eastern province. It was also quickly put down. But these events presaged the emergence of a much more serious threat from other religious dissidents in the 1990s. Shi'i protest, mostly from Saudis abroad, reappeared. More significantly, a small number of radical salafi clerics, both inside and outside the Kingdom, began to agitate for reforms of what they saw as a regime corrupted by Western—especially American—influences. Among these activists was a young man from one of Saudi Arabia's most successful business families whose name was Osama bin Laden. Finally, on 16 July 1979 Saddam Hussein consolidated his personal authority in Iraq upon the resignation of President Ahmad Hassan Al-Bakr, a decade after their Ba'th nationalist party had taken power in a military coup. At this juncture Iraq was well placed to assume the leadership of the Arab world, especially since Egypt had been ostracized after President Anwar Sadat had signed the peace treaty with Israel without having achieved any gains for the Palestinians. Iraq's abundant oil revenues were actually used quite effectively to build the country's socio-economic infrastructure as well as support an ambitious military programme. Saddam Hussein's ambition and ignorance of political realities led him to go to war with Khomeini's Iran. In Washington the Reagan administration (some of whose officials resurfaced in the administration of George W. Bush), attempting to play Realpolitik, offered military intelligence assistance to Saddam in the hope of preventing an Iranian takeover of the vulnerable pro-Western Arab oil monarchies; but it was also pleased that the war lasted a long time (from 1980 to 1988), giving Iraq a pyrrhic victory and weakening both of these big and unfriendly Gulf countries. But Washington's satisfaction was short lived, for in 1990 Iraq suddenly overran its small and oil-rich neighbour Kuwait. The administration of George H.W. Bush refused to countenance Saddam's takeover, and US armed forces led an international coalition to expel the Iraqis from Kuwait. It was the first—but not the last—major US military action in the Arab world.

Following Iraq's expulsion, for just over a decade Washington sought to maintain Gulf security through a strategy of 'dual containment' of both Iraq and Iran, with the emphasis on pervasive and debilitating sanctions against Iraq intended to diminish its military threat potential against its neighbours and to eliminate its capabilities to produce or deploy weapons of mass destruction.

Perhaps the most important and disturbing development in the period after 1979 was the emergence of a new kind of phenomenon, one that was not readily comprehensible in terms of traditional state-oriented approaches to international relations. This was the phenomenon of transnational Islamist networks prepared to utilize terrorist tactics against the United States especially and the West in general. Although its political discourse was couched in Islamic terms, it took two fairly distinct forms. The dominant one was Shi'i-driven movements sponsored by the revolutionary Iranian regime. It manifested itself most dramatically in Lebanon, which was in the throes of a civil war. Americans and other Westerners were taken hostage in Beirut, and some were killed. Groups affiliated with what would become Hezbollah twice bombed the American embassy and, in a suicide truck bombing, killed 241 US Marines on a peacekeeping mission in 1983. Other such incidents occurred outside Lebanon.[4]

The second strand, marked by fundamentalist salafi and Wahhabi Sunni Islam, traced its lineage to the anti-colonial struggles between the two world wars but then was overshadowed by the relatively secular nationalist movements of the 1950s and 1960s. Inspired by radical offshoots from the Egyptian Muslim Brotherhood, it resurfaced in Egypt and Syria in the 1970s and was responsible for the assassination of Egypt's President Anwar Sadat in 1980 and a bloody confrontation with the Syrian regime of President Hafiz al-Asad in the late 1970s and early 1980s. Islamist organizations also began to play a major role in Palestinian politics. In the 1990s Islamist movements successfully mobilized large numbers of followers in many Arab countries, leading in some cases, such as Algeria, Tunisia, and Egypt, to violent confrontations. The movement assumed a transnational aspect, inasmuch as its leading ideologues, such as the Sudanese activist Dr. Hassan al-Turabi, sought to build a loose, broad-based front across the entire Arab world. All these developments were deeply worrying to American officials, because of the anti-Israeli and anti-American tone of their discourse.

Meanwhile, a new strand of networked Islamist terrorism—exemplified by fundamentalist Sunnis like Osama bin Laden, was gaining ground. In the 1990s there were several terrorist attacks on American targets, including one on New York's World Trade Centre in 1993. In the late 1990s American personnel in Saudi Arabia and embassies in Africa were also targeted. Although increasingly aware of this serious new threat, the Clinton administration responded in a relatively ad hoc manner.[5] After the bombing of American embassies in Kenya and Tanzania in 1996, President Clinton ordered limited military strikes in Afghanistan and on what turned out to be a legitimate pharmaceutical factory in Khartoum. Following the bombing of American military facilities in Saudi Arabia in 1998, administration officials became even more alarmed but were unable to fashion an effective counter-terrorism strategy. And President Clinton made no military response at all to the bomb attack on the USS Cole in Aden harbour in October 2000, just a few months before the end of his term. To its credit, Washington undertook efforts to reassure the Islamic world that America was not anti-Islamic. For example, American Muslim leaders were invited to the White House for the iftar (fast-breaking meal) in the month of Ramadan. But such gestures were mainly symbolic, and America's attitude towards rising political Islam remained ambivalent at best, if not hostile.

The American response to the devastating attacks in New York and Washington on September 11, 2001 was encapsulated in the term 'global war on terror'. Now, with a vengeance, the US undertook to respond to an enemy whose field of action erased all traditional areas, like the Middle East or West Asia. This was a global enemy with networks apparently extending from the Arab Middle East in all directions—Central, South and Southeast Asia, Europe, and Africa. Eschewing a law-enforcement strategy, the administration advanced a military approach, focusing initially on regime change in Afghanistan, where the Taliban rulers had given sanctuary and protection to Osama bin Laden and al-Qa'ida. Washington deployed its intelligence agencies to hunt down radical Islamist terrorists around the world and established special prisons in Guantanamo Bay, Cuba, and elsewhere to detain 'enemy combatants' indefinitely without charges or legal recourse. Next the administration turned its attention to a long-time objective of the neo-conservatives—invading and occupying Iraq. What had been expected to be a quick military and political operation turned out to be a swamp. One consequence of America's misadventure in Iraq was the strengthening of Iran's influence throughout the region, and the administration came to view 'Iranian-sponsored terrorism' (Shi'i) along with al-Qa'ida and related terrorist groups (Sunni) as an existential threat to America and its Middle Eastern allies—Israel, Egypt, Saudi Arabia, and Jordan among others. As Bush's second term came to an end, even his supporters were conceding that the 'global war on terrorism' was far from over. And the manner in which Washington was prosecuting this 'war' was creating intense and widespread hostility toward the USA throughout the Arab and Muslim world.

President Barack Obama made a special effort to reach out to the Muslim world when he took office in 2009 with an eloquent speech at Cairo University. But his administration continued to take vigorous military and counterterrorism steps against Al-Qa'ida and its allies, especially in Afghanistan and Pakistan. When Obama announced in May 2011 that American Special Forces had killed Bin Laden in Pakistan he took pains to warn Americans that the struggle against Al-Qa'ida and transnational radical Islam was not over, and it remained to be seen whether Al-Qa'ida's far flung affiliates would have the ability to exact revenge.

Conclusion

The Middle East, observed the French scholar Gilles Kepel, is best defined as a zone of crises rather than by traditional geographic conventions.[6] By that reckoning the region, from the American strategic point of view, has expanded mostly eastward during the past decades. The US and its allies invaded Afghanistan in pursuit of Bin Laden and the Taliban. The US invaded Iraq partly in pursuit of Al-Qa'ida and partly to protect Israel. The US launched the "global war on terror" and sent its operatives to many countries in Asia, Africa and Europe in pursuit of the elusive enemy. Today the

US deploys over 5,000 military personnel, nearly half of them "afloat", across the traditional Middle East and Indian Ocean area. Bahrain is the home of the Fifth Fleet. The US Central Forces Command (CENTCOM) has delineated Egypt, the Fertile Crescent and Arabian Peninsula, along with Sudan, Ethiopia, Kenya, Iran, Afghanistan and Kazakhstan as within its "area of responsibility." Since 2002 the CIA Directorate of Intelligence has maintained an office covering the area from Morocco to India.

In the meantime, new information technologies like satellite television and social media seem to be hastening the construction or reconstruction of communal identities, and in the Arab world the wave of protests that began in December 2010 seem to facilitate the spreading of common concerns. American officials recognize this: for example, in 2010 General David Petreaus told a Congressional committee that "due to perceptions of US favouritism for Israel" the ongoing conflict in Palestine was having a negative effect on US interests in CENTCOM's area of responsibility.[7]

Over the long term will shifts in the global balance of power lead to a redefinition of the Middle East? It is now commonplace to speak of China and India as emergent players in this region—today mainly in economic terms, but tomorrow perhaps in strategic terms as well. At the same time perceptions of the decline of the United States, while perhaps premature, are beginning to raise questions of whether "America's Middle East"—a domain of American hegemony stretching over a zone of conflicts from the Atlantic to the Indian Ocean—may give way to "Asia's West Asia."

Notes

1. See Charles Kurtzmann, "Cross-Regional Approaches to Middle East Studies: Constructing and Deconstructing a Region," *Middle East Studies Association Bulletin,* 41/1/2007, 24-29. For a comprehensive set of maps depicting different conceptions of the region see also the Carolina Centre for the Study of the Middle East and Muslim Civilizations at http://mideast.unc.edu/where/mahan-1902.shtml.
2. Robert D Kaplan, "Centre Stage for the 21st Century: Power Plays in the Indian Ocean," *Foreign Affairs,* March/April 2009.

3. See Ussama Makdisi, *Faith Misplaced: The Broken Promises of U.S.-Arab Relations, 1820-2010* (New York: Public Affairs Press, 2010). See also James A Field, *America and the Mediterranean World, 1776-1882* (Princeton: Princeton University Press, 1969).
4. See J. K. Cooley, *Unholy Wars: Afghanistan, America and International Terrorism* (London: Pluto Press, 2002).
5. F. A. Gerges, *America and Political Islam: Clash of Cultures or Clash of Interests?* (Cambridge: Cambridge University Press, 1999).
6. Prof. Gilles Kepel, University of Paris, comments made at the seminar at the Singapore Ministry of Foreign Affairs, jointly organized by the Middle East Institute, National University of Singapore and Sciences-Po, January 14, 2011
7. General David Petreaus, testimony before the US Senate Armed Services Committee, March 16, 2010.

6

South Asia, West Asia, and the Centre: Edge Dialectics of Modern Islamic Networking

Itzchak Weismann

In the Muslim geographical imagination West Asia has always been regarded as the centre. This is all too natural considering that the Arabian Peninsula was the cradle of Islam: there the Prophet received the call and thence he and his followers spread the new faith far and wide. The image has been sustained throughout the ages in the consciousness of the *umma* by the direction of the daily prayer to Mecca (*qibla*), the annual pilgrimage (*hajj*), and the privileged status accorded everywhere to the alleged descendents of the Prophet (*sada*, *ashraf*). It seems to have become further strengthened in premodern times through such institutions as al-Azhar University in Cairo, which attracted students from all over the Muslim world; the Ottoman Sultanate-Caliphate with its increasing claims to universality; and the Arabian puritan Wahhabi creed, which became a generic term for militant fundamentalist Islam.

In this essay I argue that in modern times in some significant respects South Asia has come to fill the place of West Asia as a centre in the rapidly expanding and ramifying networking of the Muslim *umma*. A relative latecomer to the community of believers, and long "at its edge," from the seventeenth century on, and more evidently in the nineteenth and twentieth centuries, Indian Islam became a major source of influence for West Asia and other Muslim regions in both terms of innovative religious trends of thought and in new modes of organization. The rise of South Asia as a major Islamic centre took place in the setting of the political and cultural crisis of Indian Islam—from the disintegration of the Mughal Empire to British rule to partition, and was facilitated by the improvement of the means of communication. Since the crisis was earlier and deeper than that in the Ottoman Empire and its successor states, the Indian men of religion were quicker and more profound in responding to the challenge and in formulating new ideas and institutions to overcome it. These would later be adopted and adapted in West Asia and other parts of the Muslim world.

The essay begins with a brief theoretical discussion in the Muslim context of the major components of my conceptual framework: the centre, the edge, and the network. I then demonstrate the influence exerted in the past two centuries by each of the major Islamic trends and movements of South Asia on their counterparts outside India. Lastly I discuss the reasons for the ascendency of South Asia over West Asia in the modern era and offer some preliminary observations on the reconfiguration being undergone by the worldwide Islamic network under the impact of globalization.

Centre, Edge, and Network

Two pertinent tropes have been proposed in recent scholarship in the field of Islamic studies for analyzing socio-spatial developments in modern Islamic civilization in general,[1] and in relations between South Asia and West Asia in particular. One of them is Richard Bulliet's notion of the edge, which "exists wherever people make the decision to cross a social boundary and join the Muslim community." Bulliet suggests a view of Islam from the edge complementary to its habitual view from the centre. While Islamic history is normally portrayed as an outgrowth from the single nucleus of the Arabian Caliphate, he maintains, a view from the edge highlights the role of the great variety of non-Arab localities in the formation of the universal *umma*.[2] Bulliet's work itself focuses on the medieval Iranian world. Of particular relevance for us is his description of the creation in the eleventh and twelfth centuries of a diaspora of Iranian scholars, who in the wake of the political crisis of the Iranian cities at the time moved to the Iraqi centre and brought with them the new educational institution of the *madrasa*. Iranian scholars were also prominent in the cultural opening up of two new regions of Muslim settlement at that time: Anatolia and India.[3]

South Asian Islam would in due course follow Iran in this dialectical movement from the edge to the centre. After its conquest at the beginning of the thirteenth century, conversion to Islam took place especially at the edge of the edge—on the Subcontinent's peripheries of Punjab, Bengal and the Deccan. As beautifully demonstrated by Richard Easton, this was a centuries-long process, primarily conducted by *pirs* through local shrines.[4] Still, it was never complete, and Muslims have never constituted more than a quarter of the total population. Even at the heyday of Muslim rule in India the Mughal Emperors—at the centre of the edge—opted for inclusion regarding the Hindu majority, a policy that occasionally drew the criticism of the more orthodox men of religion.[5] The disintegration of the Mughal Empire early in the eighteenth century and the subsequent fall of India at the hands of the British led such men of religion to turn their energies to finding ways to resuscitate and reform Islam.[6] Unlike medieval Iran, they generally did not leave India, but they had ample means at hand to spread their innovative ideas and institutions outside the Subcontinent through travel and print, and today through the Internet.[7]

This brings us to our second conceptual tool, the network. In their study of Islamic renewal and reform movements of the (long) eighteenth century John Voll and Nehemia Levtzion identified an underlying informal network, which "consisted of scholars who had a variety of contacts with each other, sharing educational experiences." The centre of this ramified network was at Mecca and Medina, where everybody converged for the hajj, but most teachers, who taught a combination of Hadith, Law and Sufi studies, came from the "middle ring" of North Africa, Kurdistan and India, while their most dramatic impact was felt in the conversion and jihad movements of the "outer ring," in West Africa and South East Asia.[8] Taking a broader view, Miriam Cooke and Bruce Lawrence regard Muslim networks—academic, commercial or aesthetic—as a key term for highlighting transnational connections, interactions and exchanges within the global Muslim community, the *umma*. For them this is the only prism through which one can gain a perspective on how over the past fifteen centuries diverse groups of Muslims have contested and rearticulated what it means to be Muslim.[9]

As elsewhere, in South Asia Islam has progressively been integrated down the ages into the network of the global Muslim *umma*. This process gained momentum from the sixteenth century on, not least due to the introduction of Western navigation to the Arabian Sea;[10] by the eighteenth century Indian ulama-Sufis had acquired a prominent place in the Islam-wide scholarly network of revival and reform movements. Prototypical figures were Shah Waliullah, the Muhaddith of Delhi, who returned from the hajj to become the forefather of practically all subsequent religious reform trends in India;[11] Murtada al-Zabidi, the itinerant who eventually proved a major inspiration for religious reform in Egypt;[12] and Hayah al-Sindhi, who stayed in Mecca and is principally remembered as a teacher of Ibn 'Abd al-Wahhab.[13] These were to be followed by the trends and movements that are the subject of this article: the Naqshbandi Sufi brotherhood and the Modernist and Ahl-i hadith trends in the course of the nineteenth century, and the ideological formulations of Abu al-Hasan 'Ali al-Nadwi and Abu A'la al-Mawdudi in the twentieth.

The dialectics of centre and edge and the concept of network together indicate that the flow of religious ideas and institutions between South Asia and West Asia in the past two centuries has by no means been unidirectional; perhaps it was also largely unconscious. The enfeebled Indian Muslims looked more than ever westward for spiritual and political support, as the Khilafat movement in particular shows.[14] But at the same time, the desire to stem the rapidly deteriorating situation at home forced the Indian scholars to exert themselves and take the lead. Their influence on the course of Modern Islam has been crucial and continues so to this day.

South Asian Origins of Modern Islamic Reform

In this section I present five of the major Islamic reform trends of the nineteenth and twentieth centuries: Sufi reformism, Islamic modernism, Islamic fundamentalism, the Islamic movement, and radical Islam. Each emerged at a different point in time, so together they represent the trajectory of modern Islamic reform. Each transpired at the "centre" of West Asia and spread to other parts of the Muslim world to acquire universal validity. Yet each in turn was first formulated in South Asia as a reflection of the experiences and agonies of its Muslim community.

Sufi Reformism

The Khalidi Sufi brotherhood represents a culminating point in the Islamic revival and reform network of the (long) eighteenth century on the one hand, and an early manifestation of modern Islamic activism on the other. The brotherhood derives its name from its founder, Diya' al-Din Khalid (1776-1827), who combined Sufi experience with profound religious learning. Khalid spread his way in the early decades of the nineteenth century in the Ottoman lands, in the rural and tribal areas of his native Kurdistan and in Anatolia and the major cities of Baghdad, Damascus, and finally Istanbul.[15] His deputies in the Ottoman capital gave their support to Sultan Mahmud II's efforts to resuscitate and modernize the Ottoman state in face of the gathering European menace and backed the elimination of the moribund Janissary corps that stood in the way of his reforms.[16]

The Khalidiyya was an offshoot of the major Naqshbandi Sufi brotherhood, which throughout history distinguished itself in its orthodoxy and activism.[17] The Naqshbandiyya was founded in the fourteenth century in Bukhara, spreading from there in the following centuries to all corners of Asia. One of its main branches, the Mujaddidiyya, was established in India at the height of Mughal rule by Shaykh Ahmad Sirhindi, who regarded himself as the renovator (*mujaddid*) of the second Muslim millennium. Sirhindi forged a fresh combination between the mystic path and the Law, and emphasized the duty of the Sufi shaykh to guide the ruler on the path of the shari'a.[18] His successors during the Mughal decline were forced to abandon the endeavour to influence rulers, and focused their attention on protecting the integrity of the Muslim community. Under British rule they also began to seek sustenance by spreading the brotherhood outside India.[19]

Khalid's brotherhood derived directly from the Mujaddidi branch of the Naqshbandiyya. His attention was drawn to India while on the hajj in 1806, the year the Wahhabis took over Mecca. He himself tells us how while he was praying in the Ka'aba a mysterious man pointed that direction out to him, and told him that only there would he find enlightenment. Departing to India three years later, Khalid landed in Delhi, where the leading contemporary Mujaddidi master in the city, Shah Ghulam 'Ali, is said to have been waiting for him. Khalid trod the path in the short span of a year, at whose end the master conferred on him "full and absolute succession" and instructed him to spread the path in Western Asia.[20]

Khalid's work in the eastern provinces of the Ottoman Empire and the influence exerted by his deputies on the upper echelons in the capital attest that he was faithful to Ghulam 'Ali's instructions and to the Naqshbandi-Mujaddidi legacy in general. The innovations he introduced were practically designed to enhance them in the different circumstances of the Ottoman Empire. These lay mainly in the organizational field and included a concentrated form of retreat (*khalwa*) which allowed him to ordain swiftly a large number of disciples, a spiritual focus on his figure (*rabita*) designed to consolidate the new offshoot under his central leadership, and closing the door during the *dhikr* session (*ghalq al-bab*) which secured its exclusivity. Together, these innovations helped Khalid turn his brotherhood into an effective socio-religious movement, whose aim was to support the Ottoman government's effort to modernize while keeping it within the bounds of the shari'a in the service of the Muslim community.[21]

Islamic Modernism

The Modernist trend consists of elite religious reformers who advocate the adaptation of Islam to modern ideas and institutions in Western terms. Its emergence in the latter half of the nineteenth century is generally associated with the names of Jamal al-Din al-Afghani and his once disciple Muhammad 'Abduh. Afghani (1838-

1897),[22] who was actually an Iranian Shi'ite, arrived in Istanbul in 1869 and two years later moved to Egypt. He gathered around him a group of admiring disciples, to whom he imparted Islamic philosophy and the principles of rational *ijtihad*. He also encouraged them to engage in politics.[23] In 1884 Afghani together with 'Abduh (1849-1905) established in Paris the short-lived but influential Pan-Islamic journal *al-'Urwa al-Wuthqa* (The Firm Bond). Thereafter the two parted ways. The conspirator Afghani wandered around the European capitals in search of allies, and ended up in Istanbul in the service of Sultan Abdülhamid II. 'Abduh spent the rest of the 1880s in Beirut, until he was allowed to return to Egypt. Accommodating himself to British rule, he was appointed chief mufti and rector of al-Azhar to promote religious reform.[24]

South Asia was a major source for Afghani's revolutionary ideas. His first stay in India was in the late 1850s, in the formative period of his late teens. It was here that Afghani became acquainted with modern Western science—perhaps even to the point of becoming sceptical about religion. Here, in the wake of the Great Revolt of 1857, to which he was apparently witness, he also developed fierce opposition to British imperial rule. Of most relevance for us, during this stay of several years in India Afghani must have learned of the reformist ideas of Shah Waliullah and his successors in favour of practicing *ijtihad*, an evolutionary scheme of history, and *jihad* in alliance with outside Muslim rulers.[25]

Afghani's second visit to India was likewise in a crucial point in his life, between 1879 and 1882, just before the publication of *al-'Urwa al-Wuthqa*. During this period he became acquainted with the ideas of Sir Sayyid Ahmad Khan, the leading Islamic modernist in South Asia, and wrote his major work, "The Refutation of the Materialists," against him. Ahmad Khan (1817-1898) sought rapprochement between the British rulers of India and their Muslim subjects, reinterpreted the Qur'an in light of modern reason and science, and advocated the adoption through *ijtihad* of Western ideals and standards.[26] As Keddie has shown, Afghani's motivation in writing the refutation was not Ahmad Khan's religious ideas as such; it was rather the recognition that religion is a major tool for political mobilization and his opposition to the Indian reformer's cooperation with the British.[27]

Jamal al-Din al-Afghani's West Asian career—in Egypt and as a global revolutionary—shows clear marks of his Indian experiences. Its peculiar features lay in the adaptation of the principles of Shah Waliullah and Sayyid Ahmad Khan to the global struggle against Western, particularly British, imperialism.[28] Afghani shared the Indian modernists' reformist ideas about a return to the Qur'an and *sunna*, the practice of *ijtihad*, and Islam's compatibility with reason and science. For him, however, religious reform was secondary to the primary goal of political unification and strengthening of the Muslim *umma*. In Egypt of the 1870s Afghani spread a liberal interpretation of Islam as a means to face the encroaching West. In the 1880s and 1890s he absorbed himself in the Pan-Islamic idea and in scheming, which ultimately led him to the court of Sultan Abdülhamid. About this time, ironically, his erstwhile disciple Muhammad 'Abduh decided to follow Ahmad Khan's political legacy and cooperate with British rule in Egypt.'[29]

Islamic Fundamentalism

The modern Salafi trend, which closely followed Islamic fundamentalism, and like it initially consisted of elite reformers, espoused a return to the fundamental principles of the ancestors of Islam (*al-salaf*) as the mechanism for Islamic modernization. The emergence of the Salafiyya is usually associated with the name of 'Abduh's disciple Rashid Rida (1865-1935), editor of the first major Islamic journal *al-Manar* in Cairo, but its foundations had already been laid by groups of religious reformist intellectuals in the Arab provinces of the late Ottoman Empire. One of the earliest proponents of the new Salafi creed was Nu'man Khayr al-Din al-Alusi (1836-1899) of Baghdad. In 1881 Alusi published a book in defense of the purist medieval thinker Ahmad ibn Taymiyya, in which he censured the popular Sufi practices of seeking the intercession of saints (*tawassul*) and tomb visits (*ziyarat al-qubur*), as well as the juristic practice of blind imitation of past authorities (*taqlid*).[30] His colleagues in Damascus, 'Abd al-Razzaq al-Baytar (1837-1917) and Jamal al-Din al-Qasimi (1866-1914), further elaborated on the harmony of revelation and reason and opposed the divisiveness of the legal schools (*madhhabs*),[31] while in Aleppo

'Abd al-Rahman al-Kawakibi (1849-1902) added a sharp critique of the autocratic Sultan and the subservient conservative ulama, before he escaped to Egypt.[32]

The Salafiyya claims a long pedigree, which passes through the Hanbali School, Ibn Taymiyya, and the Wahhabis. But its modern reformation was triggered by parallel developments in South Asia. The connection was established by Nu'man al-Alusi, who while on a visit to Cairo in 1878 came across the Qur'an exegesis of the Indian Ahl-i Hadith leader Siddiq Hasan Khan. Deeply impressed by its reformist import, Alusi began to correspond with the author, and under such inspiration he undertook to write the defence of Ibn Taymiyya.[33] Like the Islamic Modernist trend, the Ahl-i Hadith movement emerged in India in the wake of the bloody suppression of the Great Revolt of 1857. Its proponents were imbued with the feeling that the end of the world was imminent and sought, albeit with little success, to unite all Muslims by focusing on the norms of the hadith. The Ahl-i Hadith rejected the authority of the four schools of law and all institutional forms of Sufism, which they described as accretions and deviations. Theirs was a rationalist *ijtihad* designed to free Islam of all customs that might seem ridiculous in the eyes of the Western ruling race.[34]

Early modern Salafi thought echoed the ideas of its South Asian counterpart. The ways of Alusi, Qasimi, Kawakibi, and later on Rida differed from those of Hasan Khan and his colleagues in Ahl-i Hadith because of the various circumstances in which each operated. The Indian reformers were allowed a free hand in religious matters by their British rulers; the Arab reformers were subjected to the oppressive regime of Sultan Abdulhamid II in alliance with the conservative ulama and Sufis. Like the Ahl-i Hadith movement, the Salafis thus stressed the need strictly to follow the Qur'an and *sunna*, adopted a rationalist mode of *ijtihad*, and were increasingly opposed to the Sufi brotherhoods and the legal schools. For them, however, these were part of an oppositional standing that they developed toward the modern Muslim government, hence also their resorting to a collective notion of the ancestors (*salaf*) as bearers of the "true" understanding of the scriptures.[35]

The Islamic Movement

The Society of the Muslim Brothers is the most influential popular religious movement in West Asia. It was founded in Egypt in 1928 by the charismatic teacher Hasan al-Banna (1906-1949) to propagate Islam among the oblivious masses (*da'wa*) and to combat British foreign domination (*jihad*). Banna adhered to the Salafis' call to return to the Qur'an and *sunna*, but unlike them he opted for an inclusive approach that set his movement above all parties and embraced all shades of Islamic reform under its banner. By the 1940s the Muslim Brothers was already the largest political organization in Egypt, with branches in other Arab countries. These joined the nationalist struggle to drive out colonial rule while striving to ensure that after victory independent Muslim governments would subscribe to the rules of the shari'a. The outlawing of the Muslim Brothers in Egypt and Banna's assassination by police agents in 1949 left the movement in disarray.[36]

Hasan al-Banna apparently was little aware of the Islamic reformist arena of South Asia when he founded the Society of the Muslim Brothers. There is no indication that he had any knowledge of the popular organizations of the Khilafat movement after World War I[37] or of the more enduring Tabligh-i Jama'at movement which followed it in the 1920s.[38] Only after Banna's demise did an Indian influence become felt on the course of the Muslim Brothers. This was due primarily to the Indian scholar Abu al-Hasan 'Ali al-Nadwi (1914-1999) and to the pseudo-history book *What has the World Lost with the Decline of the Muslims* he had published a few years earlier.[39] As the title indicates, in this work Nadwi accepts the general fundamentalist postulate about the latter-day decline of Islam; but he also describes the ascendency of European civilization as the contemporary parallel of the pre-Islamic era of barbarity (*jahiliyya*), hence concludes that the Muslims, under Arab leadership, must once more assume the role of saviors of humanity and of its guides to the right path.[40]

Abu al-Hasan 'Ali al-Nadwi[41] belonged to the notable family whose members were heads of Nadwat al-Ulama (the Council of Religious Scholars) and directors of its college at Lucknow, positions that he himself would inherit in 1961. These institutions were established in the late nineteenth century to promote unity among Indian religious reformers and enhance the study of Arabic language and culture in India in general.[42] Having in due course joined the Tablighi Jama'at movement, Nadwi undertook in 1951 a one-year tour of the Middle East. He was enthusiastically welcomed by the Muslim Brothers of Egypt and Syria, who, he soon discovered, had read and been much impressed by his book.[43] In 1956 he traveled to Syria again, at the invitation of Mustafa al-Siba'i, leader of the Syrian Muslim Brothers and dean of the newly-founded Shari'a Faculty of the Syrian University in Damascus; and later on contributed regularly to their organ.[44] Nadwi expressed his admiration at the political activism of the Muslim Brothers, which to him seemed to complement the quietist populism of the Tablighi Jama'at. From his Arab comrades' point of view, it was rather the historical analysis that he offered that could give them a new sense of orientation and mission which they had partly lost in those troubled times.

Radical Islam

The radical wing of contemporary Islam consists of the myriad groups that place jihad at the forefront of their action and struggle against foreign powers and indigenous Muslim regimes alike. The Egyptian Sayyid Qutb (1906-1946), the martyred spokesman of the Islamic radicals, joined the Muslim Brothers in 1951, and a year later was appointed head of the *da'wa* section of the movement. The Muslim Brothers were harshly persecuted by the military-authoritarian regime established in Egypt by Jamal 'Abd al-Nasir in 1954, and Qutb himself was detained, tortured, and later executed. In his prison years he composed his radical manifesto, *Ma'alim fi al-tariq* (signposts). The main import of the work is the proposition that contemporary Muslim societies that follow man-made laws instead of the shari'a are in a state of *jahiliyya* since they recognize the sovereignty (*hakimiyya*) of rulers, whom they worship (*'ubudiyya*) rather than God. This sparks an unprecedented urge to create a Muslim vanguard to combat impious governments even before foreign aggressors.[45] Qutb's call was heeded after his death by the Jihad group that assassinated Egyptian president Anwar Sadat, the rebels of Hama in Syria, the leaders of Hamas in Palestine, and eventually al-Qaeda.

The main concepts of Sayyid Qutb's radicalized teaching come, yet again, from South Asia. As we have just seen, the idea of a contemporary *jahiliyya* was developed by Abu al-Hasan 'Ali al-Nadwi, with whom Qutb had ample opportunity to talk during the former's visit to Egypt in 1951.[46] Still, Qutb's inclusion of Muslim societies as part of today's *jahiliyya* and its association with the conceptual pair *hakimiyya* and *'ubudiyya* are borrowed from the work of Nadwi's compatriot, Abu al-A'la al-Mawdudi (1903-1979). Mawdudi was the founder and first leader of the Jama'at-i Islami, the major Islamic movement in India and later Pakistan. Unlike the Muslim Brothers, his was a structured vanguard organization designed to encourage Muslims to embark on an Islamic revolution to re-establish the original exemplary *umma*. Mawdudi was no less a forceful ideologue, one of whose main goals was the political mobilization of Islam.[47] In 1941, the year the Jama'at-i Islami was founded, Mawdudi also published a short book, *The Four Technical Terms in the Qur'an*, with the aim of clarifying the original meaning of the most basic Qura'nic terms as they were understood at the time of Prophet Muhammad. In this work he first introduced the concepts of *hakimiyya* and *'ubudiyya*.[48]

The radical Sayyid Qutb of the late 1950s and 1960s fully adhered to the dichotomous view of societies presented by his South Asian mentor. But the different destiny of Islamic activism in Egypt and Pakistan drove him to go one highly charged step farther. Mawdudi was given ample space to develop his organization and work for the Islamization of independent Pakistan, a process that peaked under the military rule of General Zia ul-Haq from 1977 to 1988.[49] By contrast, Qutb and his comrades languished in prison in Egypt under Colonel Nasser's military regime. Their bitter experiences were mirrored in the articulation of the concepts of *hakimiyya* and *'ubudiyya* with that of *jahiliyya*. For Qutb, the main task of the Islamic vanguard was no longer merely to enhance the "true" religion of the forefathers, but to fight its formidable enemies and rescue it from total destruction.

Why South Asia?

The ascendency of South Asia as a major centre of modern Islamic reform trends may be attributed to a number of factors. One of them is the sheer demographic weight of the Indian Muslims. On the Subcontinent itself Muslims have remained a minority, a fact that fostered an existential fear of being overwhelmed by the unbelieving environment; but in the Muslim world at large they formed the largest concentration. Today about a third of the world Muslim population lives in India, Pakistan, and Bangladesh.[50] Another factor is the great improvement in the means of communication. The spread of European navigation in the Arabian Sea from the sixteenth century on facilitated broader performance of the pilgrimage to the Holy Places in Arabia and enhanced contacts with West Asia in general.[51] The introduction of print during the nineteenth century was closely intertwined with the coeval Muslim religious revival.[52]

Yet as with Iran in the earlier period, it was primarily the political crisis experienced by Indian Muslims from the eighteenth century on that gave this edge community such a central role in the modern network of Islamic reform movements. From the Indian scholars' point of view the disintegration of the Mughal Empire and the subsequent subjection of the country to British colonial rule had nothing to do with Western technological progress and military prowess as such; it was rather the deviation of the Muslims from the path of God that brought such calamities upon them. From this perspective the Indian men of religion set out to analyze the causes of Muslim decline and prescribe the ideological and organizational means for revival. Their "solutions" developed over time with the change of circumstances, while also reflecting the major divisions within their ranks: Sufis and scholars, westernizers and traditionalists, organizers and thinkers, communitarians and statists. Taken together, they represent a remarkable intellectual and organizational effort that through the introduction of new means of communication easily spread to other parts of the Muslim world. As the Ottoman Empire and its Arab provinces and later successor states underwent their own political crises in the face of the encroaching West, their Muslim men of religion had at hand ready solutions, which they then adapted to the specific problems of their own countries.

In the last decades of the twentieth century the informational revolution of "the age of globalization" brought in its wake a tremendous expansion of the networking component in worldwide human society. This amounts to a transplant of the old dialectics of centre and periphery (or edge) into a new one of the global and the local, aptly described through the trope of glocalization.[53] For many contemporary westerners the Muslim image has been shattered by the atrocities of the Taliban in Afghanistan and Pakistan, and even more by the global terrorism of al-Qaeda. Less known is the intellectual activity of moderate Indian Muslim thinkers such Asghar Ali Engineer and Wahiduddin Khan in India itself and in the South Asian diaspora in Britain and elsewhere.[54] Through such liberal thinkers Indian Islam may well continue to play its role as a major centre of modern Islamic reform.

Notes

1. For a broad historical conceptualization of Islam as civilization, also defined as Islamdom, see Marshal G.S. Hodgson, *The Venture of Islam: Conscience and History in a World Civilization* (3 vols. Chicago and London: University of Chicago Press, 1974), 1, 57-60. Hodgson, incidentally, was opposed to the use of the term West Asia, because for him "Asia" was equivalent to the term "Orient."
2. Richard Bulliet, *Islam: The View from the Edge* (New York: Columbia University Press, 1994), 7-9.
3. Ibid, 147-152.
4. Richard Eaton, *Sufis of Bijapur 1300-1700: Social Roles of Sufis in Medieval India* (Princeton: Princeton University Press, 1978); "The Political and Religious Authority of the Shrine of Baba Farid," in Barbara Metcalf (ed.), *Moral Conduct and Authority: The Place of Adab in South Asian Islam* (Berkeley, University of California Press, 1982), 333-356; *The Rise of Islam and the Bengal Frontier, 1204-1760* (Berkeley: University of California Press, 1993).
5. Opposition to the inclusive, syncretistic, religion of Akbar, the actual founder of the Mughal Empire, is usually associated with the arrival on the Subcontinent of the orthodox Naqshbandi brotherhood. See Aziz Ahmad, *Studies in Islamic Culture in the Indian Environment* (Oxford: Oxford University Press, 1964), 167-181.

6. See Barbara D Metcalf, *Islamic Revival in British India: Deoband 1860-1900* (Princeton: Princeton University Press, 1982); Dietrich Reetz, *Islam in the Public Sphere: Religious Groups in India, 1900-1947* (New Delhi: Oxford University Press, 2006).
7. Francis Robinson, "Technology and Religious Change: Islam and the Impact of Print," *Modern Asian Studies* 27 (1993), 229-251.
8. Nehemia Levtzion and John O Voll (eds.), *Eighteenth-Century Renewal and Reform in Islam* (Syracuse: Syracuse University Press, 1987). For criticism concerning the innovation and unity of such a network, see R.S. O'Fahey and Bernd Radtke, "Neo-Sufism Reconsidered," *Der Islam* 70 (1993), 52-87; and Ahmad Dallal, "The Origins and Objectives of Islamic Revivalist Thought, 1750-1850," *Journal of the American Oriental Society* 113 (1993), 341-359.
9. Miriam Cooke and Bruce Lawrence (eds.), *Muslim Networks from Hajj to Hip Hop* (Chapel Hill and London: University of North Carolina Press, 2005), 1-28.
10. Sayyid Athar Abbas Rizvi, *A History of Sufism in India* (New Delhi: Munshiram Manoharlal Publishers, 1983), 2:.319-347.
11. J.M.S. Baljon, *Religious and Political Thought of Shah Wali Allah Dihlawi, 1703-1762* (Leiden: Brill, 1986).
12. Stefan Reichmuth, "Murtada al-Zabidi (d. 1791) in Biographical and Autobiographical Accounts: Glimpses of Islamic Scholarship in the 18th Century," *Die Welt des Islams* 39 (1999), 64-102.
13. John O Voll, "Muhammad Hayya al-Sindi and Muhammad ibn 'Abd al-Wahhab: An analysis of an Intellectual Group in Eighteenth-Century Medina," *Bulletin of the School of Asian and African Studies* 38 (1975), 32-38.
14. Gail Minault, *The Khilafat Movement: Religious Symbolism and Political Mobilization in India* (New York: Columbia University Press, 1982).
15. Butrus Abu-Manneh, *Studies on Islam and the Ottoman Empire in the 19th Century, 1826-1876* (Istanbul: The Isis Press, 2001), 13-22. The first scholar to note Khalid's prominence was Albert H. Hourani in his "Sufism and Modern Islam: Mawlana Khalid and the Naqshbandi Order," *The Emergence of the Modern Middle East* (Berkeley and Los Angeles: University of California Press, 1981), 75-89.
16. Ibid, 46-71.
17. Itzchak Weismann, *The Naqshbandiyya: Orthodoxy and Activism in a Worldwide Sufi Tradition* (London and New York: Routledge, 2007).
18. Yohanan Friedmann, *Shaykh Ahmad Sirhindi: An Outline of His Thought and a Study of His Image in the Eyes of Posterity* (Montreal and London: McGill University Press, 1971).
19. Warren Fusfeld, "The Shaping of Sufi Leadership in Delhi: the Naqshbandiyya- Mujaddidiyya, 1750-1920," (Ph.D. Dissertation, University of Pennsylvania, 1981).
20. Muhammad ibn Sulayman al-Baghdadi, *Al-Hadiqa al-nadiyya fi adab al-*

tariqa al- Naqshbandiyya wa'l-bahja al-Khalidiyya (Cairo: al-Matba'a al-'ilmiyya, 1313/1895), 33-39.

21. Itzchak Weismann, *Taste of Modernity: Sufism, Salafiyya, and Arabism in Late Ottoman Damascus* (Leiden: Brill, 2001), 29-55.
22. The definitive biography is Nikki R. Keddie, *Sayyid Jamal al-Din "al-Afghani": A Political Biography* (Berkeley: University of California Press, 1972).
23. Juan R.I. Cole, "New Perspectives on Sayyid Jamal al-Din al-Afghani in Egypt," in *Iran and Beyond: Essays in Middle Eastern History in Honor of Nikki R. Keddie*, eds. Rudi Matthee and Beth Baron (Costa Mesa CA: Mazda Publishers, 2000).
24. Muhammad Rashid Rida, *Ta'rikh al-ustadh al-imam al-Shaykh Muhammad 'Abduh*, vol. 1 (Cairo: al-Manar, 1931).
25. Keddie, *Sayyid Jamal*, 22-32
26. See Wilfred Cantwell Smith, *Modern Islam in India*, 2nd ed (London: Victor Gollancz, 1946), 15-28.
27. Nikki R. Keddie, *An Islamic Response to Imperialism: Political and Religious Writings of Sayyid Jamal al-Din "al-Afghani," Including Translation of the Refutation of the Materialist from the Original Persian* (Berkeley: University of California Press, 1968), 36-45.
28. Aziz Ahmad, *Studies in Islamic Culture in the Indian Environment* (Oxford: Oxford University Press, 1964), 55-62.
29. Albert Habib Hourani, *Arabic Thought in the Liberal Age 1798-1939* (Oxford: Oxford University Press, 1962), 130-160.
30. Itzchak Weismann, "Genealogies of Fundamentalism: Salafi Discourse in Nineteenth-Century Baghdad," *British Journal of Middle Eastern Studies* 36 (2009), 267-280.
31. David Dean Commins, *Islamic Reform: Politics and Social Change in Late Ottoman Syria* (New York: Oxford University Press, 1990), 65-78.
32. Hourani, *Arabic Thought*, 271-273.
33. See Muhammad Bahjat al-Athari, *A'lam al-'Iraq* (Cairo: al-Matba'a al-salafiyya, 1345 AH), 60-61.
34. Barbara Dali Metcalf, *Islamic Revival in British India: Deoband 1860-1900* (Princeton: Princeton University Press, 1982), 268-296; Claudia Preckel, "Islamische Reform in Indien des 19, Jahrhunderts: Aufstieg und Fall von Muhammad Siddiq Hasan Khan, Nawwab von Bhopal," in *Die Islamische Welt als Netzwerk: Möglichkeiten und Grenzen des Netzwerkansatzes im Islamischen Kontext*, ed. Roman Loimeier (Würzberg: Ergon, 2000), 239-256.
35. Weismann, *Taste of Modernity*, 3.
36. The classic study of the movement is still Richard Mitchell, *The Society of the Muslim Brothers* (London: Oxford University Press, 1969).
37. Gail Minault, *The Khilafat Movement: Religious Symbolism and Political Mobilization in India* (New York: Columbia University Press, 1982).

38. Muhammad Khalid Masud ed., *Travellers in Faith: Studies of the Tablighi Jama'at as a Transnational Islamic Movement for Faith Renewal* (Leiden: Brill, 2000); and the excellent study by Yoginder Sikand, *The Origins and Development of the Tablighi Jama'at* (1920-2000): *A Cross-Country Comparative Study* (New Delhi: Orient Longman, 2002).
39. Emmanuel Sivan, *Radical Islam: Medieval Theology and Modern Politics* (New Haven and London: Yale University Press, 1985) 23.
40. See Abu al-Hasan, 'Ali al-Hasani al-Nadwi', *Madha khasira al-'alam bi-inkhitat al-Muslimin*, 2nd ed. (Lucknow: al-Majma' al-Islami al-'ilmi, 2001).
41. Jan-Peter Hartung, *Viele Wege und ein Ziel: Leben und Wirken von Sayyid Abu l-Hasan 'Ali al-Hasani Nadwi (1914-1999)* (Würzburg: Ergon Verlag, 2004).
42. Metcalf, *Islamic Revival*, 335-347.
43. See Abu al-Hasan 'Ali al-Hasan al-Nadwi', *Mudhakkirat sa'ih fi al-sharq al-'arabi* 2nd ed. (Beirut: Muassasat al-risala, 1975), 26-33, 86-89, 99-103.
44. See Abu al-Hasan, 'Ali al-Hasani al-Nadwi, "Bayni wa-bayna faqid al-Islam al-Ustadh al-Duktur al-Siba'i," *Hadarat al-Islam* 5, 6 (1384/1964), 8-15.
45. Gilles Kepel, *Muslim Extremism in Egypt: The Prophet and Pharaoh* (London: Al-Saqi Books, 1985), 38-59.
46. Nadwi, *Mudhakkirat Sa'ih.*
47. Seyyed Vali Reza Nasr, *The Vanguard of the Islamic Revolution: The Jama'at-i Islami of Pakistan* (Berkeley: University of California Press, 1994).
48. See Abu al-A'la al-Mawdudi, *al-Mustalahat al-arba'a fi al-Qur'an* (numerous editions). Also appeared in English translation as *Four Basic Qur'anic Terms* (Lahore: Islamic Publications, 1979).
49. Seyyed Vali Reza Nasr, *Islamic Leviathan: Islam and the Making of State Power* (New York: Oxford University Press, 2001), 130-157.
50. Yohanan Friedmann , "Islamic Thought in Relation to the Indian Context," in *Islam et Société en Asie du Sud*, ed. Marc Gaborieau (Paris: École des Hautes Études en Sciences Sociales, 1986), 79-80.
51. M.N. Pearson, *Pious Passengers: The Hajj in Earlier Times* (New Delhi: Sterling Publishers, 1994).
52. Francis Robinson, "Technology and Religious Change: Islam and the Impact of Print," *Modern Asian Studies* 27 (1993), 229-251.
53. Roland Robertson, "Globalization: Time – Space and Homogeneity and Heterogeneity," in *Global Modernities,* eds. Mike Featherstone, Scott Lash and Roland Robertson (London: Sage Publications, 1995), 25-44.
54. Yoginder Sikand, *Muslims in India since 1947: Islamic Perspectives on Inter-faith Relations* (London: Routledge, 2004).

7

Politics of Resistance in the GCC States: A Theoretical Framework

Sima Baidya

Defining Resistance

The trajectory of resistance reflects different shades and forms of politics. The word 'resistance' connotes the power to resist or protest against the status quo. Any change to break the status quo can be termed as resistance. Resistance refers to collective action against existing norms or power. The power of collective or unified action makes it a norm in many political systems and becomes an integral part of the system. West Asia is a conflict prone zone. Politics of resistance is not hitherto non-existent. Sporadic outburst of protest or dissent is a regular phenomenon here. This paper would like to highlight, whether resistance politics is an integral part of the system or not. Resistance is a loaded term. Politics of resistance in West Asia does not follow a linear path, more so, in the case of the six Persian Gulf countries or GCC i.e. Gulf Cooperation Council states. Resistance in GCC states take a diverse path. Nature of the economy of these countries is rentier. Persian Gulf polity is rentier-authoritarian in nature. Rentier economy promotes rentier polity. Authoritarian nature of politics gives birth to different kind of state-citizenship relations. It needs to be examined at different levels—whether it is resistance or diffused opposition or only dissent. Small grievances convert into dissent and dissident movements. The term resistance is more specific and used in case of external powers or occupier or aggressor. As is the case always, dilemma or dialectical relations determine the course of its action. Resistance in GCC states works at certain levels. The word 'resistance' originates from the meaning 'to resist'. What is to resist? Resisting the system, which is antithetical or resisting the regime, which is repressive or anti-people. The concept resistance connotes a holistic approach. Several terms, like dissent, oppositional politics, resistance etc. reflect the real situation in Persian Gulf countries. In most of the cases, dissent is the more appropriate term.

Rentier-Authoritarian Nature of the GCC States

All six Gulf Cooperation Council states are rentier states. The term rentier comes from the word 'rent'. All these countries earn their economic wealth from rent. Gulf countries are rich in hydro-carbon resources. Income from the state is from oil extraction. In the literary sense of the term, it is extraction and not production. Hydro-carbon resources cannot be produced or manufactured. If a country or region is endowed with natural hydro-carbon resources, then only it can claim to possess hydro-carbon resources. As a result of extraction, there is no mode of production nor can production relations be constituted. Incipient capitalism and its elements/ components are absent in case of Persian Gulf region.

In the absence of economic capitalism, rentier economy creates a different type of political space or specifically leaves no political space. In the absence of production relations client-patron relations gained momentum and became the rule of the day. To be in power for decades, rulers and regimes create client-patron relations.

Like a welfare economy or more than that these Persian Gulf countries offer diverse sets of social security network. States are the social security provider in the GCC region, ranging from education to marriage to child birth to employment. Basic differences between a welfare state and rentier state reflect in the form of 'tax'. The more appropriate expression of capitalist system vis-à-vis democratic system is 'no tax without representation'. The linkage between economic system and political system is more prominent. Thus, upside down situation is also very much possible.

In the case of the Persian Gulf countries, no taxation and no representation is viable and the norm of the existing political system. A flurry of literature is available on the antithetical relations between oil and democracy. Sometimes, it can be regarded as oil curse instead of oil as a boon.

Existing political relations in the Gulf region reflect the authoritarian nature of politics and democracy deficit. It is not democracy gap, but democracy deficit, which speaks volumes about the state-citizenship relations. Ground reality of these countries reveals that it is basically feudal relations between the ruler and the ruled. Like the monarch/king and subject. Concept of people/citizen to have equal rights in the affairs of the state is not accepted. Citizens are given enough social security to fulfil the vacuum in the political sphere. The Aristotelian epithet, 'Man is a political animal' has never become the first priority. In a sense GCC region differentiates itself from the Third world countries. Vibrant national movements for its independence is absent in the case of Persian Gulf countries. Thus, the bond or thread to unite people against a visible enemy is absent hitherto.

Linkages between Authoritarianism and Protests

Many analysts argued that a decade of activism is very much visible in West Asia since 2000. This new found activism can be attributed to basically three factors, like political protests, political reforms and pressure from external actors for more political reforms.[1] Apart from the external pressure, internal pressure is also mounting in the Persian Gulf region. Authoritarian nature of politics does not institutionalize or legitimize the protest in their political system. In the absence of institutionalization, protests grow inside or underground. In an authoritarian polity, authoritarianism determines the nature of its political protests. Thus, underground political activities or political activities in exile have become prominent. In spite of undercurrents of grievances, in most of the cases protests are different in nature.

Nature of Oppositional Politics

Oppositional politics can be categorized into three types, i.e.:

1. Opposition to the ruler, 2. Opposition to the regime, 3. Opposition to the system.

It is like differential calculus. The question lies, whether it is the existing pattern of oppositional politics in the GCC region or the pattern is something else in the region or opposition politics is a non-existing phenomenon in the Gulf region. Oppositional politics connote an alternative system as well. It is in the same matrix, but two different poles, antagonized to face each other. Oppositional politics proposes directional politics, moves from one direction to another, creating a broadening gap.

So far as the GCC states are concerned, oppositional politics is not articulated in a formal/legal way. Nature of oppositional politics shows, it is not united or articulated against a common enemy.

Precisely, it can be said that oppositional politics is not present or almost non-existent in the system. As systems differ, so does oppositional politics. It would be wrong to hypothesize that no opposition voice comes from any corner of the system. Most of the times, it is not diffused or feeble. In terms of impact, it is less influential. Irrespective of its impact and characteristics, it cannot be denied that 'grievances'—is more important. In most of the cases, it has been observed that grievance crystallizes in the form of dissent to defy something. Dissent is the more appropriate term/concept in this context. Dissent is to defy something and dissent by nature cannot be widespread. And in terms of impact/consequences/effect sometimes may be strong, but limited and diffused within specific time period. Protest is also more appropriate. People might protest against some issue or articulate issues not acceptable to the regime.

Historical Background of Movements in the GCC States

Historical evidence shows that movements [dissent/protests] are not non-existent in the GCC countries. This region has witnessed many protests in all parts without any exception ranging from Saudi Arabia to Oman. There were/are several groups to articulate their views against the regime. Though their aims are diverse, not all the time it is comprehensive or talks about religious goals. e.g. in the context of Bahrain, 'Demonstration is an expression of popular anger at Bahrain's deteriorating economic conditions, specially growing unemployment'. In the absence of a domestic political mechanism dissident movements in exile have grown. Existence of dissident politics in exile proves the denial of political space by the state. Exclusionary politics of the government is responsible for the outgrowth of dissent in exile. Dislocation of politics has taken a different path vis-à-vis different political discourse. In recent years growth of dissent and globalization has enhanced the politics of dissent in exile. Moreover, Arab Spring in the Persian Gulf countries can be considered as a strong reflection of the not so new dissident politics in exile. Some of the groups[2] occupied prominent position in the international sphere as well, as far as their impact is concerned; like Committee for the Defence of Legitimate Rights, Al-Qaida, Movement for Islamic Reform in Arabia, Arabian Peninsula People's Union, Workers' Committee etc. in Saudi Arabia, Jidda Conference etc. in Kuwait, Islamic Front of the Liberation of Bahrain, Article 19 Organization etc. in Bahrain, Popular Front of the Liberation of Oman etc. in Oman.

Current Wave of Protests

Protests sparked off in West Asia and North Africa with the self immolation of Bua-Azizi in Tunisia. Protests spread out like fire. Tunisian President Ben Ali fled the country and the Tunisian protest was followed by the Egyptian uprising. Tahrir square became the symbol of this current movement. The impact of the popular uprising in Egypt was no different from Tunisia. Hosni Mubarak's three decades rule came to an end.

Thereafter, West Asia and North Africa have started witnessing waves of protests all over the region and GCC states are no exception. Though it can be argued, GCC states in comparison with other states have witnessed less protests or battles for change. Certainly oil money is the main reason.[3] But it is not beyond the ring of protests in the region. It has been expected that Persian Gulf region will be witnessing more and more protests in comings days and months. Even Saudi Arabia is not far behind[4].

Bahrain

Bahrain is in flames. Among all six Gulf Cooperation Council countries, Bahrain is really burning. Protests are fierce. The Government had to destroy the Bahraini tower in Pearl round about. Situation is not like Libya, but GCC states/heads of GCC states took security measures. Bahrain is a very important country in the Persian Gulf. Moreover, the United States of America's Fifth Fleet is in Bahrain. As a result of collective decision, Saudi Arabia has sent ground troops in Bahrain. Iran has conveyed its protests and wanted Saudi Arabia to withdraw its troops from Bahrain. Not only the security aspect, but the sectarian Shi'a-Sunni divide has come to the fore. It is not clear, whether actual Shi'a-Sunni divide prevails or it is ascribed identity, projecting itself as Shi'a-Sunni divide, when it could be a popular uprising demanding basic needs. Among GCC states, Bahrain occupies the most prominent position. But other countries cannot escape the heat.

Kuwait

Kuwait is also facing the heat of protest movements. Kuwait reflects the most vibrant political culture. Political behaviour of people is mature and argumentative. Already people are vocal for their socio-political and economic rights. Among all the Persian Gulf countries, Kuwait is the only country where people practice democratic norms. As a political system, it is not democratic, but some unique practices, like, diwaniyaa etc. make Kuwait an argumentative political entity. But there is no reason that the Arab Spring will be out of bounds in this small Gulf country. Kuwait has avoided the Arab Spring in its soil, but is facing its impact in the form of fierce opposition from the parliament, which is unusual in the region.[5] No doubt fear of the Arab Spring has gripped Kuwait. Kuwait banned people from Syria, Pakistan, Afghanistan, Iraq and Iran from entering the country.[6]

Saudi Arabia

The most conservative country Saudi Arabia is not far behind. People have also assembled and given a call to articulate their grievances. Friday prayer could be a symbol of protest, where grievances could be articulated in a large gathering. People in large numbers gathered for Friday prayers and eventually turned into protesters[7]. The

Government has taken altogether different steps. Apart from stopping all the protests by physical means, the Government offered huge sops to its citizens.

Shi'as are the vanguard in the protest movement in Saudi Arabia. In the Saudi system, Shi'as are discriminated a lot. But it would be wrong to analyze that this is only a Shi'a revolt and against the Sunni majority regime. In the current spell of protests, Shi'as and Sunnis are protesting jointly and have called for reforms[8]. The Saudi Arabian youth is more agitated[9] and they derived inspiration from other countries from the region. In the absence of an institutional mechanism to redress the grievances, the Saudi youth is taking a different path. To organize protests, use of technology plays a very important role. With the help of technology, Saudi Arabian protesters are spreading out the protest and have really become bold to articulate their demands and ask for political reform. In the recent petition signed by protesters from almost all walks of life, they have demanded 'a transition to constitutional monarchy, greater accountability in state spending and elections to a council that advises the king'[10].

Oman

This small Gulf state also cannot save itself from the fire of protests. People are vocal and against the regime. In this small Gulf state, protests have not gone so far that the regime's survival will be in immediate danger, but people here are following the same path as the other protesters in the region. Protesters are setting camps outside Government houses in Oman. Their main demand is political reform[11]. And this protest is not limited only to the capital, but it is spreading out in different cities as well. Protest in Oman has also turned violent. At least two people died in the industrial city of Sohar. Their demands are more specific and reflect the sharp division among citizens and foreign people and discrimination against its own people in terms of wages[12]. Protesters also confronted the police directly, which has not been witnessed in recent years in this Gulf kingdom[13].

Main Issues

Reasons behind dissent or protests in the GCC states vary ranging from religious to basic necessities. 'Go back to the basics' or a fundamentalist discourse has gained international recognition after Al-Qaida etc. But many times it has been observed that the modernist approach in terms of defining necessity has come into the picture. Grievances are present in Persian Gulf states. Economic well being does not guarantee equal distribution of wealth as well as power. Tedd Gurr termed this phenomenon as 'relative deprivation'. But other ills of economy are not totally absent in the region. Unemployment is not totally absent.

The involvement or presence of religious element in the movement has always been misunderstood. But the purpose and objectives of these movements are not religious at all. Dissident movements and the issue of religious revivalism are intermingled. More so the usage of the term fundamentalism i.e. go back to the 'basic or book' gains currency. It is difficult to differentiate between the two, i.e. movements with religious nature and dissent against the existing regime. Nevertheless, political aspirations have been articulated through these movements. It might not be Islam per se, but Islam can be used as a political idiom.

Analyzing the recent protest movements, one thing has come out that basic necessities rule the grievances. Rather than religious considerations and ideological orientations, on the one hand, it is economic criteria from deprivation to wage difference to corruption and misappropriation of country's wealth. And, on the other, only economic criterion is not the basis. e.g. in Saudi Arabia, the King is ready to disburse happily billions of dollars to make its citizens happy and in a way to quell the protests. But Saudi protesters are not looking forward to get the sop and not to protest, but they understood freedom and human dignity are more important than a few bucks, of which they don't have any dearth in their own country. It is also surprising that on 19 April, 190 intellectuals across the globe wrote, 'the conduct of some GCC governments in stifling peaceful demands for freedom, justice and democracy'.[14]

Golamreza Vatandoust has articulated the cause, 'the globalized world of information and internet age and the expression of people around the world and citizens have a greater role to play in the Arab Spring. As people demand more accountability, transparency has increased and citizens can no longer tolerate Mokhabarat states'.[15]

Arab Spring is Different

History has witnessed Arab protest movements in the past. There is a debate about the nature of the Arab protest. Many have interpreted this as the phenomenon of social movement. Social movement in the Arab context can be defined as "an instance of claims making as a unit of strategic action in the public sphere that consists of the purposive and public articulation of political demands, calls to action, proposals, criticisms or physical attacks, which actually or potentially affect the interests or integrity of the claimants and/or "other collective actors" (Koopmans *et al.* 2005).[16] Many have argued about the nature of the Arab Spring. As it has happened or has been happening in the West Asian region, many analysts have termed it and made an effort to equate it with Islamic movements. Invariably any movement in the West Asian region can be linked with Islamic values. Sometimes, if not overtly but implicitly any protest can be interpreted as an attack on Arab values that very well can be connected with identity as well.[17] Arab Spring cannot be termed as Islamic movements for the simple reason as Edmund Burke articulated; Islamic movements use Islamic concepts and rhetoric in different political and economic environment.[18] Burke was cautious enough to express other criteria or parameters to judge social movements 'regardless of the cultural idiom in which grievances are expressed.' Thus, loads of criticism against Arab Spring as an Internet Revolution or Twitter Revolution cannot diminish its importance in the political spheres. If Internet Revolution can change the regime of decades, then it should be equated with other strong methods of protests. Recently a study[19] has been done to understand the impact of social media on West Asia. West Asia has the largest number of new face book users. This study has specifically highlighted on three Persian Gulf countries, like, Saudi Arabia, Bahrain and Oman. It shows the calls for protest on Face book with actual demonstration. It has impacted Saudi Arabia by 12.9 per cent, Bahrain by 32 per cent and Oman by

7.8 per cent. Earlier protesters had used information technology to protest against the regime. Persian Gulf states have witnessed 'petition fever' or sending fax as a method of protest long back. But in most of the cases the use of information technology was used in exile politics. And it was considered as a safe way of protest to avoid severe political punishment. Globalization has impacted upon the dissident movements in the GCC states. Use of conventional methods, like, internet, other modern communication systems etc. have become an important tool to mobilize people and consolidate the movements. Dialectical nature of the state-citizenship relation indicates a sharp contrast and is a reflection of the duality. The difference is wide open between the Arab states and the Arab streets.

Implications for GCC States

As well known Sociologist Khalid al-Dakhil commented, 'Saudi Arabia cannot run away from the ripples and ramifications of what is happening in the region'; it has been well accepted that same can be applied to the whole Persian Gulf region. GCC has been playing a very active role in the whole situation. Right from helping Bahrain to mediate even in Yemeni protests. GCC states have invited both the Yemeni Government and the protesters to talks in Saudi Arabia.[20] If it is true, it can be observed as a larger role for GCC than envisioned by the organization itself.

Even if GCC is ready and has been playing a pro-active role, other powers i.e. Iran is also gaining importance in the whole scenario and is turning out to be the most powerful country in the whole equation. And the implications are enormous[21] . Some people have argued that Iranian influence is linked with the Shi'a factor. It could be proved as a fallacy as well. While role of Shi'a factor cannot be denied in West Asian protests, it would be naïve to term it as Shi'a protests. There has been an attempt on the part of the regime to project it as the sectarian divide/clash and hence detrimental to the people of West Asia. Shi'a is minority in the Persian Gulf region except Iran and Bahrain. Thus, like any other minority in any system of the world, face discriminatory treatment. So the Shi'a outburst against the system should be regarded as a normal phenomenon of any political protest. But in all the countries, Shi'as and Sunnis are protesting together and have raised their voice against the regime.

Moreover, it has different implications also, as Persian Gulf states didn't ask for the help of the Western powers and the Western powers also didn't offer unsolicited help. Instead, all GCC countries came together to help Bahrain to overcome the crisis. Even if repressive measures are total and complete, still GCC has not been successful in curtailing the movements.

In other words, it would have been a very difficult situation for all the GCC countries, if they would not have acted collectively. As they themselves are not immune to the situation and political upsurge, it is very much for their benefits, they come forward to help Bahrain and in a way have shown the collective strength to the region or the protesters. GCC is cautious that protests should not spread in their neighbouring countries. At this point of time, situation is really bad for Yemen. Yemen is on the verge of collapse. President Saleh has been injured and there is no respite from the current spell of protests. Though, GCC offered mediation two months back, calling both the government and opposition.[22] But ultimately it is of no use.

Significance of the Current Movement

This is neither a revolution nor revolutionary change. People don't talk about structural changes. People don't talk about structural changes as their main goal. In most of the cases, it is not a leadership driven movement. The world has been witnessing a wave of protests without a recognizable rank of leadership. People are protesting for their basic necessities. The most important recognizable factor is people across any kind of divide or barrier. So, in recent times, strength of the people is absent in the West Asian domain. People as an important political category have never been taken into account as a valid component.

In the recent Arab protests movements, people have come up with their aspirations. It is not important whether these movements are recognized or not, originated from the bottom or grass root level. There was no doubt and no dearth of literature that people were suppressed and oppressed. Citizens as a necessary component have been neglected for decades. Though there should not be any doubt that political role playing on the part of its citizens is absent. It was almost like a feudal political structure, where people were treated more like a subject than a citizen and the ruler plays the role of a guardian and takes care of the people's necessity. Relation between ruler and ruled is not being established on the basis of rights. Thus, uprising of the people is very important and should be taken note of. Arab Spring has left its imprint upon the political soil and would have implications in the years to come.

Notes

1. Oliver Schlumberger, *Debating Arab Authoritarianism: Dynamics and Durability in Non-democratic Regimes* (U.S.A.: Stanford University Press, 2007), 2.
2. Sima Baidya, *Dissent in the Land of Arab* (New Delhi: Academic Excellence, 2007).
3. www.usip.org. Gregory F. Gause III, "Arab Spring: Bahrain and Saudi Arabia," May, 2011.
4. www.jpost.com. Reuters and Oren Kessler, 'Surge in Arab Protests expected in Gulf States,' 03 February 2011.
5. www.au.ibtimes.com. "Political crisis shifts to Kuwait as ruling family is "split," 7 June, 2011.
6. www.syrianemergencytaskforce.org. Joanne Bladd, "Kuwait blacklists Syria nationals," 22 May, 2011.
7. www.boston.com. 12 March, 2011.
8. www.ft.com. "Saudi Protesters stage fresh rallies," Abeer Alam, 23 March, 2011.
9. Janine Zacharia, "Signs of dissent becoming more visible among Saudi Arabian Youth," *Washington Post Foreign Service*, 10 March, 2011. www.washingtonpost.com.
10. Janine Zacharia, "In Saudi Arabia, activists push more boldly for reform," *Washington Post Foreign Service,* Monday, 7 March, 2011.
11. www.saudigazettte.com. "Omani protesters set up camp," *Saudi Gazette,* 23 March, 2011.
12. www.ft.com. Simon Kerr, "Protests awaken sleepy Sultanate of Oman," 28 February, 2011.
13. www.ft.com. "Protests turn violent in Oman port," 27 February, 2011.
14. www.opendemocracy.net. Kristen C. Ulrichsen, "Gulf States: Studies Silence falls on Arab Spring," 25 April, 2011.
15. www.kuwaittimes.com. Ben Garcia, "Arab Spring breaks some famous myths," 17 May, 2011.
16. Joel Beinin and Frederic Vairel, *Social Movements, Mobilization and Contestation in the Middle East and North Africa* (U.S.A: Standford University Press, 2011), 146.

17. Jacques Waardenburg, "Islam as a Vehicle of Protest," in Ernest Gellner, (ed.), *Islamic Dilemmas: Reformers, Nationalists, Industrialization* (Oxford, UK: De Gruyter, 1985), 37.
18. Edmund Burke III and Ira M Lapidus, (ed.), *Islam, Politics and Social Movements* (U.S.A: University of California Press, 1990), 19.
19. www.dsg.ae. Dubai School of Government. Arab Social Media Report, 2011
20. www.arabtimesonline.com. "Gulf states launch Bid to mediate in Yemen crisis," 04 April, 2011.
21. www.jpost.com. Jonathan Spyker, "Gulf Regimes: The real game—Saudi Arabia," 11 March, 2011.
22. Ibid, 21.

8

The "Tehran" Factor in West Asia

Doomed to Destabilise?

Kingshuk Chatterjee

From the time that the Islamic Republic of Iran came into being, it has seldom been considered in a favourable light in terms of the role it plays in the arena of international relations in West Asia. The list of international grievances against Tehran has grown steadily since 1979: the fledgling Islamic Republic had professed an agenda of exporting its revolutionary ideology, which had caused some flutter in its immediate neighbourhood, particularly in those states with a noticeable Shi'i component in their population; it fought a prolonged war against Iraq in the 1980s; it aided and abetted Syria and Hizballah during the Lebanese civil war and since then, which has contributed to instability in Lebanese politics; that it has supported the HAMAS in Israeli-occupied Palestine all through the 1990s. In the first decade of the 20th century, Iran was found to be surreptitiously developing a nuclear programme, which was greeted with consternation in its neighbourhood, and raised the prospect of disturbing the stability of the Gulf region at best, and nuclearisation of the entire region at worst. Tehran's potential to destabilise was perceived to have increased after the Gulf War of 2003, leading to the removal of its greatest geo-political challenger in the region, Ba'athist Iraq. The threat potential of Tehran is considered to have increased further with the bellicose posturing that characterises the Ahmedinejad presidency—ranging from its vocal, financial and logistical support of the militant HAMAS and its declared opposition to the right of the state of Israel to exist, to Tehran's projection of its determined opposition to US power in the region.

In more abstract terms, Tehran is seen to be behaving like a revisionist power in the international order, with particular reference to the Middle East as a whole and the Gulf region in particular. This marked a reversal in Tehran's standing in the international order: after being considered an oasis of stability in the region since the end of the second world war and a close ally of the USA, Iran fell foul of Washington D.C., being subjected to a policy of 'containment' in the 1980s which became a policy of 'dual containment'. Iran's support for HAMAS militancy in the 1990s won for it the label of a 'rogue state'. The impression of the Islamic Republic being a revisionist regime was further reinforced in the post-9/11 world once suspicions about Tehran's nuclear programme allegedly in violation of her NPT commitments came to light, and particularly in the wake of President Bush's 'Axis of Evil' Speech, which equated Tehran with Baghdad and Pyongyang. To be fair, many in the US administration were initially uncomfortable with Washington's sweeping claims about Tehran's mala fide, because for a revisionist power Tehran was doing precious little. But many among them have increasingly found such doubts difficult to reconcile with the hard revisionist position evinced by President Ahmedinejad.

This paper proposes to interrogate the general assumptions of this discourse on Tehran as a factor of instability in the politics of West Asia. The paper advances the contention that there are elements in Tehran's foreign policy that have been either misunderstood, or neglected; and that such elements, if addressed differently might actually serve to stabilise the region in the medium term. It further makes the contention, that hard revisionism is possibly only a passing phase in Tehran's policy towards the region, and subjected to watchful indifference might not leave much enduring impression in the politics of the region.

Useful Questions about Tehran's Revisionism

Standard allegations of the revisionist character of the foreign policy warrant a few useful pointers. In the three decades since the Islamic Revolution, Iran has not started a single war, nor fought one aiming at territorial expansion or restoration. Nor, indeed, does Iran have any irredentist agenda towards any of its neighbours. This is not to say that Iran has no disputed frontiers altogether or indeed that all territorial issues are settled. Iran has unsettled frontiers to the north, west and south of long vintage, viz. the dispute over Abu Musa and Tonb islands with UAE, over the Shatt al-Arab with Iraq and over the Caspian Sea with the Caspian littoral states. In each of the three cases, however, Tehran has been an avowedly status quo power, and is itself the target of revisionist designs of its neighbours.

Iran's claim on the islands of Abu Musa, Tonb-i Bozorg (Greater Tonb) and Tonb-i Kochak (Lesser Tonb) has been disputed by the United Arab Emirates since 1971.[1] Located on the Persian Gulf between the southern Iranian coastline and the Hormuz, the Tonb islands and Abu Musa were part of a cluster of islands that had changed hands repeatedly down the centuries. This was largely because, given their strategic locations on the Gulf just past the straits of Hormuz, whoever commanded these islands would be in a position to oversee shipping in and out of the Gulf. Hence, whenever any strong central authority emerged in the Persian Gulf region, it tended to assert its authority over the islands, and whenever it weakened they tended to slip away. At least from the Safavid times, parallel to the decline of the Portuguese power in the Gulf, these islands came under the sway of the kingdom of Persia although the inhabitants spoke Arabic rather than Persian. The Tonb islands used to be recognised as a part of the Persian Kingdom by London, without any reservations, as late as 1886. However, suspicious of growing influence of Russians, and later Germans, they began to raise doubts about the finality of the matter by entertaining for the first time the claims of the Qasami family of the trucial emirates of Sharjah and Ras al-Khaimah to lordship over the islands. Given the extensive strategic and economic stranglehold Britain had come to enjoy in southern Persia, Tehran deemed it prudent not to antagonise London at a time when Iran was experiencing domestic turmoil and removed its presence from the islands on 14th June 1904, subject to the reservation that neither of the parties should hoist their flags on any of the islands till such time as the matter was settled. Three days later, the emirate of Sharjah hoisted its own flag unilaterally, presumably with tacit British encouragement. While Abu Musa continued under the administration of Sharjah, the Tonb islands were handed over to the Qasemi rulers of Ras al-Khaimah when it was recognised as a separate emirate in 1921.

Iran persistently disputed the claims of Sharjah over Abu Musa and those of Ras al-Khaima over Tonb islands, and kept on negotiating with Britain over the claims. When Britain decided to wound up its military presence in the region, the seven trucial states on the Arabian coast along the straits of Hormuz (Abu Dhabi, Dubai, Sharjah, Fujayra, Ras al-Khaima, Ajnan State) constituted themselves as the UAE upon becoming independent in 1971. Iran claims that Tehran and London had come to a tacit understanding that, once Britain pulls out of the region Tehran could move in. Accordingly, when Britain left the region and the UAE came into being, Tehran repossessed the islands militarily, allegedly in accordance with that understanding. Needless to say, UAE disputes the existence of any such understanding. The Islamic Republic has steadfastly defended Tehran's action in 1971, and all bilateral meetings on the matter have so far been fruitless.

While Abu Musa and Tonb islands have involved Tehran in protracted diplomatic disputes with UAE, the dispute over the Shatt al-Arab has involved Iran in "the longest war" with Iraq.[2] The Shatt al-Arab waterways comprises of the Tigris-Euphrates river system along with that of the Karun river.[3] Till the end of the First World War, usage of the river system was guided by the Ottoman-Persian understanding which was acceptable to both sides for generations. After the Great War, Britain changed the rules of the game by introducing the Thalweg principle, which rests on a line drawn between the deepest points along the stream bed, effectively sharing the waterway down the middle. The principal problem for Iraq has been that when it was carved out of Ottoman Mesopotamia in the 1920s, its access to Gulf coast was denied by the creation of the emirate of Kuwait as a British protectorate. Hence the riverine port of Basra on the Shatt al-Arab is Iraq's only access to the Gulf, whence vessels have to ply part of the way through marshy waterways upto Umm Qasr. The alternative of plying down the more navigable eastern channel of the Shatt al-Arab is not available because that passes through Iranian territory, past the ports of Khorramshahr and Abadan. Upon acquiring power, Saddam Hussein had reopened the question by claiming the entire waterway right up to the Iranian shores, which occasioned minor skirmishes and tensions along the border. In 1975 Baghdad and Tehran signed the Algiers Accord, which reinstated the frontier roughly along the Thalweg lines. In 1980, as Iran was engulfed by the turmoil generated by the unfolding revolution, Saddam unilaterally (thus illegitimately) abrogated the 1975 Accord and declared war on Iran. When the war ended in 1988, the terms of the Algiers Accords were reinstated after the loss of millions of lives, and ruination of Iraqi and Iranian economy.

Similarly, the issue of a final demarcation of jurisdiction over the Caspian Sea among the littoral states has proven highly elusive, largely because there is no single established legal framework for resolution.[4] The only legal framework available for any resolution is based on a series of treaties signed between Iran (Persia) and Russia (Soviet Union) in 1813, 1828, 1921, 1935, 1940 and 1956, dealing with the sharing of the Caspian and its resources between the two. In 1935 it was agreed that territorial waters fishing provision would apply to 10 km from the coastline, but no definitive demarcation of the coastline was undertaken. In 1956, for the first time Moscow and Tehran explored the issue of demarcation of the Caspian, marginally addressing the sharing of sea-bed resources. In general, all the treaties of the 20th century worked with the general principle that territorial jurisdiction would hold for 10 miles from the coastline—beyond that, condominium. The problem began after the collapse of the USSR as bilateral demarcations became invalid, with the newly emerged littoral republics registering their claims. Needless to say, Tehran's original position—that Russia and the Soviet-successor states share the area designated for the USSR—understandably found no takers.

The usual international legal instrument for such territorial disputes, the UN Convention on Law of the Seas (UNCLOS), does not apply in this case because the Caspian is actually a lake.[5] The most logical solution is supposed to be to divide the Caspian among the five littoral states—viz. Iran, Azerbaijan, Russia, Kazakhstan and Turkmenistan. But major differences exist even over the modality of such division. Tehran advocates equitable division among the division, of 20 per cent each. Azerbaijan, Kazakhstan and Turkmenistan seek allocation commensurate to littoral length of the respective states on the Caspian—i.e. Kazakhstan 29.9 per cent; Azerbaijan 20.7 per cent; Turkmenistan 19.2 per cent; Russia 15.6 per cent and Iran 14.6 per cent. Had this been a mere territorial issue, the demarcation may not have proven so intractable a problem. However, the Caspian is a proven reservoir of oil and natural gas. According to one estimate, in terms of a rough five-way division of the Caspian resources in proportion to the littoral regions, Kazakhstan, Turkmenistan and Azerbaijan are likely to be the greatest beneficiaries, while Tehran and Moscow are slated to lose out.[6] Understandably, Iran and Russia are not very keen on the littoral-wise division. Also reasonably large concentration of such reserves is to be found along the areas disputed between Iran, Turkmenistan and Azerbaijan. Tehran therefore adamantly resists any arbitrary demarcation of the maritime frontier, and resists attempts at exploration of disputed areas. Tehran has even carried out skirmishes and air-raids on areas claimed by Azerbaijan in 2002 over exploration by BP. The matter continues to be discussed; Iran prefers the settlement to be limited to the Caspian Sea level, not to have it internationalized.

It is noteworthy that despite Tehran's image as a "rogue" regime, Tehran has exercised moderation quite consistently in the face of revisionism on the part of its neighbours. It is also worth mentioning that despite shifts in the domestic balance of power inside the Islamic Republic, Tehran's policy on these issues has remained consistently status quo in character.

Iran the Troublemaker: Lebanon and Palestine

Iran's reputation as a troublemaker in the region goes back to the early days of the Republic, not merely because it had given a call to the oppressed peoples in the neighbourhood to rise in rebellion against their rulers, but more because of its involvement in the bloody and protracted conflicts in Lebanon and occupied Palestine, and also on account of her implacable opposition to the state of Israel.

Tehran has backed Syrian involvement in Lebanese civil war in the 1980s, and has provided the militant Hizballah movement from 1983 with a broad range of financial, military, logistic and political support.[7] While both Tehran and the Hizballah find it convenient to deny Tehran's involvement, Iran is considered to have been the principal source of arms and ammunitions for the Hizballah right from 1983 and to have operated training camps for the Hizballah under the prominent Iranian revolutionary Mostafa Chamran.[8] After the end of the Lebanese civil war, Iran has continued to provide Hizballah with logistical support to emerge as the principal force of opposition in Lebanon. Even Hizballah's television and propaganda network, Al-Manar, was set up with support from Iran.[9]

Iran has also been involved in the Israeli-Palestine conflict from the latter part of the 1980s. Tehran has financed and possibly also trained the HAMAS (Harakat al-Muqawwamat al-Islamiyya or the Islamic Resistance Movement) from the late-1980s, and definitely from the mid-1990s. Estimates vary, but the general agreement has been that the quantum of Tehran's assistance to HAMAS has not been insignificant. US sources have estimated Iranian support to the HAMAS to have ranged between $30 million and $50 million during the 1990s; Canadian intelligence estimates the transfer for the same period to have been between $3 million and $18 million.[10] Despite the considerable difference in the two figures, the substance of Iranian assistance is yet to be disputed. US intelligence believes that Tehran's support for HAMAS operated on pay-for-performance principle, which peaked in 1995-96 with a plethora of suicide bombings. In 1995-96 alone, Tehran is supposed to have transferred between $25 million and $50 million.[11] The Intelligence and Terrorism Information Center at the Israel Intelligence Heritage and Commemoration Center suggests that Tehran's support for the HAMAS was pivotal in the latter's increased ability to launch its swathe of rocket attacks during 2006-07.[12]

While Iranian involvement with Hizballah and HAMAS need not be disputed, the rationale behind such intervention needs be put in perspective. The usual explanation proffered was that the revolutionary regime was keen on exporting its revolutionary ideology, and that the Alawite Shi'i rulers of Syria and the Shi'ite organization of Hizballah in Lebanon were natural constituencies for Tehran to address. This argument, to put it mildly, is silly. It does not explain Tehran's interest in HAMAS. Indeed it is not necessary that Tehran's support for all forces everywhere must be motivated by the same reason. That in fact was the reason pedlar's of "export of ideology" thesis stood their ground, and explained away Tehran's support for HAMAS by contending that Khomeini had always taken his stand in favour of the Palestinian struggle, while the support for Hizballah and 'Alawite rulers of Syria were motivated by ideological considerations.

It is possible, however, to give a strategic explanation for Tehran's involvement in Lebanon and Palestine, without resorting to ideological preferences. Iran's war with Iraq had Tehran completely isolated in the neighbourhood with Saudi Arabia, Kuwait, UAE and the USA actively supporting Iraq at various stages of its war effort in various ways. Tehran's bid to break out of this diplomatic isolation took it to Damascus, where Syria's intervention in the Lebanese civil war had already made Damascus very unpopular with the West and its Arab neighbours. Tehran began supporting Syria, and then (once Israeli invasion of Lebanon made the Hizballah mount a gallant resistance to the invaders) Hizballah, principally in order to open a second front that could distract American interest and therefore concentrate less on Iraq.[13] Iran's interest in the HAMAS also was presumably driven by similar concerns of keeping the second front open after the Lebanese civil war was over—US preoccupation with the Arab-Israeli dispute would serve to reduce the heat on Iran. Additionally, in the light of the funding of Iraq during the Iran-Iraq war by Arab governments in the name of Arab solidarity, Tehran's espousal of the Palestinian cause was meant to send a powerful message to the Arab streets—that on the crucial question of Palestine Tehran remained more true to the Arab cause than all the Arab regimes.

How does this reading square with the relentless hostility that the Islamic Republic has been showing to Israel over the last three decades? To answer that question, one needs ask two more. Does Iran and Israel have any territorial disputes they need resolve? No, because they don't even have any common boundary, nor ever had. Second, does Iran and Israel have any other disputes (not involving any third party like the Hizballah or HAMAS) that need be resolved? That is to say, if the two *wanted* to resolve their mutual issues, what would they negotiate over? The answer is, once again, there is no such issue. In that case, what drives this enmity between Tehran and Tel Aviv? Israel's position is clear that the Islamic Republic has been supporting Hizballah and HAMAS, and the Ahmedinejad administration poses an existential threat for Israel—Tel Aviv is yet to cause any such offence against Tehran. So why does Tehran behave towards Israel the way it does? A strategic explanation would suggest that Tehran is targeting the *Shaitan-e Kochak* (the Lesser Devil, i.e. Israel) to hurt the *Shaitan-e Bozorg* (the Great Satan, i.e. USA). Such an argument would explain why Iran supports Hizballah and remains more Palestinian than the Palestinians. It would also explain why such support escalates whenever Tehran is under international (read, US) pressure on any issue (as in the 1980s, between 1994-96, during 2003, and 2006-08). To the issue of the anti-Zionist ranting of Ahmedinejad we will turn later.

Iran, the Troublemaker? Iraq and Afghanistan

Tehran's role in supporting militant movements in Lebanon and occupied Palestine is of quiet an old vintage. In the last decade, however, Tehran has been repeatedly accused of functioning as a force abetting instability in her immediate neighbourhood, especially in Iraq and Afghanistan. Such allegations, though, are not as substantive as those pertaining to the case of Hizballah and HAMAS, largely because there is not general consensus within the accuser-in-chief, the US administration. Nevertheless, as it would frequently happen, Bush's labelling of Tehran as a part of the axis of evil has gained a longer shelf-life than it warranted.

Iraq's neighbours as much as the USA has persistently accused Iran of trying to destabilise Iraq ever since Saddam Hussein was toppled in 2003. Iran's Arab neighbours fear that Iran is trying to create a series of Shi'i centres of power in the Arab heartland by propping up various Shi'i forces in Iraq, Lebanon and, in 2011, in Bahrain. King Abdullah II's comments about "the rise of a Shi'i crescent" out of the Iraq war have been periodically echoed by Saudi diplomats that US intervention in Iraq is effectively handing over the country to Iran.[14] The American case is that once Saddam was toppled, Tehran became particularly active in trying to gain leverage in Baghdad, backing various factions (mostly Shi'i) at different points of time: viz. Ahmed Chelabi, the Supreme Council of Islamic Revolution in Iraq (SCIRI), the Badr militia of Muqtada al-Sadr and even Sunni insurgent groups. The strongest such indictment came from the US Ambassador to Iraq, Zalmay Khalilzad in February 2006, when he charged with a "mixed policy towards Iraq", blending normal diplomatic relationship with making available the arms and ammunition that have kept the trouble brewing in Iraq.[15]

Such allegations beg a few obvious questions. First, why would Iran want to destabilise Iraq? Second, does Iran gain from instability in Iraq? Conventional wisdom would suggest that since Tehran had fought the most destructive war in Iranian history with Iraq, it makes sense for Iran to keep her powerful neighbour considerably weakened. More pertinently, there is a very good case to argue that Iran is uncomfortable having the USA in its backyard, and would prefer the Americans out of Iraq quickly lest they start using Iraq as their base for any potential invasion of Iran. This mood was reasonably pervasive in the early part of 2006 as US rhetoric against Tehran began to grow particularly bellicose. Thus, it would certainly make strategic sense for Tehran if the Iraqi situation went out of hand for USA, bogging America down in Iraq to an extent that Washington DC would be neither willing nor able to launch an invasion of Iran in the near future.

There is little reason to doubt that Tehran would want at the very least a friendly regime in Baghdad. Having already fought the most destructive war in living memory with her western neighbour, Iran would be extremely uncomfortable with either an inimically disposed regime in Baghdad or even one that might allow the US a strategic depth against Tehran. Thus while Tehran tried to develop friendly relationship with the Nuri al-Maliki regime, it was equally keen on developing mileage with both forces in power and those in opposition, which might give it some strategic depth in Baghdad for the duration of US presence in the region. Tehran seems to believe that its best chances of success would come with the Shi'i elements in Iraqi politics that have been hitherto repressed by the Sunni minority, but not by trying to establish a "theocratic" regime in Baghdad, which would be guaranteed to provoke Sunni Arab and Kurdish hostility. Iran is determined however to prevent the rise of a Saudi-backed Sunni insurgency in Iraq that would lend strategic depth to any anti-Tehran disposition. Hence, while Tehran disputes the allegations of its military and logistical support to Sunni and Shi'i insurgency in Iraq, and while no substantive evidence exists justifying either of these charges, the probability of Tehran's support for Muqtada al-Sadr and the Badr militia loyal to the SCIRI remains fairly high.[16]

To argue, however, that such measure purports to destabilise Iraq is to miss the plot completely. Unstable Iraq, with a central authority unable to control the regions, would invariably amount to greater autonomy for the Kurds in the north. This is against the interests of Tehran (as also Ankara), because the very introduction of autonomy for the Kurdish regions of Iraq had resulted in similar aspirations and demands in the adjacent Kurdish regions of the Islamic Republic. Further strengthening of the autonomous character of Kurdish autonomy would provide a fillip for the demand for independent Kurdistan that is almost certain to destabilise Iran as much as Turkey. Hence, it might be safe to contend that, Iran would prefer a weak Iraq to strong Iraq, and a stable Iraq to an unstable one.[17]

USA has also occasionally charged Iran of subverting the stability of the Karzai regime in Kabul (not that Karzai needs much help). However, Iran has a much better and demonstrable record in Afghanistan than in Iraq, because Iran suffered considerably from the problem caused by the Afghan civil war which drove hundreds of thousands of refugees into Iran. When the civil war broke out in Afghanistan in the early 1990s, Tehran backed Burhan al-din Rabbani hoping for a quick stabilisation. It paid the price for that support when the Taliban came to power and unleashed subjected the Hazara Shi'i to severe persecution. After the fall of the Taliban, Tehran has constantly cooperated with the creation of the successor regime. Tehran needs stability in Kabul because it cannot take any more refugees,[18] and also because instability in Afghanistan accentuates Iran's narcotic problem.[19]

The US authorities have been accusing Tehran for some time, though, of talking and even supporting regional forces in Afghanistan that are working to undermine Karzai in Kabul. Such efforts by Tehran to open up a second line in Afghanistan is prompted by the failure of the Karzai administration in striking genuine roots in Afghan politics, prompting fears that in the event of any US pull-out, Karzai would go the same way as the Najibullah regime. For Tehran's part, it has no preference for one faction over any other. If Karzai cannot deliver, Tehran would back anyone who can serve to stabilise Afghanistan. It would not confine itself to co-operating with Karzai alone—hence the suspicion against Tehran.

The Nuclear Question: Undeniable Right or Strategic Imperative?

The principal reason why Tehran generates the attention that it does, in its neighbourhood as much as in the international community as a whole, is on account of its nuclear programme. Tehran, a signatory of the NPT as a non-nuclear weapon state, has always denied having a nuclear weapons programme. It also insists that the Iranian nuclear programme is for civilian power generation, which is its inalienable right under the NPT. However, in 2003, the USA brought to light a range of intelligence data and satellite photos that indicated the existence of nuclear weapons programme. Since then, the question of the emergence of Iran as a nuclear power has caused nothing but consternation among her neighbours as well as in the international arena in general.

Iran's nuclear programme had begun under the Pahlavi dynasty, with benign neglect of Washington DC, since Tehran was America's greatest ally in the Middle East, ahead even of Israel. At the initial stage, Iranian nuclear establishment was even working in collaboration of Stanford University; Tehran's principal collaborators in the construction of its nuclear reactors were France and Germany. In the wake of the Islamic Revolution of 1979, as USA imposed sanctions on Iran, and Tehran was undecided on whether to carry on such a costly venture. After the project was put on hold, the French and German associates decided to pull out, refusing to work under new conditions imposed by the Republic as also sanctions imposed by USA. Their withdrawal from nuclear cooperation compelled Tehran to suspend her nuclear programme.[20] All through the 1980s, owing to the war with Iraq as also the consequent financial hardship, the nuclear programme remained in a deep freeze. However, after the Gulf War of 1991, as the full extent of Baghdad's WMD programme came to light, the nuclear programme was revived, with (it later appeared) an eye to militarisation of the nuclear capacity. Upon Germany's refusal to cooperate with the programme on account of US sanctions on Iran, Russia came forth to start the Bushehr reactor.[21] Tehran has also allegedly sought assistance from China and nuclear rogue regimes like North Korea and Pakistan to move in the direction of developing its military programme.

Tehran's nuclear programme (civilian and/or military) has been the one common strand running through the domestic and foreign policies during the Rafsanjani (conservative-pragmatist), Khatami (liberal-reformist) and Ahmedinejad (conservative-hard-line) eras. Initiated under Rafsanjani during the 1990s with full support of the conservative forces that dominated Tehran's defence establishment, pace of the programme was escalated forth clandestinely till its existence was revealed in 2003 during the Khatami era. Under intense international pressure the Khatami administration suspended the weapons related activities of the nuclear programme, and negotiated with the EU-3 (European foreign ministers), accepting the Additional Protocol and suspended enrichment of uranium voluntarily.[22] Resumption of the programme under President Ahmedinejad is suspected to have escalated the pace of uranium enrichment to critical levels, indicative of its military character.

The USA contends Tehran's nuclear programme to be a major threat to the stability of the region, and fears that a nuclear Iran would trigger a massive weapons race in the region at the very least and nuclear arms race at the worst. This would make one of the world's most volatile regions even more volatile. Washington DC therefore considers prevention of Iran's emergence as a nuclear weapon state a strategic imperative for the Middle Eastern region.

Ironically, the Iranians too look upon their own nuclear programme as a strategic imperative. Given the hostility of the various US administrations since 1979, the Iranian establishment views with alarm what appears to them as an encirclement of Iran—with presence of US troops in Iraq, Afghanistan, Kuwait, Turkmenistan, and strategic alignment with Saudi Arabia, Oman, UAE, Bahrain, Pakistan, Turkey, Turkmenistan. Additionally, the discovery of the extent of Iraq's WMD programme had sharply escalated defence expenditure of virtually all the Arab states in the Gulf. But US sanctions ensure that Iran is unable to develop its defence preparedness at par with its neighbours. Hence, strategically as much as militarily Iran has had a feeling of being under siege. The advocates of developing nuclear weapons capability argue that given US determination to prevent any change in the regional balance of power against itself, Iran could easily become the target after Iraq and Afghanistan are settled. Thus Iran should develop nuclear weapons capability while the USA is not looking hard enough.[23]

Further, if aspiring for nuclear capability was the reason why Iraq, Iran and North Korea were painted in the same brush of 'Axis of Evil', Iran was at one point seriously considering abandoning its nuclear option if that allowed things to cool off. President Khatami was among those in the Iranian establishment who argue that Iran should become a "near-nuclear" power like Japan and Germany who have the capacity to develop nuclear weapons capability but do not exercise that option unless compelled to do so.[24] He took a major gamble in this direction by suspending Tehran's nuclear programme pending resolution of all issues with the IAEA. But the US ouster of Saddam Hussein while letting Pyongyang off the hook made Tehran suspicious. By the closing months of the Khatami era an idea was gaining ground that Saddam could be ousted *because* he had already been disarmed; Pyongyang was spared *because* North Korea could not be disarmed—in other words, the USA heeds only the strong and tramples over the weak(ened).[25] By the time Ahmedinejad came to power, the prevalent opinion in Tehran's defence establishment seems to have been that the nuclear arsenal is like an insurance against military intervention and regime change. That it has no genuine commitment to making the Middle East genuinely nuclear weapons-free, Tehran argues (with some substance), is clear from US refusal to look into the nuclear arsenal of Israel years after Mordechai Vanunu blew the whistle on it.

The Bus that was Missed: The Khatami Era

Despite all the adverse publicity that Tehran has received from the

West, Iran had made genuine efforts to bridge the gulf caused by the Islamic Revolution of 1979 right from after the end of the Iraq-Iran war. Tehran's attempts at normalisation of its relations with the world under the stewardship of President Akbar Hashmi Rafsanjani (1989-2007), with his policy of economic liberalisation, were very convincingly thwarted by the policy of 'dual containment' of Iraq and Iran that Washington pursued at that time. But probably the best chance at reconciliation since 1979 had come during the presidency of Sayyid Muhammad Khatami (1997-2005), which was badly squandered.

President Khatami had made serious manoeuvres towards normalisation with the international community, driven by domestic economic compulsions. With the global decline in the price of oil, Iran was earning an average price of $9.50, as against the average of $12 per barrel projected for the period 1995-99. As against an average oil income of $9-12 billion, the projected import bill was set at $14 billion, with provision for its upward revision subsequently.[26]

In this context of economic hardship, Khatami decided to step up the structural adjustment policies recommended by World Bank and IMF during the Rafsanjani era, and launched a charm offensive aimed at accomplishing normalisation of relations with the west, especially the USA that had been begun by Rafsanjani. Khatami's 'constructive engagement' with the EU was rapidly followed with feelers being sent out by his foreign minister, Kamal Kharrazi to the USA, so that normal relations with Washington DC could be restored. In return it was hoped that the US opposition to Iran's entry in the WTO would be dropped, Iran would become integrated into the world economy and that the resultant expansion of the country's economic horizons would help the embattled economy recover. The response he received from Europe, known as constructive engagement', strengthened Khatami's hand in the arena of Iran's domestic politics to such an extent that he and his foreign minister Kamal Kharrazi were able to push vigorously for a revision of many of the cardinal postulates of Tehran's foreign policy, including the confrontationalist posture that Tehran had maintained towards the USA. Fresh grounds, very clearly, were being broken when Khatami spoke of the imperative of *Guftogu-ye Tamaddunha* (Dialogue of Civilisations) during his address to the UN General

Assembly in September 1998.[27] Candlelight vigils taken out in Tehran after the tragic events of 9/11 indicated the strength of the positive vibes Khatami had unleashed, increasing the hopes of such normalisation.

When USA invaded Afghanistan to topple the Taliban regime, Tehran cooperated extensively with Washington and was instrumental in promoting the Karzai-Northern Alliance coalition. In January 2002, Tehran pledged $540 million (as against $290 million pledged by USA) at an international donors' conference; Tehran even volunteered to train 20,000 Afghan soldiers under US leadership.[28]

Khatami sought to use the overtures in January 2002 as an opening gambit in normalisation of relations with Washington, but opponents of Khatami tried to undermine such overtures with arms shipments to Palestine. Two weeks later, President Bush's 'Axis of Evil' speech made no mention of Iranian contribution in Afghanistan. This was seen in Tehran widely as an indication that Khatami's olive branch was being spurned. Nevertheless, as USA began to move against Iraq, Khatami and Kharrazi pressed for cooperation with USA. At one stage, Khatami and Kharrazi even considered allowing USA the use of Iranian airspace for operations against Iraq, because by weakening Iraq USA was in a way serving Tehran's interests.[29]

But the dynamics of domestic politics prompted the Rahbar (Supreme Leader) 'Ali Khamenei to go against such cooperation, citing the Axis of Evil Speech as his evidence of American feelings towards Iran, foiling Khatami-Kharrazi duo. USA's discovery of evidence indicating Tehran's nuclear weapons programme and the consequent international pressure on Tehran, coming as it did alongside the ouster of Saddam, gave Khatami his last opportunity to bring about reconciliation. He suspended the nuclear programme pending resolution of the issue by negotiation with the IAEA, hoping that Tehran's nuclear weapons programme being in its infancy such resolution would not be difficult. Once that happens, normalisation of relations with the international community could follow with some ease. However, by 2004, there was a growing consensus in Tehran that USA was not responding to any of Iran's conciliatory gestures. Presidential hopeful, 'Ali Larijani, attacked the concessions made by Rowhani under instructions from the President, compelling Khatami resume some of the suspended nuclear activity, but stopping well short of uranium enrichment, which remained an extended olive branch even after Tehran began to harden diplomatic positions with the EU-3 in 2004.[30] The writing on the wall, however, was clear: Khatami had lost the gambit, opening the way for Ahmedinejad.

The Ahmedinejad Phenomenon: An Exercise in Brinkmanship

Mahmoud Ahmedinejad, who was elected President in 2005 and re-elected in 2009, reflects the hard-line backlash against the Khatami phenomenon in Iranian body-politic. In terms of domestic politics as much as foreign policy, Ahmedinejad is virtually the polar opposite of President Khatami. In domestic policy he stands for a brand of economic populism and social conservatism that has halted the tide of liberalisation of Iranian economy and society that Khatami and to an extent Rafsanjani had championed for the decade and a half after the end of the Iraq war. On the global stage, quite unlike the conciliatory mood of his last two predecessors, Ahmedinejad stands for a revisionist approach to Iranian foreign policy. Two things have worked for him so far. First, Ahmedinejad has had a windfall surge in oil revenue, which has allowed him to distribute largess at home and peddle for influence abroad. Second, there is a growing assumption about the relative balance of power in the Middle East: that the USA is stuck in a no-win situation in Iraq and Afghanistan; and that Tehran is gaining in influence in the region as USA loses its grip. An assumption that the growing turmoil in the Arab world from the beginning of 2011 and fall of close US associates like Hosni Mubarak of Egypt has continued to endorse.

The principal point of difference between the Ahmedinejad era and those that went before is the increased resources at the disposal of the government. In 2005 alone Iran's oil export revenue stood at $46.6 billion, double the high point of the Khatami era of $23.7 billion in 2003.[31] Given the sharp appreciation in global oil prices, fluctuating between $55 per barrel to as high as $147 per barrel, the windfall Ahmedinejad began to enjoy was staggering in its proportions. In 2007-08, Iran's oil exports revenue stood at $70 billion, and despite the global economic slowdown in 2008-09, Iran's oil revenue fell to only $64 billion—more than two and a half times over the average for the Khatami period.[32]

This steady increase in the finances at his disposal has served to reinforce Ahmedinejad's trademark style in politics: brinkmanship, be it in the matter of domestic politics, economy or foreign affairs. In 2006 he reopened the nuclear option for Iran in association with the conservatives (who had resented Khatami's suspension of the nuclear programme)—an alliance forged with the appointment of 'Ali Larijani as the chief nuclear negotiator and Manouchehr Mottaki as foreign minister. The assumption underlying this gesture was that the nuclear issue could be settled in Iran's favour only from a position of strength. The consequent international pressure and prospect of war in 2006 arguably resulted in Tehran's decision to reopen a second front in Lebanon and Palestine. Funds and military support from Tehran abetted Hizballah's reinvention of itself; Tehran also offered HAMAS financial support after being elected to power in the Palestinian Authority, when Israel refused to disburse fund that Palestinian Authority was entitled to.[33] This was also the time that Tehran presumably lent support for those forces in Iraq and Afghanistan that are opposed to US occupation/presence.

In 2007, as Larijani and Mottaki finally began to headway in nuclear negotiations (arguing enrichment would be carried out outside Iran, so that Iran could not divert the enriched uranium for military purpose), Ahmedinejad removed Larijani in internal power struggle, to retain his posture as resolute defender of the Iranian people.[34] In 2010, Mottaki was also removed in a bid to finally eliminate the traditional conservative establishment's influence on his hard-line policy.[35] There is considerable disquiet in the corridors of power in Tehran over Ahmedinejad's nuclear brinkmanship because even according to the most 'alarmist' western assessment about the state of Iranian nuclear programme, Tehran is unlikely to be able enrich enough uranium to produce nuclear weapons before 2015 at the earliest.[36] It is thus self-defeating for Tehran to step up the ante in this manner unless the undisclosed objective is to force substantive concessions from the international community in general and USA in particular.

Ahmedinejad's brinkmanship is not limited to the nuclear issue alone. In 2005, soon after coming to power, Ahmedinejad expressed the view that the "Zionist state of Israel should be wiped off the map," and arranged international conferences denying the historicity of the Holocaust. The barrage of international criticism that followed had to be responded to by Tehran at great length, clarifying that the President 'meant' the "Zionist" state had to be replaced by a state which was not Zionist in its orientation; it was not a comment on the state of Israel. Needless to say, such clarifications had come too late.[37]

Ahmedinejad had further proposed to switch Iran's trade in oil from Dollar to Euro, and also exhorted the OPEC to do so, ostensibly because of the weakening of the dollar in global market in 2007, but actually to end America's global economic hegemony.[38] He also very demonstrably began to cosy up to regimes that had no love lost for Washington, such as Venezuela and Cuba, determined to carve out a space in the global arena outside the ambit dominated by the USA.

Largely with this aim in mind, Ahmedinejad began to play the China card in Iran with much greater vigour than anyone else before him. China's involvement with Iran has grown steadily since the 1980s, with Iran becoming China's second largest supplier of oil and gas during the period of President Khatami.[39] Since the closing months of 2005, Tehran has drifted increasingly closer to Beijing. In 2006, as the apprehension of a US invasion had begun to grow, there was a widely held belief doing the rounds on the streets of Tehran that the grant of increasing stakes in Iranian oil and natural gas reserves to China would persuade Beijing to provide Tehran with a shield against any US invasion.[40] China has plans even of building a $2 billion railway network that would run from Kermanshah in the south to Khosravi on the border with Iraq, with an eye eventually to head into the centres of Shi'i pilgrimage in Iraq, and maybe even someday into Syria.[41] China's stake in Iran has grown to such an extent during the Ahmedinejad era that some in the Tehran establishment are growing uncomfortable with the idea of being sucked into the Chinese orbit.[42]

As a result of all these factors, President Obama's gesture of offering unconditional talks failed to cut any ice with Iran. Tehran under Ahmedinejad is firmly of the opinion that US influence is diminishing by the day in the Middle East as a whole, thus Ahmedinejad is unlikely to refrain from brinkmanship—unless the Majlis elections of 2011 results in major reverses for the President.

Given the persistence of Ahmedinejad in the game of brinkmanship, there are some likely scenarios which may play out in the next few years. First, Tehran continues to play the China card, bypasses US and EU sanctions imposed in 2010 with Chinese assistance, goes nuclear as a sort of insurance, triggering a new round of arms race in the Gulf. Such a scenario is not very likely, but not impossible either. Iran has indeed kept growing closer to China even after the sanctions, and is now increasingly relying on SINOPEC to refine Iranian crude and sell it back to cater to the Iranian market.[43] This has given China even greater stake in the Iranian economy, as evident in the concessions given in March 2011 for the Azadegan oil-field. But it remains doubtful to what extent China would be willing to shield Tehran if it goes nuclear, and thereby invites the wrath of the international community. Given the existing situation in the international political and economic arenas, China is unlikely to provoke or endorse any total breakdown of the existing international order that might jeopardise its steady rise to global pre-eminence—and that is precisely what is likely to happen if China militarily or otherwise confronts the USA. Hence China may choose to defend Iran diplomatically at the UN, IAEA and other fora, but if push comes to the shove, Beijing may not oblige Tehran. The veterans in Tehran would be mindful of this consideration, and have, since 2005, repeatedly had the occasion to rein in the President.

A second possibility is that Israel feels existential threat posed by Iran attaining critical mass, and tries to take out Iran's nuclear facilities while it can—the way it did with Iraq in 1981. This would be nothing short of disaster. Bearing in mind the example of Israel's strike against Iraq (which delayed the Iraqi WMD programme by at least a decade), Iran has taken good care to not have its nuclear establishment concentrated in any one location, nor in any locations removed from populated areas.[44] It would not be possible to attack all the Iranian nuclear facilities simultaneously without alerting the country's defences. In case of any Israeli strike on any one of these, security in the rest would be heightened automatically. Either way, any attempt at complete neutralisation of Iranian nuclear programme is very unlikely to be fully successful. Moreover, such an attempt is almost certain to result in massive loss of lives by way of collateral damages, as Iranian nuclear facilities are located near major populated areas. Such an action virtually guarantees substantive long-term hostility towards Israel, and may even escalate the slide towards nuclearisation. Largely mindful of such considerations, Washington does not consider any such preemptive strike by the USA and discourages any such adventurism by Israel as well.

There is a third possibility which is perhaps a shade more likely. The economic sanctions imposed by USA and the EU have been having its toll on Iran's embattled economy. Iran's oil exports fell by 24 per cent and its revenues fell by $19 billion in 2009-10. Far more sinister is the problem that during the period of windfall profits from sale of oil, Ahmedinejad was keener on handing out government largess in populist gestures in domestic arena, and in order to buy diplomatic and strategic mileage in the international one. This was despite repeatedly voiced concerns about the dire need of reinvestment in Iran's petroleum infrastructure—one of the concerns that had propelled the economic reforms under Khatami. The impact of such a disastrous policy is becoming increasingly clear as the rate of attrition of Iran's petroleum infrastructure is quickening. The Paris-based International Energy Agency estimates that Iran's capacity to pump oil would reduce by 18 per cent, falling to 3.3 million barrels per day by 2015, at the present rates of production, consumption and investment.[45]

In tell-tale signs of the problem, Ahmedinejad has been compelled to take some unpleasant steps. In June 2007, he had announced a monthly quota for purchase of oil at subsidised rates, which resulted in major furore.[46] With the fall in oil revenues touching 40 per cent in the last quarter of 2010, in December that year fuel subsidies were cut by $20 billion (pushing ex-pump fuel prices up by 400-900%).[47] There is some likelihood that this fresh round of hardship would compel Ahmedinejad to abandon his trademark populism, which would in turn weaken him politically. This can happen in two ways: first, the hard-line faction close to

Ahmedinejad lose the 2011 Majlis elections to conservative-pragmatist forces, who, led by people like Larijani and Mottaki press for settlement of the nuclear issue in return for substantive concessions from USA, underwritten by Russia and EU (i.e. reduction in the antagonistic posturing in return for acceptance of overseas enrichment for civilian power generation); second, the hard-line faction diminishes in strength, and conservative-pragmatists and reformists together push Ahmedinejad for nuclear settlement in return for the end of the sanctions regime.

Either way, given the particular constellation Iran's economic and political situation, the likelihood of a sustained policy of brinkmanship is unlikely to have a much longer shelf-life.

Conclusion

Foreign policy of the Islamic Republic of Iran is considerably more pedestrian than it has been frequently made out. Despite the substantive differences that exist between Tehran and its neighbours, Tehran has consistently steered away from any major revisionist agenda in its engagements with the world outside. Although Tehran has had occasion to behave in a manner that conveys the impression that Tehran has a destabilising role to play in the Middle East, a careful analysis reveals that such activities (such as the support for the Hizballah or the HAMAS) were reactions to a feeling of strategic embattlement, rather than any long-term agenda for regional hegemony. Ahmedinejad's hard revisionism is more like a tactical shift than a substantive change in this strategic reality of encirclement by less-than-friendly forces. However, hard revisionism is likely to be a passing phase at the very worst, because the Iranian economy cannot support the dynamism such policy involves. In this scenario, watchful neglect of Tehran is best suited to circumstances. If the diplomatic pressure on Tehran is reduced somewhat, it would prevent any knee-jerk drive towards the nuclear option, and will allow positions to soften on either side, and ease out the crisis in the medium term by generating mutual confidence about the non-confrontational motives of the other side.

Notes

1. For a detailed discussion, see Amirahmadi Hooshang, ed., *Small Islands, Big Politics: the Tonbs and Abu Musa in the Persian Gulf,* (New York:New Martin's Press, 1996); for a brief survey, see Fathali Ghahremani-Ghadjar, "The Status of Greater and Lesser Tonb and Abu Musa", http:/ /www.Iranian.come/History/2008/Tonb_Final_Ghahremanian.pdf. (accessed on March 18, 2011).
2. The literature on this is quite prodigious. For a narrative account, see Dilip Hiro, *The Longest War: the Iran-Iraq Military Conflict* (London: Paladin Grafton books, 1990).
3. See Kaiyan Homi Kaikobad, *The Shatt al-Arab Boundary Questions: A Legal Appraisal* (Oxford: Clarendon Press, 1988); Richard S. Schofield, *Evolution of the Shatt al-Arab Boundary Dispute* (Cambridgeshire: Middle East and North African Studies Press, 1986).
4. Haghayeghi Mehrdad, "The Coming of Conflict to the Caspian Sea," *Problems of Communism*, vol. 50, no. 3, May/June 2003, 33.
5. Ibid., 33.
6. Kazakhstan would be entitled to proven reserves of an estimated 39.6 billion barrels (bbl) of oil and 106 trillion cubic feet (tcf) of natural gas with another possible reservoir of 32 bbl of oil and 35 tcf of gas; Turkmenistan has proven reserves of only .5 bbl of oil and 102 tcf of gas (and possible deposits of 38 bbl of oil and 159 tcf of gas), Azerbaijan has proven reserves of 7 bbl of oil and 48 tcf of gas (and possible reserves of 32 bbl of oil and 35 tcf of gas); Russia's proven reserves in the region amount to about .3 bbl of oil (and possible reserves of 7 bbl); and Iran has proven reserves of .1 bbl but possible deposits of 15 bbl of oil and 11 tcf of gas 12 bbl. See Bernard A. Gelb, *Caspian Oil and Gas: Production and Prospects*, CRS Report for Congress, September 2006, 3, http:// fpc.stage.gov/documents/organization/74906.pdf (accessed on January 12, 2011).
7. See, Anthony H. Cordesman, "Iran's Support for the Hezbollah in Lebanon", http://csis.org/files/media/csis/pubs/060715_hezbollah.pdf (accessed on March 26, 2011).
8. An Iranian academic on condition of anonymity, (whose father was instrumental in the negotiations that begun Iran's military and logistical involvement with Hizballah) in conversation with the author, Beirut, 2005.
9. Mousawi Ibrahim, Director, Political Programmes, Al-Manar Television, in conversation with the author, Beirut, May 2005.
10. Matthew Levitt, *HAMAS: Politics, Charity and Terrorism in the Service of Jihad* (New Haven and London: Yale University Press, 2006), 172.
11. Ibid., 172.
12. http://terrorism-info-org.il/malam_multimedia? English/eng_n/pdf/ iran_e004.pdf (accessed on January 16 2011).

13. For a detailed argument along these lines, see Anoushiravan Ehteshami and Raymond A. Hinnebusch, *Syria and Iran: Middle Powers in a Penetrated Regional System* (London and New York: Routledge, 1997).
14. Anoushiravan Ehteshami, "Iran's Regional Policies Since the End of the Cold War," in *Contemporary Iran: Economy, Society, Politics,* ed. Ali Gheissari (Oxford and New York: Oxford University Press, 2009), 345.
15. Nelson Hernandez, "US Ambassador Criticizes Iran's Role in Iraq", *The Washington Post*, February 20, 2006.
16. Anoushiravan Ehteshami, "Iran's Regional Policies Since the End of the Cold War", in Ali Gheissari, op.cit., 360-61.
17. For a succinct analysis of Iran's policy towards the new Iraq, see Mohsen M. Milani, "Iran's Persian Gulf Policy in the Post-Saddam Era" in Ali Gheissari, op. cit., 359-63. See also, Kayhan Barzegar, "Iran's Foreign Policy Strategy after Saddam", *The Washington Quarterly*, 33:1, January 2010, 173-89.
18. Iran has approximately 1.1 million Afghan refugees, after repatriation of nearly half a million in 2001, with the coming of the Karzai administration. See *Afghan Refugees in Iran: From Refugee Emergency to Migration Management*, (Report commissioned by International Peace Research Institute, Oslo and Chr. Michelsen Institute, 2004), http://www.cmi.no/pdf/? file=/afghanistan/doc/CMI-PRIO-AfghanRefugees InIran.pdf (accessed on January 12, 2011).
19. For a detailed treatment of this question, see A. William Samii, "Drug Abuse: Iran's 'Thorniest Problem'," *Brown Journal of World Affairs,* Winter/ Spring 2003, vol. IX, issue 2, 283-99.
20. Hamid Baeidi-Nejad, "Khatami's Nuclear Policy," *The Iranian Journal of International Affairs*, vol. XVIII, no. 1, Spring 2005, 56.
21. Ibid., 57.
22. Shahram Chubin, "The Iranian Nuclear Riddle After June 12," *The Washington Quarterly,* 33:1, January 2010, 166.
23. Saideh Lotfian, "Nuclear Policy and International Relations," in *Iran in the 21st Century: Politics, Economics and Conflict*, eds. Homa Katouzian and Hossein Shahidi (London and New York: Routledge, 2008), 162.
24. Ibid.,163, 165.
25. Ibid., 161.
26. Sohrab Behdad, "From Populism to Liberalism,", in *The Economy of Iran: Dilemmas of an Islamic State*, ed. Alizadeh Parvin (London and New York: I. B. Tauris, 2000), 135.
27. For an account of Iran's engagement with the UN during the Khatami era, see Kourosh Ahmadi, "Iran and the United Nations during Khatami's Presidency", *The Iranian Journal of International Relations*, vol. XVIII, no. 1 (2005), 21-51.
28. James Dobbins, "Negotiating with Iran: Reflections from Personal Experience," *The Washington Quarterly*, 33:1, January 2010, 155-56.

29. Even when the US was preparing to invade Iraq, Kharrazi ignored repeated US violations of Iranian airspace in the run-up to the war. This provided Khamenei, Rafsanjani and other opponents of Khatami's reforms to scuttle the gestures of normalisation. www.ips.net/iranwalksonice/html
30. Shahram Chubin, "The Iranian Nuclear Riddle after June 12," *The Washington Quarterly,* 33:1, January 2010, 166-67.
31. Joint Economic Committee, US Congress, *Iran's Oil and Gas Wealth,* Research Report #109-31, March 2006, 2, http://www.house.gov/jec/studies/rr109-31.pdf
32. http://www.payvand.com/news/09/feb/1034.html
33. http://www.nytimes.com/2006/02/23/international/middleeast/23mideast.html? _r=1, (accessed on January16, 2011).
34. *Ettelaat*, October 20, 2007.
35. *Ettelaat*, December 13, 2010.
36. http://edition.cnn.com/2007/POLITICS/12/03/iran.nuclear/index.html (accessed on April 1, 2011)
37. For a discussion of the context of, and controversy about the remark, see Ali M. Ansari, "Iran under Ahmedinejad", *Adelphi Paper* 393, International Institute of Strategic Studies, London: Routledge, 2007, 51-53.
38. "Tehran dumps dollar for euro", http://www.arabianbusiness.com/tehran-dumps-dollar-for-euro-12598.html (accessed on April 1, 2011).
39. For a detailed treatment of Sino-Iranian ties, see John W. Garver, *China and Iran: Ancient Partners in a Post-Imperial World* (Seattle and London: University of Washington Press, 2006).
40. See Ali M. Ansari, op. cit., 55-56.
41. "China to build $2 bn railway for Iran," http://www.telegraph.co.uk/finance/china-business/7985812/China-to-build-railway-for-Iran.html (accessed on April 2, 2011)
42. This is partly the reason why Tehran has not agreed to extend the Iran-Pakistan-India pipeline into China. Earlier, when New Delhi broke away from the talks over higher per unit price than originally suggested, Beijing had offered to join in the project. At that stage, some people in the Iranian establishment had suggested that India should be punished for its obduracy and the negative vote in the IAEA by cutting it out and diverting the pipeline to China. Some others however were unwilling to allow China become so crucial on her own in Tehran's scheme of things, and managed to say, Iran has to be patient with India because it is an old friend.
43. Previously Reliance Petrochemicals used to perform a large share of this activity, crucial in keeping the Iranian economy running, but Reliance was in the process of reducing its transactions with Iran from 2009 under US and Saudi pressure, and has completely stopped after the sanctions were imposed in 2010.

44. The Iranian nuclear establishment is spread all over the country. Apart from the Russian-built nuclear reactor in Bushehr (on the Gulf), there is a heavy water reactor in Arak (central Iran); uranium mines are located in Saghand (east-central Iran) and Gachin (on the Gulf); uranium enrichment plants are located in Natanz and Qom (central Iran); Esfahan has a uranium conversion facility, Tehran a nuclear research centre, Ardakan a yellow-cake production facility and Anarak a nuclear waste facility.
45. Spencer Swartz and Benoit Faucon, "Iran's Falling Output Means Less Revenue, Clout," http://online.wsj.com/article/SB1000142405278470 4569204575328851816763476.html (accessed on April 2, 2011).
46. "Petrol Stations torched in Iran after Ahmedinejad rations fuel," http:/ /www.timesonline.co.uk/tol/news/world/middle_east/article1992542.ece (accessed on April 2, 2011).
47. *Kayhan*, December 20, 2010.

INDIA AND WEST ASIA

9

India, Iran and the "US Factor"

Sujata Ashwarya Cheema

Introduction

India's long-standing ties with Iran received a major fillip in the post-Cold war period as the emergent world order generated new issues that required the two states to engage more deeply than before. India and Iran not only agreed to enhance extant economic and technical relations but also decided to cooperate on security issues. The realization of the wide potential of Indo-Iranian ties, however, has been stymied by advances in India's relations with the United States. In 2005, the United States under President Bush's administration changed the international nuclear regime to accommodate India's entry into the 'nuclear club' without a mandatory membership of the NPT. Under the terms of the dramatic Indo-US civilian nuclear deal, India will receive nuclear technology from the United States and will be able to buy nuclear fuel and technology from the world market. In effect, the deal lifts more than a three-decade US moratorium on nuclear trade with India. Since the agreement for cooperation on nuclear energy was announced by the two countries in July 2005, New Delhi has been under intense pressure to align its stand with Washington on Iran's nuclear programme as well as hold back on energy and security ties with Tehran. India has voted against Iran (and with the US) at the IAEA on more than one occasion leading to an evident fraying of cooperation in energy and security areas. However, it is equally true that India does not support the US policy of isolating Iran and impeding the development of its energy sector through sanctions, which is out of step vis-à-vis New Delhi's strategic goals. Although the United States and India have found some common grounds against Iran's nuclear programme, they may not be enough to override India's long term goals of having access to Iranian energy. India would like to preserve a thriving bilateral relationship with both Iran and the United States in a "fine balance".[1] In other words, New Delhi aims to pursue bilateral relations with the two adversaries consistent with its interests and requirements, irrespective of the conflicts they might have with each other. India is eager to reclaim its "strategic autonomy"—the idea that no country can be allowed to have excessive influence over its foreign policy decisions—which has been the defining feature of the country's foreign policy decisions since independence.[2] This article attempts to examine the impact of the "US factor" on relations between India and Iran pertaining to three issues: Iranian nuclear programme, energy cooperation and emerging challenges from the Afghan imbroglio, where the American footprint looms large. These will be analysed in the backdrop of brief overviews of India's ties with Iran and the United States. It is argued that three critical areas, namely, energy security, terrorism, and access to Afghanistan and Central Asia, will keep India's ties with Iran stable in the near future, even if, there are no new agreements or initiatives and, even as, Washington's urges New Delhi to ratchet up pressure on Iran.

The Contours of Indo-Iranian Relations

The end of the Cold war presented both India and Iran with new challenges and opportunities. A reorientation of relations followed as both countries started articulating their foreign policies in light of the changed global environment. India's foreign policy witnessed an expected reorientation: ideological affiliations gave way to interest-based relations. In West Asia, India became more clear-eyed in pursuing its interests. Consequently, countries that had received insufficient attention during the years of the Cold War—Iran, Israel and Saudi Arabia—became important for India's new West Asia policy. On the other hand, the dilution of revolutionary ideology with the death of Khomeini and Iran's need of a partner to break out of its isolation caused a shift in the country's foreign policy, as the Islamic Republic searched for friends and allies in national interest. A subtle shift towards India's side on the Kashmir issue facilitated a general rapprochement between India and Iran.

Since the early 1990s, Indo-Iranian interests have converged around a number of issues: trade in energy resources, stability and opportunities in Central Asia, prospects of mutual benefit from commercial ties, terrorism emanating from Afghanistan and Pakistan, and the possibility of cooperation in defence and intelligence areas. India and Iran signed two major agreements—the Tehran Declaration (2001) and the New Delhi Declaration (2003)—which proposed the expansion of bilateral partnership on the aforesaid issues as well as, significantly, contained a commitment to forge defence linkages and develop strategic relations.[3]

India's interests in the energy sector have major overlaps with those of Iran. Indo-Iranian ties in this sector have evolved on the solid logic of demand and supply: Iran is anxious to sell its abundant hydrocarbon resources and India, deficient in domestic energy reserves, is an eager buyer. The complementary interest of India and Iran in the energy sector was recognised in the New Delhi and Tehran declarations. The former envisaged the energy sector as a strategic area of their future relationship, whereas the latter emphasized the mutual benefit that could be derived from enhanced cooperation. With high rates of economic growth and over 15 percent of the world's population, India has become a significant consumer of energy. The government hopes to maintain an annual GDP growth rate of about 8 percent over the next quarter century to meet its developmental goals, which would require India to at least triple its primary energy supply.[4] In 2006, India was the sixth largest oil consumer in the world and some observers believe that by 2025, India may become the fourth largest consumer of crude oil following only the United States, China and Japan.[5] Therefore, energy supply has become a major economic and strategic issue in India's engagement with Iran.

As the Soviet Union disintegrated, both India and Iran had an interest in maintaining stability in the Central Asian region. While Iran was mindful of the possibility of ethnic conflicts in the emerging states of this new region spilling over into its territory, India was equally eager to have stability there. New Delhi's interest lay in retrieving the region's market that was cut off for Indian goods with the collapse of the Soviet Union. Through the Iranian territory, the India-Central Asia trade not only revived, but also expanded, as oil and natural gas deposits were discovered in the region.[6] Iran, on the other hand, was eager to benefit from serving as a conduit for the Caspian Sea energy to distant lands in the east. India, in addition, committed itself to developing Iranian ports and road links, for easy access to the land-locked Afghan territory.

A shared threat from Islamic radicalism emanating from Pakistan and Afghanistan emerged as one of the most significant area of cooperation between India and Iran in the 1990s. The consolidation of power by the extremist Taliban that subscribed to Sunni jihadist ideology remains a major source of anxiety for both countries. As opposed to Pakistan that quickly recognized the Taliban regime in 1996, India and Iran backed Afghanistan's anti-Taliban Northern Alliance. Since then Iran, India, and Russia coordinated have extensively to contain Pakistan's involvement in Afghanistan and its support to the Taliban.

One of the key instruments of the New Delhi Declaration is the "Road Map for Strategic Cooperation," which envisages robust defence cooperation between the two countries, including training and exchange of visits. Though, defence ties between India and Iran have been clouded in secrecy, a number of reports from secondary sources seem to suggest that India would cooperate with Iran on upgrading the latter's Russian-supplied weapon's system, supply conventional military equipment and spare parts, provide expertise in development of military hardware, and train Iran's armed forces.[7] Some reports indicate that Iran has "allowed India to have access to its military bases in an event of war with Pakistan." If true, this could fundamentally alter regional balance of power in India's favour.[8]

Several analysts also speak of close intelligence and security ties between New Delhi and Tehran, inferring from the presence of an unusually large number of Indian consulates at strategic locations in Iran, such as those in Zahedan and Bandar Abbas. However, cooperation in this area appears to indicate a reinforcement of "strong Indo-Iranian political relations rather than a broader defence alliance."[9] While India and Iran could have built upon an earlier cooperation in areas such as nuclear energy and space, political compulsions dictate that no such engagement is in offing very soon.[10]

The prevalent view that India's attraction for Iran is primarily as a source of oil, ignores the broad-based engagement India looks at in perusal of its national interests. Iran is also important to India's strategic conception as it offers easy access to prized geopolitical theatres of Central Asia and Afghanistan.[11] Maintaining a positive relationship with Iran gives India an important Muslim ally to counter Pakistan's anti-India propaganda on Kashmir and a ready balancing power on Islambad's western border, especially at times when Indo-Pak relations is increasingly contentious. In addition, relations with Iran help India to deflect criticism from domestic Muslim constituency on its expanding ties with Israel. Many also see India's dealings with Iran as a continuation and assertion of historical relations, especially when the country's other associations appear to be straining them.

The Progress in Indo-American Relations

In pursuance of its interests-based engagements, India's relations with the United States also registered a marked improvement in the post-Cold War years. With liberalization of the economy in the early years of the 1990s, India's vigorous growth became one of the key factors in transforming India-US relationship.[12] An expansion in economic ties, with growth in trade and investment, began to bring down the wall of suspicion between the two countries, even as the prospect for strategic cooperation remained tethered to America's non-proliferation commitments in South Asia. As a matter of fact, after India tested a nuclear device for the second time on 11 May 1998, the US administration under President Bill Clinton imposed a host of military and economic sanctions. On its part, India remained adamant about keeping its nuclear option, although New Delhi reiterated its commitment to 'no-first use' of nuclear weapons.[13] The immediate effect of the sanctions was to further strain relations between the two countries, already fraught by decades of suspicions and misgivings. The situation deteriorated even further when Pakistan conducted its own nuclear tests a few days later.

In the aftermath of the South Asian nuclear tests, the United States engaged the two regional adversaries in intensive talks on parallel tracks over the next two and a half years. From June 1998 through September 2000, fourteen rounds of dialogue between the United States and India bridged many gaps in understanding between the two countries and raised the level of trust between them. It laid the foundation for an eventual reconciliation between India's nuclear ambitions and America's non-proliferation agenda. Deputy Secretary of State Strobe Talbott and Minister of External Affairs Jaswant Singh not only grappled with the urgent issue of arms control and non-proliferation, but they also discussed the potential of economic and strategic cooperation between the two countries. The process of continuous and extensive dialogue enabled the United States to play a crucial role in averting the July 1999 crisis between India and Pakistan from escalating into a nuclear conflagration. The Talbott-Singh talks paved the way for President Bill Clinton's landmark visit to India in March 2000, which opened a new chapter in Indo-US ties. It also set the ground for US cooperation with both India (and Pakistan) in the war against terror after September 11, 2001.[14]

The bipartisan agreement on the need to broaden the scope of the Indo-US partnership was taken to a much higher plane by the Bush administration when it moved forward on a quartet of core security issues involving sensitive technology transfer: civilian nuclear technology, civilian space technology, high technology trade, and missile defence.[15] The centrepiece of improved bilateral relations became the cooperation in nuclear energy announced in a joint statement on July 18, 2005 by Prime Minister Manmohan Singh and then US President George W. Bush. India agreed to separate its civil and military nuclear facilities and place all its civil nuclear facilities under International Atomic Energy Agency (IAEA) safeguards and, in exchange, the United States agreed to lift three-decade moratorium on nuclear trade with India. It also contained provisions for expansion of US-India cooperation in energy and satellite technology.[16]

Washington's willingness to consider civilian nuclear cooperation with India marked a harmonization of India's nuclear ambitions and America's non-proliferation agenda. President Bush had been able to overcome strong domestic opposition to the deal on the key assumption that New Delhi at the turn of the century was well poised to suit Washington's objectives in South Asia. With an interest in safeguarding an open international economy and secure in the resilience of its democratic institutions, senior Bush administration officials believed that, India could emerge as America's most important partner on global issues. These included maintaining a stable balance of power in South Asia, defeating global terrorism, protecting economic supply routes in the Indian Ocean, and ensuring that China's rise continues to be peaceful.

The clarity of Bush administrations' India policy has taken a beating with current US government under President Barack Obama. With his administration's focus on the problems of Afghanistan and Pakistan, India is increasingly seen as part of the problem rather than as part of the solution. India's reluctance to offer concessions on Kashmir, that might encourage Pakistan to cooperate more thoroughly in Afghanistan, is considered by officials in Washington as a serious impediment towards resolving the Afghan imbroglio.[17] This "re-hyphenation" of India and Pakistan policy after the Bush's strong efforts to downplay decades of Pakistan-centricity in the United States' approach to South Asia, does not bode well for the broad strategic partnership between New Delhi and Washington, envisioned by the previous administration. Can India at this point afford to abandon Iran, which, is New Delhi's major energy supplier and a partner in solution to the Afghan crisis? Given the growing challenges of long-term energy security and stabilization of Afghanistan, it may well be time to ask such a question. India's dilemma on Iranian nuclear programme, energy dealings with the Islamic Republic, and impediments to challenges to a comprehensive Indo-Iranian engagement on Afghanistan, illustrate the impact of the "US factor" on one of India's crucial bilateral relations.

The Nuclear Flashpoint

Ever since the secretly-built Iranian nuclear facilities at Natanz and Arak a heavy water production plant at Arak were brought to light in 2002 by a Paris-based opposition group, the National Council of Resistance of Iran (NCRI), there has been widespread apprehension about the ultimate aim of Tehran's nuclear programme. The US has alleged Iran of aiming to develop nuclear weapons. Iran, however, insists that its nuclear programme is entirely for peaceful civilian purposes. The international community, led by the United States and the European powers, has rallied to bring Iran to task for non-compliance of the non-proliferation norms through censure at the International Atomic Energy Agency (IAEA) and imposition of United Nations Security Council (UNSC) sanctions.

In September 2005, India voted for the IAEA resolution finding Iran to be in "non-compliance" of the safeguard obligation under the Nuclear Non-Proliferation Treaty (NPT) and then it voted in February 2006 (with 26 other nations) to refer Iran to the UN Security Council for violating international obligations. The votes stirred fierce controversy in India but went a long way in placating those policymakers, who questioned India's relationship with Iran during the Congressional debates on the US-India civilian nuclear deal. Even though the government denied that there was any linkage between the votes and the then developing Indo-US nuclear cooperation, policymakers in New Delhi understood that the fate of the initiative depended upon making a choice between Iran and the US at the IAEA. That the Indian officials were indeed pushed hard by their American counterparts in New Delhi and Washington to support the US/EU resolution at the IAEA or give up on the nuclear deal has now been corroborated by the India Cables—despatches from the US Embassy in New Delhi to Washington—accessed through the Wikileaks.[18]

Prime Minister Manmohan Singh and his government faced a barrage of criticism nationally, from a wide range of analysts and politicians, for capitulating under US pressure and abandoning the "autonomy" of India's foreign policy. Though the government officials argued strenuously that the country's votes was cast "independently" and in step with India's opposition to a nuclear

Iran, the "change in stand" on Iran was widely received as a display to loyalty towards the US.

The pressure on India remained throughout the period that the deal was being finalized. A few weeks into the September vote, a diplomatic cable of October 20, 2005 reveal that Washington officials were worried about India's future course of action on the Iran issue in the face of "growing pressure to backtrack from its earlier stance... and abstain in any future IAEA votes". In a secret cable of January 12, 2006, the then US Ambassador to India, David C. Mulford noted that "the US would like to seek an affirmative vote from India on referring Iran to the UNSC. Abstaining at this stage is not enough, he said, highlighting the importance of India's September 24 BOG [Board of Governors] vote, and the fact that an abstention now would be seen as walking back the GOI's non-proliferation commitment."[19] Mulford later publicly warned that the pact could "die in the Congress," if New Delhi did not back Washington's bid to bring Iran before the UNSC, in the forthcoming meeting of the IAEA in January 2006. State Department spokesman Sean McCormack in Washington said while Mulford was expressing his own opinion in the remarks, he was reflecting the "the very strongly-held feelings" in Congress about the Iran issue.[20] Even before the Wikileaks cables brought into clear light the connection between India's "anti-Iran" vote and the fate of the Indo-US nuclear deal, a former US government official of the Bush administration, opined, in a talk in 2007 in New Delhi (at a premier security-related think tank-IDSA) that India's votes against Iran at the IAEA were "coerced."[21] That India's votes brazenly dovetailed with the US policy of isolating Iran was not lost out on the critics of the nuclear deal.[22]

Despite its repeat vote against Iranian nuclear programme, the leaked diplomatic cables divulge that there was no let up in pressure on India to fall in line with the American stand. And the civil nuclear deal was both the carrot and the stick. Referring to US and Indian press reports of India-Iran joint naval exercises and training of Iranian navy in Cochin in February 2006, the Americans, in one of the cables, "stressed that the US would see military cooperation with Iran fundamentally more worrying than simple economic ties. It could also seriously complicate efforts to convince the US

Congress to approve the Civil Nuclear Cooperation initiative." When clarified that the visit was just a "routine port call, and training was not part of the planned visit", the bottom line from the American side was that "dallying with Iran [is] not only dangerous for regional stability but also put at risk Congressional support for the civil nuclear deal."[23] In a bid to put pressure on the Indian government, the Bush administration had highlighted India's Iran policy in Congressional hearings on the Indo-US nuclear deal[24] and American Embassy officials in India were vigorously doing their part in getting India to choose between Iran and the US.[25]

Even as India joined the United States in voting against Iran in an IAEA resolution in November 2009, in accord with its earlier position on non-compliance and opposition to Iran's nuclear ambitions, it asserted that Iran had a right to peaceful use of nuclear energy under the NPT. New Delhi's position has been to support Iran's right to a civilian nuclear programme under the global non-proliferation norms, hold Iran accountable to its obligations under the NPT, IAEA and UNSC guidelines and "encourage" the country to address questions on its nuclear matters to the satisfaction of the international community. Although Indian leaders and analysts have for decades been critical of the non-proliferation treaty, for creating nuclear "haves" and "have-nots" as it pursued its own nuclear programme, India's upholds that Iran as a member of the NPT has certain obligations that it must fulfil.

As Iran's nuclear standoff continues and as the Islamic Republic suffers the fourth round of the UN Security Council-imposed sanctions, India is clearly in a quandary. When Foreign Secretary Nirupama Rao in a speech in July 2010 expressed New Delhi's disapproval of additional sanctions (which takes off from the UNSC Resolution) by individual countries against the Islamic Republic's energy sector, and referred to their detrimental impact on India's energy security, India demonstrated that it is conscious of its equities with Iran notwithstanding the IAEA votes. The official's comment was political in nature, intended at imparting a fresh momentum to Indo-Iran bilateral relations, which had been losing pace for some years now. The message could hardly go unnoticed at a time when Iran was under intense pressure from the Western powers, led by Washington, to roll back its nuclear programme. Such a position puts India at odds with the United States and lays bare the dilemma posed by continuous pulls and pressures of a strategic partnership with Washington.

Further, while on the one hand, India cannot wish away the unfavourable impact that economic sanctions can have on its energy security and trade relations, policymakers in India are well aware of the importance of a strategic alliance with world's superpower. In the last two years India has made substantial gains in areas such as military-to-military ties and counter-terrorism: defence trade between the India and United States has expanded to three billion worth and the FBI has been coordinating with the Indian intelligence on Mumbai terrorist attacks.[26] With the nuclear deal, India is also poised to have access to high technology in areas of energy, space and communication. Ideally, India would like to maintain a parallel relationship with both the United States and Iran, but this is evidently not happening. The United States is firmly between India and Iran, undermining the realization of the full potential of their ties and driving them apart on various other issues. Indo-Iranian relations have suffered and remain 'underdeveloped'.[27] This is not-so-subtly manifest in the Indo-Iranian energy ties.

The Energy Highs and Lows

Ever since India embarked on a high growth trajectory with economic liberalization, the country is acutely aware of its lack of adequate domestic sources of energy to meet ever-growing demand. Already India imports more than two-third of its hydrocarbon requirements and any further escalation would adversely affect its energy security. Placing current import dependency at 72 per cent, a Planning Commission report warns that the country faces "formidable challenges" in meeting its energy needs and that our "import dependence is growing rapidly."[28] In this scenario, India's policymakers are well aware of the need to diversify sources of energy supply. This is where Iran comes into play: the Persian Gulf nation accounts for roughly 10 per cent of the world's total proven petroleum reserves.[29] Iran in 2007 accounted for 17 per cent of India's crude oil imports making it the second-largest supplier of oil after Saudi Arabia at 23 per cent.[30]

In addition to seeking new suppliers for energy, India is also looking into energy resource diversification. This accounts for the increasing use of natural gas, largely driven by demand in the power sector. Although India's natural gas production has consistently increased, demand has already exceeded supply and the country has been a net importer of natural gas since 2004.[31] Iran has an enormous reserve of natural gas, which according to a 2008 estimate stands second only to Russia.[32] However, Iran's tremendous potential as a source of natural gas for India is yet to materialise.

Since the mid-1990s, Indian and Iranian officials had been involved in negotiations to construct a gas pipeline stretching from the South Pars fields in Iran via Pakistan to Gujarat in India. The proposal, also known as the Iran-Pakistan-India (IPI) pipeline project, however, came into Washington's spotlight only in 2005. During her visit to India in March 2005, the then-Secretary of State, Condoleezza Rice, publicly expressed her misgivings about India's interest in pursuing a gas pipeline project linking Iran with India. The Indian government had promoted the project as a confidence building measure with Pakistan and this could have benefitted the US as well, but the Bush Administration opposed it on the ground that it had the potential for revitalizing the Iranian energy sector, as well as opening up new possibilities for the export of oil and gas from the wider Caspian sea region through Iran. This would give crucial revenues to Tehran, which has been facing punitive economic sanctions for its controversial nuclear programme and undermine the US policy of isolating the Islamic Republic in global polity and economy.

Soon after the announcement of Indo-US civilian nuclear cooperation agreement in July 2005, Prime Minister Manmohan Singh was quoted as saying that he was not aware "if any international consortium of bankers would probably underwrite this,"[33] which gave away the pressure on New Delhi to abandon the project. As a commentator argues, "Given the improved financial situation of India, even a medium level private company could easily underwrite the $7 billion project. Singh's statement was, therefore, largely political."[34] The US government reportedly warned leading oil companies as well as governments of various nations—including India—that sanctions were possible if they pursued energy deals with Iran. Amid the growing global isolation of Iran, Indian government is now suggesting that its participation in the gas pipeline deal might not give any strategic advantage to the country, given the very low quantity (30 million standard cubic meters per day) of gas involved. On the other hand, on account of India's stand at the IAEA, Iran has put off the IPI project by raising several technical and financial issues. In the context, the Indian side has pointed out that the Iranian gas is not the lowest priced option at the current price structure. Also many in India advocate buying gas at the Pakistan-India border as a better alternative.[35]

Even though Washington is no longer actively opposing the pipeline project, India's collaboration with Iran over the IPI project could now trigger sanctions under the Comprehensive Iran Sanctions, Accountability, and Divestment Act of 2010 (CISADA) should foreign companies that invest more than $20 million in a single year in Iran's energy sector.[36] At the same time, the Indian government does not want to disavow interest in the project lest it be accused by domestic critics of bowing to US pressure. After Pakistan signed an agreement with Iran in June 2010 to procure 750 million cubic feet of natural gas per day through the pipeline (without New Delhi's participation in the negotiations), India has indicated its willingness to resume negotiations on importing gas directly from Iran via the sea route to the Indian shores.[37] The Indian government does not want to disavow interest in the project lest it be accused by domestic critics of bowing to US pressure. The stalemate surrounding this pipeline project is considered to be yet another impact of the US factor on Indo-Iranian cooperation.

Another mega Indo-Iranian energy deal suffered a similar fate as the pipeline project. India had signed a 22 billion dollar deal with Iran for the export of Liquefied Natural Gas (LNG) five-million-ton a year in June 2005, with deliveries scheduled to begin in 2009 for a 25-year period. In the immediate aftermath of India's IAEA vote against Iran, the latter cancelled the agreement to supply India with LNG and called for renegotiation of price of gas.[38] In a recent move, Iran has sought at least one billion dollar in advance for a supply beginning 2012, which has not been entertained at the Indian end.

India's international energy strategy has also been to acquire stakes in energy production facilities in Iran, in order to ship back liquefied natural gas (LNG). In November 2009, the overseas arm of state-run Oil and Natural Gas Commission (ONGC), ONGC Videsh Limited (OVL) and Ashok Leyland Projects Services, a private company, signed agreements to take 40 per cent stake in South Pars field-phase 12 (SP-12), offered by the state-run National Iranian Oil Company (NIOC). OVL has also submitted a $5.5 billion plan to bring to production the Farzad-B gas find in Farsi gas fields in the Persian Gulf. Besides, in December 2009, OVL agreed to take twenty per cent stake in the liquefied natural gas export facility that Iran LNG (a subsidiary of NIOC) is building at the southern Iranian coast. Though this plant is to turn gas produced from phase-12 into LNG for exports, India is eying it for turning gas from the Farzad-B gas field into LNG. The Indian companies are expected to receive up to 6 million tonnes per annum of LNG for its efforts in both the gas fields. However, the two projects are stuck for the fear of inviting US sanctions.[39] The ONGC-Hinduja Group joint venture also suffered a setback in Azadegan oilfield in which the Indian combine was previously offered 45 percent interest, after China having won the right for exploration, by offering multibillion dollar soft loans.[40] The soft loan approach for securing energy assets is not high on India government's agenda as it is also fearful of its firms being banned for investing past the CISADA threshold and attracting sanctions. Moreover, the American authorities are generally opposed to Indian involvement in exploration in the energy sector in Iran.

The Afghan Conundrum

A shared threat from Sunni radicalism emanating from Pakistan and Afghanistan has emerged as one of the most significant area of cooperation between India and Iran. In fact, the two countries cooperated as far back as the early 1990s to limit the march of the Taliban. India and Iran with large Shia Muslim populations were wary of Sunni-Wahabi extremists in their proximate neighbourhood. India was, also, deeply apprehensive of Taliban's 'jihadist' ideology and its potential for fomenting trouble in Kashmir and other parts of the country. As opposed to Pakistan that quickly recognised the

Taliban regime, India and Iran backed Afghanistan's anti-Taliban Northern Alliance. Throughout the last decade, Iran, India, and Russia coordinated extensively to contain Pakistan's involvement in Afghanistan and its support to the Taliban. When the Taliban was routed by the Northern Alliance in November 2001, both New Delhi and Tehran welcomed its demise and made Afghanistan's reconstruction and development a common critical goal.

Iran pledged US$ 560 million at the Tokyo Conference on the Reconstruction of Afghanistan in 2002, and an additional US$ 100 million at the 2006 London Conference. Much of Iranian aid to Afghanistan has been utilised on infrastructure project—mainly transportation links between Iran, Afghanistan, and the Central Asian Republics—something that works in the national interest of Iran. The present level of India's assistance to Afghanistan is US$ 750 million, making it the 5th largest bilateral donor after the US, UK, Japan and Germany. According to the Indian Embassy at Kabul, of the total pledge of US$ 750 million between 2002 and 2009, the fully committed amount is US$ 758.21 million and cumulative disbursement up to 2006-07 has been US$ 278.94 million.[41]

In the New Delhi Declaration, Tehran and New Delhi, resolved to "broaden their strategic collaboration in third countries", in a clear reference to Afghanistan. In recent years, India and Iran have been targets of suicide bombings by the Taliban, al-Qaeda and their terrorist associates based on the Pakistani territory.[42] The Tehran Declaration castigates terrorism "in all its forms" condemning "states that aid, abet and directly support international terrorism" in a barely veiled allusion to Pakistan. Afghanistan and Pakistan are, then, the principal frontiers in combating terrorism targeted against India and Iran. Through joint working groups, India and Iran have been working out ways and means to combat terrorism and narcotics trade—the main source of revenue for the insurgents in Afghanistan.[43]

The issue of terrorism was central to the bilateral discussions during Iranian Foreign Minister Manouchehr Mottaki's visit to India in November 2009 and during his meeting with Indian Foreign Minister S.M. Krishna along the sidelines of the G-15 meets in May 2010.[44] Presently both the countries share similar concerns about the role of Pakistan in fostering a number of terror groups, such as, Lashkar-e-Taiba, Jaish-e-Muhammad, Jamaat-ud-Dawa and al-Qaeda, on its soil, and providing support and haven to Taliban, particularly the 'Haqqani network,' on its western and southern borders (the North Waziristan and FATA areas). India has repeatedly called international attention to Pakistan's military and intelligence establishments' backing of their operations in the subcontinent as well as attacks on India's embassy in Kabul and other India-related targets.[45] The Mumbai blasts of November 2008 and those in Pune in February 2010 have brought this connection to full light. The Pakistani military considers them as counterweights to India's presence in Afghanistan and as means to deepen its strategic depth. Iran is also feeling the heat from increasing Sunni militancy within its territory. A spate of suicide bombings has rocked Zahedan in recent years, a predominantly Sunni city along Iran's frontier with Pakistan. The October 2009 attack on Iran's Islamic Revolutionary Guard Corps in this restive city was attributed to Pakistan-based Jundullah (with possible links to Taliban or al-Qaida or elements within the Pakistani government).[46]

Although, India and Iran have a common strategic interest in countering the Taliban, the "US factor" impedes a full-bodied cooperation in this area. The emerging wisdom on resolving the Afghan imbroglio is of a "regional solution," which is not a high priority with the US administration, as it would involve Iran's participation. Six of the seven neighbouring regional powers with a stake in Afghanistan's future—Russia, Iran, India, China, Uzbekistan, and Tajikistan—share the U.S. goal of preventing the return of a Taliban dispensation in Kabul. Only one, Pakistan, which helped install and sustain the Taliban regime that ruled from 1996 to 2001, wants to see it back in power. Given their collision over the nuclear issue, Iran is not willing to be engaged in a situation which has the US at the helm of affairs. Where does that leave India that maintains a belief in diplomatic initiative by the United States to mobilize support of Afghanistan's neighbours? Can New Delhi persuade both Washington and Tehran to participate in a regional conference of the kind proposed by Secretary of State Hillary Clinton in March 2009[47] that would include Iran? The answers may not be easy, given that India and Iran hold divergent views on the US role, even though, both have been isolated by the American acknowledgment of Pakistan as a critical partner in search for an

Afghan settlement. Furthermore, India has also lost a lot of leverage with Iran with the IAEA votes and, therefore, may not be in a situation to play the role of an effective mediator. Iran may also be looking for a direct US request in this regard as was the case in 2001, rather than that passed on by India, even as the interest of the three countries intersects on this issue.[48]

Both India and Iran face an uneasy scenario of a Taliban dispensation in Kabul, given the United States' policy of negotiating with insurgent leaders, the so-called 'good' Taliban. A rapidly-expanding Taliban insurgency against the US-led NATO forces has made Washington realize that there can be no easy victory in the Afghan war. The United States has opened the door to a reconciliation process in which the American military would reach out to moderate elements of the Taliban, much as it did with Sunni militias in Iraq. This policy also reflects Afghan President Hamid Karzai's own inclination to integrate Taliban fighters who renounce violence into the Afghan armed forces.[49] Islamabad has already offered to help the Americans and Karzai government negotiate with the Taliban and other insurgents. Iran and India have joined hands to oppose the distinction between "good" and "bad" Taliban, dismissing the adoption of a $ 500 million Peace and Reintegration Trust Fund at the London Summit in January 2010, to bring Taliban fighters into the civilian fold, as absurd and destabilizing.[50]

While India is worried that a Taliban regime in Kabul will lead to an increase in Pakistan-based terrorism and deepen Islamabad's "strategic depth," Iran fears that such a scenario would strengthen the Sunni Jundullah separatist movement in Iranian Baluchistan and Wahabi militants in neighbouring regions. It is, therefore, in the interests of the two countries, to intensify coordination with each other and with other regional players such as Russia and Central Asian Republics, to stabilize Afghanistan. Indo-Iranian Joint Working Group on Terrorism is a ready instrument to begin renewed cooperation on combating the Taliban insurgency and the narcotics trade that sustains it. However, it would be foolhardy to assume that a regional initiative on Afghanistan can be sustained without the sanction and assistance of the United States and herein rests the dilemma of Indo-Iran cooperation on Afghanistan, notwithstanding its immense imperative.

Indo-Iran Relations and the Impact of the "US Factor": An Assessment

In the preceding sections, we have seen the scope and limitations of Indo-Iranian ties. This paper argues that India's relations with Iran are founded on pragmatic considerations and bolstered by complimentary interests in energy and strategic areas and, hence, here to stay. India's success in securing its ties with the United States has not deterred it from defending its relations with Iran. The February 2007 visit of India's then Foreign Minister Pranab Mukherjee to Iran and Iranian President Mahmoud Ahmedinejad's visit to India in April 2008—both amid heightened US-Iranian tension on the nuclear issue and clandestine Iranian involvement in Iraq—are pointers that India will continue to pursue its relations with Iran in view of its interest and requirements.

Tehran with its vast oil and gas reserves remains is crucial to New Delhi's growing energy needs, including an access to the Central Asian oil and gas reserves. Further, in the context of the projected and possibly prolonged instability in Pakistan and Afghanistan, both India and Iran Tehran share a common strategic objective of regional stability in south-west Asia, which makes them a long-term strategic partner. Containing extremism and militancy of Taliban in Afghanistan and Pakistan remains integral to that goal. Indo-Iran strategic cooperation has acquired renewed salience in the light of the United States' "exit strategy" in Afghanistan involving negotiations with "moderate" elements of the Taliban. With the possibility of a Taliban regime in Kabul, both India and Iran have equities to defend in the region. It is in the interest of India and Iran to support Karzai's government with all possible developmental and technical support. A coordinated effort in this direction with other regional powers that have a stake in containing extremism in Afghanistan needs to be explored by the two countries.

Besides, Tehran is an important ally of New Delhi in Islamic world, especially as a counter-weight to Islamabad's anti-India rhetoric. India's growing relations with Israel and its diminishing support for the Palestinian cause have compelled India to cultivate its relations with Iran, as a step towards fortifying its relations with other Muslim countries. The United States under Obama administration appears to have adopted a more nuanced foreign policy towards India-Iran relations. Thus, Washington has refrained from publicly expressing disapproval of the ties between the two countries. India on the other hand comprehends the areas where its relations with Iran might run afoul of the American interests: any cooperation on Iran's nuclear and military programme and defence enhancements would be crossing explicit redlines here. Such a position not only fulfils Washington's major objectives but also takes into consideration India's national interests.

Some analysts lament that India's propensity to walk the thin line by balancing its relationship with Iran and the United States, does not contribute constructively to the solution of Iran's nuclear imbroglio. They argue that India could be more proactive in persuading Iran out of its confrontationist posture vis-à-vis the western powers. In effect, India can serve as an effective interlocutor on a range of issues, beyond the enrichment question. So far India has desisted from assuming such as role, perhaps, in appreciation of the fact that it would have no real influence on the domestic constraints of Iranian foreign policy towards the United States and the West. However, India can work with the GCC states in securing an accommodation with Iran. If elements of security assurances are added into any agreement among the parties, it would allay Iran's fears to a great extent and make the Persian Gulf more secure. Such an initiative requires bold diplomatic moves on the part of New Delhi.

By maintaining its ties with Iran and US, India has demonstrated a resolve to protect its interests with both the Tehran and Washington without becoming drawn into their conflict. India's relationship with Iran enjoys across the board acceptance, whereas the same cannot be said about Indo-US relations. The Left parties and a section of Indian public opinion have been highly critical of India's strategic relationship with the United States, arguing that it would clench New Delhi into doing the superpower's bidding and undermine autonomous diplomatic initiative on international issues. While it is true that India set aside its traditional position on Iran by voting in tandem with the US over the nuclear wrangle at the IAEA, it did not restrict the scope of New Delhi's interest in Tehran. Apart from the fixtures in India's relations with Iran, other, less talked-about concerns also animate Indo-Iranian bilateral ties. A security conception and power projection beyond the perimeters of South Asia is essential as India seeks to be recognised as a global power with a decisive voice in international affairs. In keeping with this ambition, New Delhi aims to consolidate its presence in Afghanistan and Central Asia states and Tehran is pivotal to this endeavour. Iran offers easy land access to these countries, thereby, conferring India the strategic depth in much of its proximate neighbourhood. Any destabilisation in the Persian Gulf or weakening of India's ties with Iran can only jeopardize New Delhi's interest in south-west Asia. This would be an unaffordable scenario, considering the importance of the region to India's security in the post-NATO scenario. Above all, continued ties with Iran helps India to reclaim the space of autonomous decision-making withered with the nuclear deal.

Notes

1. See Harsh V. Pant, "A Fine Balance: India Walks a Tightrope between Iran and the United States," *Orbis*, vol. 51, no. 3 (Summer 2007), 495-509.
2. For an elucidation of the independent/autonomous strain in Indian foreign policy and its impact on India's future international relations, see Sumit Ganguly, "India's Alliances 2020," in *South Asia in 2020: Future Strategic Balances and Alliances*, ed. Michael Chambers (Carlisle, Penn.: Strategic Studies Institute, 2002), 363-79.
3. See C. Christine Fair, "Indo-Iranian Relations: Prospects for Bilateral Cooperation Post-9/11," in *The Strategic Partnership' between India and Iran Asia Program Special Report*, no.120 (April 2004), ed. Robert M. Hathaway, 10; Harsh V. Pant, "India and Iran: An "Axis" in the Making?"*Asian Survey*, vol. 44, no. 3 (May/June 2003), 371; "PM's Opening Statement at Delegation-Level Talks," April 10, 2001, http://meaindia.nic.in//speech/2001/04/10spc01.htm; "The New Delhi Declaration, 25 January 2003," signed between the Republic of India and the Islamic Republic of Iran, http://meaindia.nic.in//declarestatement/2003/01/25jd1.htm.
4. Carin Zissis, "India's Energy Crunch," *Council on Foreign Relations*, October 23, 2007, http://www.cfr.org/publication/12200/indias_energy_crunch.html.
5. See Vipul Tuli, "Regional Cooperation for Asian Energy Security", *RIS Discussion Paper*, no. 112 (August 2006), http://www.ris.org.in/dp112_pap.pdf, 2.
6. With Central Asian energy reserves being estimated at 2.7 percent of total world oil reserves and 7 percent of total natural gas reserves, the

region has a huge potential as a future energy source for India. Nivedita Das Kundu, "Hamid Ansari's Visit to Turkmenistan and Kazakhstan," April 24, 2008, http://www.idsa.in/idsastrategiccomments/HamidAnsarisVisittoTurkmenistanandKazakhstan_NDKundu_240408. On the importance of Central Asian region to India, see Stephen Blank, "India's Rising Profile in Central Asia," *Comparative Strategy*, vol. 22, no. 2 (April-June, 2003), 139-157; and Teresita C. Schaffer and Vibhuti Haté, "India's 'Look West' Policy: Why Central Asia Matters," *South Asia Monitor*, no. 110 (September 5, 2007), http://csis.org/files/media/csis/pubs/sam110.pdf.

7. More specifically, Indian aeronautical engineers will help Iran maintain and provide mid-life upgrade for its MiG fighter aircraft. Iran has also sought India's help to refit and maintain tanks, infantry fighting vehicles, and artillery guns. India is also planning to sell Konkurs anti-tank guided weapons and spare parts. In the past, India has helped Iran adapt four Russian-built Kilo-class submarines for warm water conditions in the Persian Gulf. Iran is also seeking combat training for missile boat crews and hopes to purchase simulators for ships and submarines from India. See Rizwan Zeb, "The Emerging Indo-Iranian Strategic Alliance and Pakistan," *Central Asia Caucasus Institute Analyst*, February 12, 2003, http://www.cacianalyst.org/?q=node/902; Ehsan Ahrari, "As India and Iran snuggle, Pakistan feels the chill," February 11, 2003, Asia Times Online, http://www.atimes.com/atimes/South_Asia/EB11Df01.html; John Calabrese, "Indo-Iranian Relations in Transition," *Journal of South Asia and Middle Eastern Studies*, vol. 25, no. 3 (Summer 2002), 75-76.
8. As cited in Donald L. Berlin, "India-Iran Relations: A Deepening Entente," *Asia-Pacific Center for Security Studies Special Assessment* (October 2004), 1. See also, Ahrari, "As India and Iran snuggle..."
9. Ronak D. Desai and Xenia Dormandy, "India-Iran Relations: Key Security Implications," March 26, 2008, www.belfercenter.org/india.
10. See C. Christine Fair, "Indo-Iranian Ties: Thicker than Oil," *Middle East Review of International Affairs*, vol. 11, no. 1 (March 2007), 51-2.
11. India strives to consolidate a strategic presence in Central Asia and the neighbouring areas, illustrated in air bases in Tajikistan and expanding presence in Afghanistan, in order to deny Pakistan the much-sought-after strategic depth. See Christine Fair, "India and Iran: New Delhi's Balancing Act," *Washington Quarterly*, vol. 30, no. 3 (Summer 2007), 148.
12. Teresita C. Schaffer, "The United States and India 10 Years Out," *The US-India Initiative Series Working Paper*, October 2010, http://www.cnas.org/node/5128.
13. See, Sumit Ganguly and Andrew Scobell, "India and the United States: Forging a Security Partnership?" *World Policy Journal*, vol. xxii, no. 2 (Summer 2005).
14. For an objective and insightful book that provides an insider's perspective

on the ground-breaking efforts to build a cordial relationship between the world's two largest democracies, see Strobe Talbott, *Engaging India: Diplomacy, Democracy, and the Bomb* (New Delhi: Penguin, 2004).

15. Ganguly and Scobell, "India and the United States..."
16. For the text and terms of the Agreement, see "Joint Statement Between President George W. Bush and Prime Minister Manmohan Singh," http://georgewbush-whitehouse.archives.gov/news/releases/2005/07/20050718-6.html;
For a discussion of the factors that facilitated the agreement, the roadblocks that were encountered, and its implications for the future of India's foreign policy, its energy security and the international non-proliferation regime and impact on Indo-US relations, see, P.R. Chari, ed., *Indo-US Nuclear Deal: Seeking Synergy in Bilateralism* (New Delhi: Routledge, 2009), and Jayshree Bajoria, "The US-India Nuclear Deal," November 5, 2010, http://www.cfr.org/india/us-india-nuclear-deal/p9663;
For arguments for and against the deal, see Hari Sud, "India–US Nuclear Deal: The Benefits," March 20, 2006, http://www.southasiaanalysis.org/%5Cpapers18%5Cpaper1740.html; Siddharth Varadarajan, "The truth behind the Indo-U.S. nuclear deal," July 29, 2005, http://www.globalresearch.ca/index.php?context=va&aid=756;
Ashley Tellis, "India as a New Global Power: An Action Agenda for the United States," 2005, http://www.carnegieendowment.org/files/Tellis.India.Global.Power.FINAL.pdf;
George Perkovich, "Faulty Promises: The US-India Nuclear Deal," September 2005, http://carnegieendowment.org/files/PO21.Perkovich.pdf.
17. For India's scepticism at designation of Islamabad as a critical partner in this endeavour, see Evan A. Feigenbaum, "Obama's India Problem," *Council on Foreign Relations*, April 9, 2010, http://www.cfr.org/india/obamas-india-problem/p21862.
18. The cable sent on September 6, 2005, noted that the then US Ambassador to India, David C. Mulford, told Foreign Secretary Shyam Saran that "the time was drawing near for fence sitters to make hard decisions...Many in Congress and throughout Washington he reminded Saran, were watching India's treatment of Iran prior to Congressional debate on the US-India civilian nuclear initiative...India had a key voice in the NAM and could swing opinion in the BOG; it was time, he said, for us to know where India stood." A comment titled "Smelling the coffee" in a cable sent three days later, notes wryly that "the September 8 HIRC statements on Iran by members of Congress served as a wakeup call to India and its Iran stance would directly impact its desire to for legislative fixes that would implement the July 18 POTUS-PM Singh agreements, especially on civilian nuclear technology. India is sufficiently

concerned to restate its position on Iran's nuclear weapons. We have an opportunity as a result. The Indians believed that they have been helpful in the IAEA on Iran, but we should press for more." Cable No. 39910 (secret), "A nuclear Iran still unacceptable to India, but Delhi questions eventual armed confrontation," dated 9/6/2005 published by *The Hindu*, March 15, 2011, www.thehindu.com.

19. Cable No. 49618 (secret), "India could vote against Iran," dated 1/12/2006 published by *The Hindu*, March 17, 2011, www.thehindu.com.
20. "Landmark nuclear deal between U.S. and India could 'die in Congress'," *Pravda.Ru*, January 26, 2006, http://english.pravda.ru/news/world/26-01-2006/74741-0/
21. Stephen G. Rademaker, a former official of the Bush administration, opined in a talk in 2007 in New Delhi (at a premier security-related think tank-IDSA) that India's votes against Iran at the IAEA were 'coerced'. Siddharth Varadarajan, "India's anti-Iran votes were coerced, says former U.S. official," *The Hindu*, Feb 16, 2007, http://www.hindu.com/2007/02/16/stories/2007021605671200.htm.
22. Manmohan Singh was criticised by the Opposition parties for bowing to the dictates of the United States on Iran and ignoring the national interests associated with India-Iran ties. For example, see "Congress defends vote, JD(S) criticises," *The Hindu*, September 27, 2005, http://www.hindu.com/2005/09/27/stories/2005092705341200.htm; "India's shameful vote against Iran," The Hindu, September 26, 2005, http://www.hindu.com/2005/09/26/stories/2005092606071000.htm; John Cherian, "The Indian volte-face," *Frontline*, vol. 22, issue 2 (October 8-21, 2005), http://www.frontlineonnet.com/fl2221/stories/20051021007113000.htm.
23. Cable No. 58266 (confidential), "India's relationship with Iran should not trouble U.S.," dated 3/27/2006 published by *The Hindu*, March 17, 2011, www.thehindu.com. Tom Lantos, the senior-most Democrat of the House International Relations Committee, was particularly disturbed by the exercise and opined that, "... in order to become a strategic ally of the United States, he said, India must recognise some basic facts, specifically some facts with respect to Iran: It is a terrorist state whose current regime strives to develop nuclear weapons. At this committee's first hearing on the proposed nuclear deal, I and others on this committee made it clear that a 'business as usual' relationship with the current terrorist regime in Tehran is unacceptable behaviour by any country seeking to be our strategic partner." Aziz Haniffa, "India Not a Threat to NPT," *Rediff.com*, April 6, 2006, http://www.rediff.com/news/2006/apr/06ndeal1.htm.
24. The then Secretary of State Condoleezza Rice argued in a Congressional hearing for the nuclear deal that it will help India "meet its rising energy needs without increasing its reliance on unstable foreign sources of oil

and gas, such as nearby Iran." See The Honourable Condoleezza Rice at the US Senate Committee on Foreign Relations on "U.S.-India Atomic Energy Cooperation: The Indian Separation Plan and the Administration's Legislative Proposal," April 5, 2006, http://foreign.senate.gov/hearings/hearing/?id=d2fe308b-f34d-83ee-1e10-83b3d9e70f8e.

25. While speaking on a televised discussion on WikiLeaks revelations, Mulford gamely fielded a number of questions on some of the other cables, most notably whether the U.S. had "arm-twisted" India into voting against Iran at the International Atomic Energy Agency (IAEA) in 2005. While observing that the "prospects of a civil nuclear deal would [have been] immeasurably damaged" had India chosen "to abstain or sit on the fence," Mr. Mulford went to the extent of justifying his actions as reported in the cable, saying "it was a key thing to do and do well." "I would not call it arm-twisting," said the former Ambassador, "but it was appropriate for me to reflect to the Indian government the dangers of not supporting a vote on Iran." S. Arun Mohan, "U.S. Embassy reports are generally accurate: Mulford," *The Hindu*, March 19, 2011, http://www.hindu.com/2011/03/19/stories/2011031962241000.htm
26. Anirudh Bhattacharya, "Status Quo on Indo-US Ties," *Hindustan Times*, January 21, 2010.
27. Harsh V. Pant, "India's Relations with Iran: Much Ado About Nothing," *Washington Quarterly*, vol. 34, no. 1 (Winter 2011), 62.
28. *Integrated Energy Policy: Report of the Expert Committee* (New Delhi: Planning Commission, 2006), http://planningcommission.gov.in/reports/genrep/rep_intengy.pdf, 9.
29. Country Analysis Briefs, "Iran," *Energy Information Administration (EIA) Official Energy Statistics from the US Government,* 2010, http://www.eia.doe.gov/emeu/cabs/Iran/Full.html.
30. *World Trade Atlas*, quoted in, Country Analysis Briefs, "India," *Energy Information Administration (EIA), Official Energy Statistics from the US Government*, March 2009, http://www.eia.doe.gov/emeu/cabs/India/Full.html.
31. Ibid.
32. *Oil and Gas Journal* quoted in "Iran," http://www.eia.doe.gov/emeu/cabs/Iran/Full.html.
33. "Indo-Iran pipeline full of risks: PM," Rediff.com, July 21, 2005, http://www.rediff.com/money/2005/jul/21pm.htm.
34. P.R. Kumaraswamy, "Delhi: Between Tehran and Washington," *Middle East Quarterly*, vol. XV, no. 1 (Winter 2008), 41-47.
35. The deal has faced numerous hiccups during the negotiations of which the United States' opposition to it proved to be decisive factor. These have been discussed in different details by diverse source. For example, see Teresita C. Schaffer and Suzanne Fawzi, "India and Iran: Limited Partnership, High Stakes," *South Asia Monitor*, no. 114 (December 20,

2007) 2; "India", *Energy Information Administration Official Energy Statistics from the US Government*, March 2009, http://www.eia.doe.gov/emeu/cabs/India/Full.html; Shiv Kumar Verma, "Energy geopolitics and Iran–Pakistan–India gas pipeline", *Energy Policy*, vol. 35, issue 6 (June 2007), 3280-3301; Harsh V. Pant, "Pakistan and Iran's Dysfunctional Relationship," *Middle East Quarterly* (Spring 2009), http://www.meforum.org/2119/pakistan-and-irans-dysfunctional-relationship; Alidad Mafinezam and Aria Mehrabi, *Iran and its Place among Nations* (Westport, CT and London: Praeger, 2008), 78.

36. See also "investment" http://www.iranwatch.org/government/US/Congress/CRS/us-congress-crs-indiairanrelations-usinterests-080206.pdf. CISADA was passed by Congress on June 24, 2010 and signed into law by President Obama on July 1, 2010. The Act expands upon the restrictions of the Iran Sanctions Act of 1996 (the ISA) and the Iranian Transaction Regulations administered by the Department of Treasury's Office of Foreign Assets Control (OFAC). CISADA covers a significantly broader range of areas than the ISA that makes it of particular interest to companies with, or considering business activities related to Iran. For full text of the Act, see "Comprehensive Iran Sanctions, Accountability, and Divestment Act of 2010," *The Library of Congress*, June 24, 2010, http://thomas.loc.gov/home/gpoxmlc111/h2194_enr.xml.
37. Syed Fazl-e-Haider, "Pakistan seals pipeline deal with Iran," *Asian Times Online*, June 15, 2010, http://www.atimes.com/atimes/South_Asia/LF15Df02.html; "India out of 'peace pipeline' as Iran, Pakistan seal gas deal," *Times of India*, June 14, 2010; Daniel Graeber, "IPI pipeline deal signed in Istanbul," *Energy Daily*, June 8, 2009, http://www.energy-daily.com/reports/IPI_pipeline_deal_signed_in_Istanbul_999.html.
38. "India signs mega LNG import deal with Iran," *Energy Bulletin*, January 7, 2005, http://www.energybulletin.net/node/3929; Sujay Mehdudia, "India-Iran LNG deal hits roadblocks," *The Hindu*, May 21, 2007, http://www.hindu.com/2007/05/21/stories/2007052104541300.htm.
39. "ONGC to use Iran LNG facility for Farsi gas," *Business Standard*, December 8, 2009. http://www.business-standard.com/india/news/ongc-to-use-iran-lng-facility-for-farsi-gas/80224/on; Utpal Bhaskar, "US sanctions on Iran have OVL wary," *livemint.com*, Jan 12, 2011, http://www.livemint.com/2011/01/11235319/US-sanctions-on-Iran-have-OVL.html?atype=tp.
40. "Iran seeks $1 bn 'Advance' For LNG," *Financial Express*, November 17, 2009, http://www.financialexpress.com/news/iran-seeks-1bn-advance-for-lng/542262/2.
41. For a comprehensive analysis of Iran's interest in Afghanistan, see, "Iran and Afghanistan," *Institute for the Study of War Report, Institute for the Study of War*, http://www.understandingwar.org/themenode/iran-and-afghanistan (undated). For India's investment in Afghanistan, see, Sudha

Ramachandran, "India drawn deeper into Afghanistan," *Asia Times Online*, April 24, 2008, http://www.atimes.com/atimes/South_Asia/JD24Df03.html; Kanchan Lakshman, "The Cat's Paw in Nimroz," April 16, 2008, http://www.outlookindia.com/article.aspx?237228; and Harsh V. Pant , "India in Afghanistan: The "Soft Power" Question," Oct 15, 2009, http://www.isn.ethz.ch/isn/layout/set/print/content/view/full/73?id=108562&lng=en

42. A spate of suicide bombings has rocked the Iranian city of Zahedan in recent years. Zahedan is a predominantly Sunni city and is the capital of Sistan-Baluchestan province, which shares a border with Pakistan. The bombings have been attributed to a Sunni Muslim group, Jundullah, with possible links to elements in Pakistan (Taliban or al-Qaida) or elements possibly even within the Pakistani government. See "Bombing Kills Iran's Revolutionary Guard Commanders," October 18, 2009, http://www.npr.org/templates/story/story.php?storyId=113911959. In addition to the bombings on the Indian Embassy in Kabul in July 2008 and October 2009 and the killing of Indian workers stationed in Afghanistan by the Taliban, India was subject to the worst ever terrorist attack from militant group, Lashkar-e Tayyiba based in Pakistan on its financial hub, Mumbai. See the final form of the report on the attack, February 25, 2009, http://www.hindu.com/nic/mumbai-terror-attack-final-form.pdf.

43. Afghanistan is responsible for more than 90 percent of the world's illicit opium production, and more than half of that product is smuggled across the Iranian-Afghan border. Furthermore, a third of Afghan heroin, which accounts for more than 90 percent of world supply, is trafficked through Iran. However, Iran is not just a transit point for these drugs as they are smuggled into the Middle East, Europe, and beyond; it itself has a significant drug problem with the highest rate of opiate abuse in the world. Iran has committed itself to combating the drug epidemic within its borders, cracking down on domestic opium cultivation and interdicting drug shipments from Afghanistan. Tehran has also developed a constructive relationship with Kabul in the field of counternarcotics, though questions remain about Iran's role in impeding Afghanistan's entry into the saffron market as an alternative to the poppy crops. "Iran and Afghanistan," *Institute for the Study of War Report*, http://www.understandingwar.org/themenode/iran-and-afghanistan (undated). For revenue incurring to the insurgents from narcotics trade, see Jonathan Goodhand, "Conditioning Peace? The Scope and Limitations of Peace Conditionalities in Afghanistan and Sri Lanka," 2006, http://www.clingendael.nl/publications/2006/20060800_cru_goodhand.pdf, 5.

44. See "India-Iran Relations," February 2011, http://meaindia.nic.in/meaxpsite/foreignrelation/iran.pdf; "India, Iran discuss ways to enhance ties," *Times of India*, May 18, 2010.

45. For an account of the support and haven that extremists have received from the Pakistani government's on the Afghan-Pakistani frontier and the political difficulties in forging a political settlement in Afghanistan, see, Ahmed Rashid, *Descent into Chaos: The United States and the Failure of Nation Building in Pakistan, Afghanistan, and Central Asia* (New York: Viking Press, 2008). A valuable description of today's most active jihadi movements in Pakistan is provided by Hassan Abbas, *Pakistan's Drift into Extremism: Allah, the Army, and America's War on Terror* (New York: M. E. Sharpe, 2005). A critical view of America's reliance on Pakistan as a front-line state for war against terrorism, see, Craig Cohen and Derek Chollet, "When $10 Billion Is Not Enough: Rethinking U.S. Strategy toward Pakistan," *The Washington Quarterly*, vol. 30, no. 2 (Spring 2007), 7-19; Ashley J. Tellis, "Pakistan and the War on Terror: Conflicted Goals, Compromised Performance," *The Washington Quarterly*, vol. 31, no. 2 (Spring 2008), 7-32. An overview of Taliban insurgency in Pakistan and America's policy in the region under Obama administration, see Kenneth Katzman, "Afghanistan: Post-Taliban Governance, Security, and U.S. Policy," *Congressional Research Service*, February 18, 2011, www.crs.gov.
46. Michael Slackman, "Iran Blames US and Britain in attack," *New York Times*, 19 October 2009, http://www.nytimes.com/2009/10/20/world/middleeast/20iran.html; "Profile: Iran's Jundullah militants," June 20, 2010, http://news.bbc.co.uk/2/hi/middle_east/8314431.stm; Raja Karthikeya, "Jundullah a wedge between Iran, Pakistan," *Asia Times Online*, Aug 7, 2009, http://www.atimes.com/atimes/South_Asia/KH07Df04.html.
47. Selig S. Harrison, "How to Leave Afghanistan without Losing," *Foreign Policy*, August 24, 2010, http://www.foreignpolicy.com/articles/2010/08/24/how_to_leave_afghanistan_without_losing.
48. For arguments on the importance of rapprochement between the US and Iran and the significance of India 'factor' see Mohammed Ayoob, "South-west Asia after the Taliban", *Survival*, vol. 44, no. 1 (Spring 2002), 10-15.
49. For a comprehensive account of this policy shift of the US administration and Karzai's policy of negotiating with senior insurgent leaders, see Kenneth Katzman, "Afghanistan: Post-Taliban Governance, Security, and U.S. Policy," *Congressional Research Service*, February 18, 2011, http://www.fas.org/sgp/crs/row/RL30588.pdf.
50. In fact, it was Pakistan that first floated the notion that the Taliban could be categorized as 'good' and 'bad' The 'good' Taliban were those who could cut ties with al-Qaeda and other terrorist groups and pursue their political goals peacefully. However, the irony is that there can be no such neat distinction as both al-Qaida and the Taliban in Afghanistan are surviving and flourishing with the connivance of the Pakistani establishment. It is no surprise that the Talibanization of Pakistan is

taking place rapidly and US-led NATO forces are increasingly losing ground in Afghanistan. See, Jane Perlez, “Pakistan is said to pursue role in U.S.-Afghan talks,” February 9, 2010, http://www.nytimes.com/2010/02/10/world/asia/10pstan.html; Prakash Nanda, “The Elusive Search for ‘Good Taliban’,” February 3, 2010. http://www.upiasia.com/Security/2010/02/03/the_elusive_search_for_good_taliban/5951/; Kanchan Gupta, “US legitimising the Taliban,” *Sunday Pioneer*, January 31, 2010, http://www.dailypioneer.com/232672/US-legitimising-the-Taliban.html. On the other hand, India, disfavours any negotiations with Taliban, either in Afghanistan or Pakistan, saying there are no good elements in the fundamentalist militia. New Delhi feels that efforts should be made to create ‘secure areas’ and promote developmental activities in such areas, a process that would alienate the Taliban. See, for example, Dharam Shourie, “Good Taliban, Bad Taliban? India Disagrees,” March 20, 2009, http://news.outlookindia.com/item.aspx?656268; Satish Chandra, “London Conference on Afghanistan: Implications for India,” *Rediff.com*, Feb 08, 2010, http://news.rediff.com/column/2010/feb/08/afghan-conference-implications-for-india.htm.

10

The Impact of Domestic Politics on India's Attitudes towards Israel and Jews

Navras Jaat Aafreedi

The only chair for Hebrew Studies in India, at the Jawaharlal Nehru University in New Delhi, funded by the Government of Israel, remains vacant even after a number of years of its being founded, because of its being reserved for the visually challenged. While Islamic Studies and Arabic and Persian are available at almost all major Indian universities and a state university devoted primarily to Arabic and Persian is being established in Lucknow in Uttar Pradesh[1] (despite the dwindling number of applicants for courses in these languages at the University of Lucknow[2]), Jewish Studies is absolutely non-existent, in spite of a continuous Jewish presence in the country for more than two millennia, a period certainly much longer than that of the Muslim presence in India. In sharp contrast to India its neighbour China, which does not have any Jewish community of its own, has Jewish Studies as an academic discipline at ten universities.[3] All this is a reflection of the apathy of the State of India towards Jewish and Hebrew Studies, in spite of the growing relations between the world's only Jewish state, Israel, and the secular state of India, the only country in the world where Jews have lived with dignity and in harmony with their non-Jewish neighbours for two thousand years.

The attitude of the State of India towards Jewish and Hebrew

Studies is dictated by domestic political concerns, just as Jews fleeing the Holocaust largely failed to obtain asylum in India, as it was made mandatory for them to give proof of guaranteed employment in India before being allowed entry. As a result of this only two thousand Jews from Nazi Europe managed to get asylum in India. "The opposition to the Jews came from the Muslim leaders in India who were pro-Arabs. For them the bonds of religion were stronger than the sufferings of Jews under Hitler. Keeping in view the sentiments of the Muslims towards this question, the government imposed many restrictions on the settlement of Jews in India. How far the policy of the Indian National Congress to appease the Muslims was also responsible for this stand of the government needs further study," writes Tilak Raj Sareen, former Director and Member Secretary of the Indian Council of Historical Research.[4] Shortly after his return from Europe, most probably at the Wardha session of the Congress Working Commmitee in December 1938, Nehru sponsored a resolution in support of the Jewish refugees, which read: "The Committee sees no objection to the employment in India of such Jewish refugees as are experts and specialists and who can fit in with the new order in India and accept Indian standards."[5]

But it was rejected by the then Congress President Subhas Chandra Bose, who, four years later, in 1942, was reported by the *Jewish Chronicle* of London to have published an article in *Angriff*, a journal of Goebbels, saying that "anti-Semitism should become part of the Indian liberation movement because the Jews had helped the British to exploit Indians (21 August 1942)."[6] Although by then Bose had left the Congress, yet he continued to command a strong influence in the party.[7] Nehru's proposal was also opposed by the Hindu Right. Savarkar, the leader of the Hindu Mahasabha, said: "...they [Indian Jews] are too few, have given us no political or cultural troubles and are not in the main a proselytising people, they will be friendly towards the Hindus who have sheltered them when homeless and can be easily assimilated in a common Indian State. But this fact must not land us again into the suicidal generosity our forefathers had been guilty of in other cases of inviting colonies of non-Hindus to India. With every sympathy with the Jews outside India, the Hindus must, therefore, oppose the present Congressite proposal of inviting or allowing any new Jewish colony to settle in

India. India must be a Hindu land, reserved for the Hindus. While our own Hindu overpopulation in some parts of India is hard pressed to find land for extention [*sic*], how absurd it is to invite non-Hindu colonies to settle in our thinly populated parts! How ridiculous it is to find some Congressites preaching birth-control to restrict our own population in order to avoid overcrowding and start straightaway to invite Jewish colonies to settle in India."[8]

In spite of the students being taught about the Second World War as part of the subject Modern European History, the students are never asked any questions about the Holocaust in any examination at any Indian university, with perhaps the exception of Jawaharlal Nehru University. When I asked the Head of the Department of Western History at the University of Lucknow, Dr. Nina David, about it, she responded by saying:

Since this is a topic which is part of the European history syllabus at the undergraduate level, we definitely discuss the Nazi persecution of the Jews, popularly known as the Holocaust, which has also been denied by many people. But the fact is that Hitler did persecute the Jews. I do discuss it at length, but we don't generally ask questions specifically on the Holocaust in the examination. It is just a part of Hitler and the Nazis, about whom I teach in the class. It is just a small segment of it. I don't sort of magnify the Holocaust while I discuss the Nazis. I cannot spend so much time on only one aspect of the Nazis... I have never thought of setting a question on it and neither have any examiners set a question on this.[9]

Until 2002, the Holocaust did not find any mention in the standard history textbook in Gujarat, which discussed in detail the terms of the treaty of Versailles. In response to complaints from the Government of Israel, the textbook was revised to only vaguely mention that many Jews were killed during the war, without mentioning the Holocaust.[10] A Holocaust films retrospective organised by the present author at two universities in Lucknow in 2009,[11] often got misrepresented in the press as a retrospective of films focussing on the Second World War.

There was, of course, the concern that Pakistan could influence the Arab world in its favour on the Kashmir issue by its anti-Israel policy, besides the considerations of energy security and employment opportunities for Indians in the Arab countries, but it was largely the Indian Muslim antagonism towards Israel that kept India from formally establishing diplomatic relations with the State of Israel for four decades, as, to put it plainly, the Indian politicians feared losing Muslim votes if the Indian state established diplomatic ties with Israel. However, in spite of all its efforts, the Muslim countries not only remained neutral during the Sino-Indian war of 1962, but even supported Pakistan during the Indo-Pakistan wars of 1965 and 1971. Shashank Joshi draws our attention to the fact "in the 1965 Indo-Pakistani War, for instance, 'Muslim' states as disparate as Jordan, Turkey, Saudi Arabia and Iran all sent military aircraft to assist Pakistan. Ironically, Israel offered covert support to India in this, as well as the 1962 Sino-Indian War before and the 1999 Kargil War after. In the latter conflict, Israel reportedly rushed ammunition to India, and assisted in the interpretation of imagery from unmanned aerial vehicles (UAVs, or drones)."[12] What is also interesting is that India continued to have relations with both China and Pakistan in spite of the wars it fought with them, but refused to have any with Israel despite the absence of any dispute or conflict with it. "India's refusal to maintain formal relations did not inhibit its leaders from seeking help and assistance from the Jewish state," discloses Kumaraswamy. "Ironically this trend began with Prime Minister Nehru. A few months after voting against the UN partition plan, he sought agricultural experts from Israel. ...During the 1962 Sino-Indian debacle, Nehru sought and obtained limited quantities of military assistance from Ben-Gurion. Likewise, anti-Israeli statements in public did not inhibit his daughter, Prime Minister Indira Gandhi, from establishing closer ties with the Israeli intelligence establishment."

"Indian Muslims have been sympathetic towards the Islamic countries and their perceived opposition significantly contributed to the prolonged absence of political relations between India and Israel," as P.R. Kumâraswâmy writes,[13] which he sees as "an aberration in India's overall attitude toward the Jewish people".[14] He correctly feels that anything that suggests the Muslim role in India's Israel policy similar to that played by Jews in America's Israel policy is generally unpopular in India. He points out, "there are a number of differences between the two communities. ...Despite these differences and obvious limitations, it is possible to draw a parallel between the roles played by American Jews and Indian Muslims. ...For the Jews, a pro-Israeli policy serves U.S. interests, and for the Muslims a pro-Arab policy promotes Indian interests. ...There is, however, a catch. The role played by the Jews in influencing U.S. Middle East policy is a hotly debated and even contested issue in the United States. Establishing a similar link between the domestic factor and India's Israel policy is a herculean task. India remains the only democratic state that does not declassify official papers. The Right to Information Act introduced in 2005 does not cover the foreign-policy domain, and much of the documentation pertaining to the Nehru era (1947-1964) remains classified. Sifting through the limited archival materials currently available in New Delhi, acrimonious debates in the Indian parliament, and declassified materials in Israel, one can reasonably conclude that the domestic factor played an important role in India's understanding of Jewish history and its policy regarding Israel. Behind the official secular discourse lies a deeply seated domestic, democratic and demographic rationale: Indian Muslims."[15]

Kumaraswamy narrates how, "while visiting the United States in November 1949, Nehru met Israel's ambassador in Washington, Eliahu Elath. ...He reminded the Israeli diplomat that over the years the question of Palestine had a deep impact upon the Indian Muslims and had been 'a constant source of agitation'. Therefore, Nehru cautioned his interlocutor that India 'must treat the thirty million Muslims most carefully.'"[16] When India was elected to the eleven-member UNSCOP, it was a Muslim, Abdur Rehman, who was selected to represent India, in accordance with Nehru's explicit desire that a Muslim personality be its representative at the UN committee, as indicated by a note prepared by the Foreign Ministry, which observed that India would have to find "*a suitable Indian Muslim with wide legal knowledge.*"[17] "Moslem leaders and intellectuals from time to time reminded the Indian government not to ignore the sentiments of the Moslem population and made it clear that the recognition of Israel would hurt them," as Dinesh Kumar writes. "Notwithstanding the differences among scholars, the sensitivities of the traumatized Moslem minority were an important concern for the Indian leadership, and constrained it from recognising Israel."[18] India established diplomatic ties with Israel only after the

1991 Middle East Peace Conference in Madrid and the end of the Cold War. According to Shashank Joshi:

> "What is notable is that each Cold War era driver of Indian enmity with Israel—rivalry with Pakistan, competition for the affections of Arab and Muslim states, a substantial domestic Muslim population perceived to be hostile to Israel and its treatment of Palestinians in the occupied territories, an Indian migrant worker community in the Middle East, and Indian dependence on the Middle East for energy supplies—remain. Some, such as the energy factor, indeed ought to have intensified as constraints on India-Israel ties.
>
> And yet, the relationship is more expansive and multifaceted than ever before. The dissolution of the Soviet Union was not unimportant, particularly in driving the India-US relationship and thereby altering India's interaction with traditional US allies. But the Soviet Union had never forced India to keep its distance from Israel, and had a turbulent relationship to its Arab allies, many of whom charted reasonably independent courses. This suggests that much of Indian policy was driven by domestic perceptions rather than rigid external constraints."[19]

Pakistan and Bangladesh still do not have any diplomatic ties with Israel, though Pakistan received humanitarian aid from American Jews during the recent floods there.[20] As far as Pakistan is concerned, Kumâraswâmy divulges that "the two countries [Pakistan and Israel] have maintained regular political and diplomatic contacts with one another for a long time, but the Islamic factor and its relations with the Middle East compelled Pakistan to keep these contacts under wraps."[21]

A Muslim League delegate once said in December 1938 that "both the British and the Hindus were Jews to Muslims, that is, their enemies. In India, Mr. Gandhi was the leader of the Hindu Jews."[22] It is also a proof of how the word Jew has come to have negative connotations among the Muslims. Another example of this is a remark made by a Muslim League delegate Abdul Khaliq, who said, "The real Jews of the West were the British and those of the East were the Hindus and both are sons of Shylock."[23] The reference to the Shakespearean character, Shylock the Jew, illustrates the argument of English fiction shaping South Asian perceptions of Jews. Most of the Indians are not even aware of the existence of Jews, and those who are, know them only through secondary sources, viz., the English language fiction, the Bible, the media reporting on the Arab-Israeli conflict, and in the case of the Muslims, also through the misinterpretation of the Qur'anic references to Jews and the Urdu press, which is generally biased against the Jews, and not as a result of any direct contact, because of their small numbers. When documentaries on Jews are dubbed in Hindi, those involved often fail to use *Yahûdi*, the Hindi term for Jews, and continue to use the English word out of their ignorance. India is the only country in South Asia with a Jewish population, which was estimated to be around 5,300 in 2002.[24]

Regarding the misinterpretation of the Qur'anic references to Jews, Suha Taji-Farouki writes:

> Adopting an essentialist approach, recent writings on the Jews in the Qur'an attribute to them an unchanging nature, which persists across the centuries. Historically conditioned polemic against *Banu Isra'il* and *al Yahud* in the Qur'an forms the basis of a generally negative construction of Jewish nature in these works. This provides a convincing explanation for current Zionist successes and abuses in Palestine, and for perceived Jewish political and economic entrenchment and domination in other parts of the world.[25]

It is worth quoting here, Edward Kessler, founder of the Centre for the Study of Muslim-Jewish Relations at the Woolf Institute in Cambridge, UK: "It seems, then, that it is not the Holy Scriptures of any religion that dictate historic behaviour, but rather the interpretation given to them, and these interpretations are, of course, the result of social, economic and political contexts."[26] Hence, a majority of South Asian Muslims, who have never had any interaction with Jews, harbour feelings of hostility and antagonism towards them, which are further aggravated by the Muslim press.

There was even a blood libel charge against Jews in the 19 May 1882 issue of the Gujarâti Muslim journal *Bombay Cassid*, which carried an article titled, "An Evil Custom amongst the Jews and their fondness of the blood of Mahomedans". The publication greatly stirred Muslim sentiments against Jews. Joseph Ezekiel Râjpurkar, an eminent member of the local Jewry, immediately served a notice to the editor of the journal, asking him to prove the charge brought against the Jews, or tender an apology for the same, while a local Jewish publication, *Israel*, refuted the charge. Moreover, the editor of *Israel*, Samuel Kehimkar, and his uncle Shalom Samuel Kehimkar, personally convinced the Qazi or Maulvi of the Jumma Masjid, that according to the Torah, Jews were prohibited from using the blood even of beasts and fowls, and that it was impossible to even consider using human blood. Subsequently, the editor of *Bombay Cassid* showed regret for the publication and carried an apology.[27]

The anti-Jewish posture of the Muslim press negatively affects the Indian Muslim perception of Jews in general. A large section of South Asian Muslims denies that the Holocaust ever took place, or raises doubts about its magnitude and scale. As a recent example, while a Holocaust films retrospective[28], the first ever in South Asia, was in progress at two universities, the Bâbâsâhéb Bhîmrâo Ambédkar University and the University of Lucknow, in September-October 2009, the largest circulated Urdu daily newspapers in Lucknow, *Râshtriya Sahâra*[29] and *Aag*[30], published stories denying the Holocaust. The articles were largely based on the arguments made by well known Holocaust deniers, viz., Arthur Butz, David Irving, Harry Elmer Barnes, David Hoggan, Paul Ressinier and Arthur R. Butz. Maulana Kalbé Sâdiq, the veteran Shia cleric is supposed to be one of the share holders of the True Media Indian Communication Ltd, which owns *Ââg*. He once said in an interview, "...the Bush administration certainly is anti-Islam. This owes, in large measure, to the power of the Zionist lobby in America. Pro-Zionist Jews control large banks, many industries and much of the media in America, and if they leave America, the country will collapse. And it is this lobby, in addition to the extreme right-wing Christian lobby, that is behind the clearly anti-Islamic and anti-Muslim policies of the Bush government."[31]

Another example is an editorial in the Indian Urdu daily newspaper *Inquilab* on 16 May 2008, titled, "Sixtieth Anniversary-Celebration of Satanism," with reference to Israel's sixtieth anniversary celebrations. Op-eds written by Abid Anwar in *Hamara Samaj* on 5 and 12 July 2010, accused Israel of trying to "destroy Muslims" in Kashmir and Maharashtra and trying to "lure Muslims into their peace trap so that they give all their ideas to these Jewish agents." The op-eds had been written with the objective of projecting the forthcoming visit of a delegation of Muslim journalists to Israel in a negative light. The articles do not cite any reference to support the accusations made against Israel. RAND Corporation, Project Interchange and India were mentioned as allies of Israel in its alleged conspiracies against Muslims. In its issue dated 13 to 19 November 2003, newsweekly *Nai Duniyâ*[32] carried a story on the present author's research on the tradition of Israelite origin among Pathans or Pashtuns, lifted straight from the Hindi edition of the 10 December 2003 issue of the newsweekly *Outlook*[33], with no credit to it. All it did except translation was that it added a few anti-Israel inputs of its own just to please its predominantly anti-Israel Muslim readers. It represented the research as a small part of a big Zionist conspiracy against Islam, aimed at depriving the religion of its bravest followers, the warlike Pathans or Pashtuns, by convincing them of their Israelite descent and then converting them to Judaism. It was the failure of his first news magazine in 1972, right after the Bangladesh struggle of 1971, that led the founder and editor of *Nai Duniyâ*, Shâhid Siddiqui, to indulge in yellow journalism, as he explains, "I went to Bangladesh at that time... I wrote the truth which was not acceptable to Muslims, because for them the creation of Bangladesh was a turning point, because [it was] the destruction of the idea of Pakistan, the two nation theory."[34] The very next year he founded *Nai Duniyâ* and benefited from a similar chance, the Arab-Israeli War of 1973. The rise in circulation to thirty thousand in just a few months time set its course of anti-Israel, anti-Zionist and anti-Jewish rhetoric. This anti-Zionist or anti-Israel rhetoric is actually a characteristic of the Urdu press. Another story on similar lines appeared on 26 May 2007 in the Urdu daily newspaper *Râshtriya Sahârâ*[35], whose editor Aziz Burney is known for "portraying the West as a self-conscious collective monolithic entity which is totally anti-Islam in its innate nature."[36] As Arshad Amanullah points outs, "the line between fact and fiction is completely blurred in the narrative world present in these editorials by Burney."[37] New Delhi based writer and filmmaker Arshad Amanullah says "the Urdu journalism, in its essence, is 'views oriented', as its role in moulding Muslim public opinion is simply incomparable to the other vernacular press".[38]

Scholarship on Muslim-Jewish relations has been focused on Middle East instead of South Asia what testifies to a failure to realise how strong the effect of South Asian Muslim attitudes towards Jews is on Muslim-Jewish relations because of the sheer number of South Asian Muslims. Also, their diaspora is larger in size and geographical spread than that of the Muslims from any other region. A number of British officials, particularly those dealing with India opposed Lord Balfour's endorsement of the Jewish demands for a state in Palestine as they were concerned that such an overtly pro-Jewish posture could antagonize the Indian Muslims, the largest Muslim population then (now divided into three South Asian countries, viz., India, Pakistan and Bangladesh). Kumaraswamy explains, "the Palestinian question gradually became part of the domestic Indian agenda, and the fervently anti-Jewish position of the Muslim League was a factor in influencing the Congress party to adopt a more sympathetic position towards the Arabs."[39] The Zionist leadership was quick to realise that active Indian Muslim involvement in the Palestine question could adversely affect their aspirations and be detrimental to the limited British commitment to the realization of the Balfour declaration. Responding to Indian Muslim opposition to the creation of Israel as the objective in view, the Zionist leadership, including Chaim Weizmann, established initial contacts with the Muslim leadership in India. The "meeting between [Shaukat] Ali and Weizmann in January 1931, was the first known direct political contact between the pre-state leadership and an Indian leader. Even though it had only modest success, the whole approach underscored the importance of moderating the position of the Indian Muslims toward the problem in Palestine."[40]

It is a measure of success that in spite of the domestic political considerations, India has managed to strengthen its ties with Israel, while continuing to support the Palestinian cause, just as it has managed to strengthen its relations with the US without weakening its relations with the Russian Federation. However, India is yet to reciprocate Israel's warmth towards it in cultural and educational terms. Although Indian Studies have found a strong base in Israel, Israel Studies or Jewish Studies still remain to be introduced in India.

Notes

1. "Urdu University seeks govt aid for its building," *The Times of India*, Lucknow, August 20, 2010.
2. "Courses in Arabic, Persian on verge of closure in LU?," *The Times of India*, Lucknow, August 1, 2010
3. Irene Eber, "Learning the Other: Chinese Studies in Israel and Jewish Studies in China," *MEI Occasional Paper*, no. 17, September 6, 2010, 4.
4. Tilak Raj Sareen, *"Indian Responses to the Holocaust,"* in *Jewish Exile in India: 1933-1945*, eds. Anil Bhatti and Johannes H. Voigt (New Delhi: Manohar in association with Max Mueller Bhavan, 2005), 59.
5. Quoted in Jawaharlal Nehru's letter to Subhash Chandra Bose, April 3, 1939, in *Selected Works of Jawaharlal Nehru, First Series*, ed. S. Gopal, vol. 9 (New Delhi: Orient Longman, 1976), 537.
6. Yulia Egorova, *Jews and India: Perceptions and Image* (New York: Routledge, 2006), 39.
7. P. R. Kumaraswamy, "India and the Holocaust: Perceptions of the Indian National Congress," *Journal of Indo-Judaic Studies*, vol. III, (April 2000), 122-123.
8. Cited in Egorova, *Jews and India*, 46-47.
9. Interviewed by the author on January 1, 2011, in her office at the University of Lucknow, Lucknow.
10. Robin David, "Fear your friend Hitler," *On the Bounce*, June 16, 2010, accessed on September 5, 2010, http://blogs.timesofindia.indiatimes.com/On-the-bounce/entry/fear-your-friend-hitler
11. Navras Jaat Aafreedi, "The First Ever Holocaust Films Retrospective in South Asia," *Journal of Indo-Judaic Studies*, vol. XI, (2010), 149-151.
12. Shashank Joshi, "The India-Israel Relationship: A Survey," *FPRC (Foreign Policy Research Centre) Journal No. 5, India-Israel Relations*, (2011), 101.
13. P. R. Kumaraswamy, "India and Israel: Evolving Strategic Partnership", *Mideast Security and Policy Studies*, no. 40, (September 1998), Publication of Begin-Sadat Center for Strategic Studies, Bar Ilan University, 4.
14. P. R. Kumaraswamy, *India's Israel Policy* (New York: Columbia University Press, 2010), 2.

15. Ibid., 16-18.
16. Ibid., 152.
17. Ibid., 145.
18. Dinesh Kumar, "India and Israel: From Conflict to Convergence of Interests", *Journal of Indo-Judaic Studies*, vol. III, April 2000,.93.
19. Joshi, "The India-Israel Relationship," 103.
20. Jonah Lowenfeld, "American Jews respond to flooding in Pakistan," *St, Louis Jewish Light*, August 26, 2010, (accessed on September 2, 2010) http://www.stljewishlight.com/news/nation/article_87d18e04-b05f-11df-a892-001cc4c03286.html.
21. P. R. Kumaraswamy, "Beyond the Veil: Israel-Pakistan Relations", *Memorandum No. 55*, Jaffee Center for Strategic Studies, Tel Aviv University, March 2000, 18.
22. Syed Sharifuddin Pirzada, *Foundations of Pakistan: All India Muslim League Documents* (Karachi: National Publishing House, 1969-70), vol. 2, 317.
23. Ibid.
24. The figure does not include the Jews who have come up in the last fifty years as a result of the Judaizing movements that have emerged in northeastern and southern India.
25. Suha Taji-Farouki, "A Contemporary Construction of the Jews in the Qur'an: A Review of Muhammad Sayyid Tantawi's Banu Isra'il Fi Al-Qur'an Wa Al-Sunna and 'Afif 'Abd Al-Fattah Tabbara's Al-Yahud Fi Al-Qur'an," in *Muslim-Jewish Encounters: Intellectual Traditions and Modern Politics (Vol. 4, Studies in Muslim-Jewish Relations)*, eds. Ronald L. Nettler and Suha Taji-Farouki (Amsterdam: Harwood Academic Publishers, 1998)15-38.
26. Edward Kessler, "Isaac and Ishmael – What's Next?" (paper presented at the Woolf Institute, Cambridge, 2009), 11.
27. H. S. Kehimkar, *The History of the Bene Israel of India*, (written in 1897), ed. Immanuel Olsvanger (Tel Aviv: Dayag Press Limited, 1937), 96-97.
28. Aafreedi, "The First Ever Holocaust Films".
29. Qutubullah, "Bīsvīn Sadi ka Sabsé Badā Afsānā," *Rashtriya Sahāra*, Lucknow, September 16, 2009.
30. "Sadī kā Sabsé Badā Jhūt? Holocaust," *Aag*, Lucknow, October18, 2009.
31. Yoginder Sikand, "Interview with Maulānā Kalbé Sādiq, Shia scholar," *Indian Muslims: Indian Muslim News and Information*, September 8 2007, http://www.indianmuslims.info/interviews/interview_maulana_kalbe_sadiq_shia_scholar.html (accessed on 10 October 2010).
32. "Malihābādi Pathānon ko Israel āné ki dāvat," *Nai Duniyā*, November 13-19, 2003 [Urdu].
33. Yogesh Mishra, "Bulāvā ā rahā hai Israel sé," *Outlook*, November10, 2003 [Hindi].
34. Robin Jeffrey, "Urdu Newspapers in India: Waiting for Citizen Kane?" in *Muslims and Media Images: News versus Views*, ed. Ather Farouqui

(New Delhi: Oxford University Press, 2009), 230.

35. Kamāl Hasan, "Chāi ki payāli mein tūfān uthāné ki baċkānā koṣiṣ", *Rāshtriya Sahārā*, May 26, 2007.
36. Arshad Amanullah, "Is Urdu Journalism in India a Lost Battle, in *Muslims and Media Images: News versus Views*, ed. Ather Farouqui (New Delhi: Oxford University Press, 2009), 276.
37. Ibid.
38. Amanullah, "Is Urdu Journalism," 273.
39. P. R. Kumaraswamy, "Beyond the Veil: Israel-Pakistan Relations", *Memorandum No. 55*, Jaffee Center for Strategic Studies, Tel Aviv University, March 2000, 21.
40. Ibid.

11

India's Historical and Cultural Relations with the Arab World

A.K. Pasha

The Asian continent has been home to great civilisations like the Indus Valley, Achamenian, Sassanian, Chinese, Mesopotamian, Dilmun and many others. Some also flourished in present-day Oman, Syria and many other parts of Asia. Throughout history there has been vigorous interaction among the peoples of Asia leading to trade and cultural links. Indian influence extended to the much of present-day South-East Asia what is known as 'Greater India'. Buddhism played a leading role in this field, which is still visible through temples and cultural influences. Similarly to the Western part of Asia, Indian influence at one time extended to the entire area inhabited by the Kurds, Central Asia and the Gulf Region. Before accepting Islam, the Kurds were followers of Buddhism. The Nabateans who established a powerful empire in much of West Asia from Petra now in Jordan are referred to as vegetarians and thought to have migrated from India. The Gulf region has seen continuous maritime contacts with Gujarat and the West Coast of India. Navigators from both sides benefited with exchange of goods and ideas thereby enriching their culture and society. Many traders and peoples from both areas especially settled (In both the regions). With the spread of Islam, Arab traders and Sufi Saints from the Gulf region added to this relationship and ties were consolidated. Many Indians converted to Islam, Christianity and Syrian Christians and monks settled in Kerala, the West Coast and other parts of India. Many Jews who could escape persecution from the Romans in West Asia also settled in Kerala and along the West Coast of India. Large numbers of Indians regularly visit religious places in the West Asian/ Gulf Region like Mecca, Medina, Jerusalem, Bethlehem, Najaf, Karbala, Mashed so on. The discovery of direct sea route from Europe by the Portuguese sailor Vasco Da Gama to Calicut in Kerala in 1498 and the subsequent European colonialism disrupted the close interaction India had with the Gulf region. After defeating Haider Ali's son Tipu Sultan in 1799 (the last Indian ruler who seriously challenged them) at Mysore, the British consolidated their rule in India. From Bombay with the assistance of Indian soldiers and administrative staff the British controlled bulk of the Gulf region (present day GCC states). Large segments of the Gulf population, who thrived on lucrative trade with India and beyond, were now virtually dependent on the British dominated trade and maritime links. The Gulf Arabs reverted to pearl fishing and the British transported their principal day-to-day requirements mostly from India. Many Indian families especially from Sind, Kutch and Gujarat settled in the entire Gulf region. People in the Gulf region now saw Indians as collaborators with British imperialism. The British deported undesirable people from the Gulf region to India. Also some Gulf merchants settled in India, mostly in Bombay. The British who promised independence to the Arabs before and during the First World War, failed to keep up their promise. The Sheriff Hussein of Mecca who was promised a United Arab Kingdom over the liberated Arab lands from the Ottoman rule found British and French rule over Palestine, Iraq, Syria and Lebanon under the mandate's rule of the League of Nations. The Sheriff's two sons were installed as Kings of Iraq and Jordan. The Jews were also promised a homeland in Palestine through the Balfour Declaration. The Mufti of Jerusalem accused the British of having a design to settle in Iraq "many million Hindus from British India". Hundreds and thousands of Indian soldiers died suppressing the Arabs who were opposed to imposition of monarchies, mandated rule and direct British/French occupation. Elsewhere in West Asia, thousands of Indian soldiers died fighting with the British during and after the war. The article makes an attempt to capture the deeper significance of the interdependent nature of history, and the linkages between military, societal, economic and political foundations of history. It focuses on Egypt as a link between Europe and Asia especially in relation to the spice trade, which formed the basis for interaction. Ottoman Turkey has also been an important link, as it had become a Eurasian power, which is studied as the basis of historical analysis. The military conquest and colonization of India and major parts of Asia by the Europeans was a consequence of superior technology. India's advantage at the moment in IT is fast changing its image around the world. India's present economic progress is linked to its past and a combination of new technology, family values, commitment to democracy and multicultural secular society.

Indus and Mesopotamian Civilisations

The oldest known civilisation identified by historians worldwide is without doubt the Nile based followed by the Indus and Mesopotamian civilisations. Both the Nile and Indus Valley civilisations were in constant contact through land with each other through the Tigris and Euphrates based civilisations as also through maritime contacts directly. According to historians from the time immemorial there existed peculiar and deeper relations between India and Egypt. "The Indus civilization was built upon the same primary inventions and discoveries as the Nilotic and the Mesopotamian. Its authors may even have included men of the same racial types".[1] Dr. M.A. Murray says: "The type of men of Punt, as depicted by Hatshepsut's artists, suggests an Asiatic rather than an African race; and the sweet-smelling woods point to India as the land of their origin. A voyage from Egypt to India by coasting vessels would be quite feasible, and undoubtedly ports for the Indian trade existed along the south coast of Arabia".[2] India's recorded interaction with Egypt started since the third millennium before Jesus Christ. In ancient Egypt, perfumes utilizing various Indian aromatics played an important role in worship, which in turn led to brisk trade. The Ishmaelites who bought Joseph from his brothers were en route to Egypt with an unspecified range of spices: They saw some Ishmaelites on their way coming from Galaad, with their camels, carrying spices, and balm, and myrrh to Egypt.[3] The Egyptians were fond of aromatics and they procured it from a semi mythical place known as "Punt". To get aromatics the Egyptians sent the first recorded merchant fleet to Punt which continued to supply to the temples and God-Kings of the Nile Pharaohs for thousands of years. The first known maritime trip to Punt took place during Pharaoh Sahure [2491-2477 BC]. Not only had the Egyptians had close trade relations it is well known that Egyptian mummies were reportedly wrapped in Bengal Muslin cloth. Some writers have tried to establish a close link between Egypt and parts of Bengal in India. These similarities led historians to conclude that there was a conquest of Bengal by the heretic kings of Egypt of the XVIII dynasty who were driven out of Egypt by the orthodox school of Amon worshippers sometime between 1358 and 1355 BC.[4]

Around 1500 BC the famous Egyptian Queen Hatshepsut sent a great naval expedition to Punt. This is visible still on the walls of the temple of Deir al-Bahri carved at the orders of Queen Hatshepsut around 1495 BC. A fleet of five ships with mariners on top of ships, rowers, and steersmen passing through a huge water body is depicted. These ancient sailors brought back to Egypt from the land of Punt, "all goodly fragrant woods of God's-land, heaps of myrrh resin, with fresh myrrh trees, with ebony, and pure ivory, with green gold of Emu, with cinnamon wood, khesyt wood, with ihmut-incense, sonter-incense, eye-cosmetic, with apes, monkeys, dogs, and with skins of the southern panther, with natives and their children".[5] The mariners also brought fragrant plants for the temple gardens. She also sent the mission to India perhaps seeking to establish commercial and diplomatic ties between India and Egypt. Not only this initiative from the Egyptian Queen led to the direct maritime communications between India and Egypt several centuries before Christ but more significantly it showed that Egyptian sailors were able to navigate the Red Sea in appropriate time to make use of the Arabian Sea monsoons to reach India and Sri Lanka and maybe perhaps beyond. From modern Somalia the ancient Egyptians continued a voyage of more than two thousand miles southward. The Egyptian ships also took Indian products like silk, perfumes, spices, medicines, rare fruits, sandalwood, incense and other items not available in the Nile valley. It is mentioned that the Egyptian sailors must have observed the Indian festival of lights—Diwali—because Egypt also has a similar state festival of lights celebrated for nine days. According to Hasan El Zayyat, this unique interaction is a proof "that the ships sailing to India did not serve the purpose of commerce only but also carriers of Indian culture."[6] Ramses III also sent an expedition to Punt. That Indian spices were an important link with Egypt is clear by the discovery of dhania (the umbelliferous fruit of the coriander plant) in the tombs of the Pharaohs especially Ramses. Its identity was confirmed in 1975-76 at Musee de L' Houmme in Paris, after long years of research that the spices came from the south of India. The Pharaoh's were obsessed with eternal life and in order to preserve the body from decomposition they used pepper as a preservative. "It was in all likelihood the supreme metaphysical importance of this end that accounts for the Egyptians extraordinary efforts to obtain a spice all the way from India".[7] Pepper was not only inserted in the nose of the Pharaoh but researchers also found traces of the spice in his abdominal cavity. Clearly this spice from India was familiar to ancient Egyptians. According to archaeological evidence, there was resemblance between a number of methods used in certain activities such as fishing, boat construction, measuring and weighing in both civilisations.

Between 200 BC and 200 AD an Indian colony existed in Alexandria which was intellectually capable of influencing the Hellenistic scholars and philosophers of Alexandria. Ashoka the Great sent an Indian diplomatic mission to the Ptolemaic court in Alexandria. In the 6th century BC the Achamenians who ruled from Iran controlled Egypt and Sind and to improve the communications built a canal linking the Nile with the Red Sea which was beneficial to trade between India and Egypt. Trade between India and Egypt under the Pharaonic rulers or otherwise greatly influenced both the societies. As we have seen earlier it carried the culture from one civilisation to another. When people move from place to place along the trade routes they carry ideas, philosophy, religions, customs, traditions, rituals as also books, handicrafts and artistic items, which familiarize people in different societies. Due to the long seacoast both India and Egypt derived considerable revenues from trade in ancient times. As during the modern period, in ancient times also culture and civilisation aspects followed trade and commerce between India and Egypt. Along with the maritime contacts referred to between India and Egypt, there existed considerable trade through the land route via Iran, Babylon, Oman, Aden, and Palestine and onto Egypt. For the ancient period, one has to rely upon direct archaeological evidence like seals made of ivory, stone, terracotta used in those lands or the use of Indian or Egyptian names for such items. In the second century BC an Indian sailor offered to show the Romans (who were ruling Egypt) the shortest direct sea route to India. Ptolemy Euergetes II (145-116 BC) the Roman ruler of Egypt welcomed the proposal and directed Eudoxus, a Greek [Cyzicus] explorer, to set out with the Indian across the high seas to India. The Greek made two trips to India to buy spices and other eastern luxuries which Ptolemy seized.[8] This was a turning point in ancient Indo-Egyptian maritime links as it heralded direct trade contacts under the Greco-Egyptian dynasty of the Ptolemies which came declined with the demise of Cleopatra. The previous maritime contacts were not regular because the sea journey was long and arduous as the small ships had to sail along the coasts and hence target of pirates.

When the Roman Emperor Augustus annexed Egypt in 30 BC he built new ports on the Red Sea and dug wells along the caravan routes crossing the desert from the Nile to the Red Sea. The Romans soon subjugated the Nabateans and the Hadhramauti merchants who had dominated the spice trade especially in the Red sea area. King Kanishka was familiar with Rome. The description of India by one Roman Apuleius [124 AD] is interesting: "The Indians are a people of great population and vast territories situated far to our east, by the Ocean's ebb, where the stars first rise at the ends of the earth, beyond the learned Egyptians and the superstitious Jews, Nabataean merchants and flowing-robed Parthians, past the Iruraeans [Palestine] with their meagre crops and the Arabs rich in perfumes-wherefore I do not so much wonder at the Indians mountains of ivory, harvests of pepper, stockpiles of cinnamon, tempered iron, mines of silver and smelted streams of gold: nor the Ganges, the greatest of all rivers and the King of the waters of the Dawn, running in a hundred streams...".[9]

During the second half of first century AD a Greek sailor, living in Egypt sailed to India through the Red Sea and along the coasts of

Arabian Sea and recorded his experiences in a book called "*The Periplus of the Erythraean Sea*". The book is a pilot's guide to sailing in the Indian Ocean telling each step of the long and perilous sea journey also highlighting the ports and harbours to halt and what goods to acquire and sell over there. The water body between Red Sea, Persian Gulf and the Indian Ocean and beyond is called as the Erythraean Sea. The Romans who controlled Egypt sent ocean-going ships to India. From the beginning of historical period, the Indian Ocean was the preserve of Arab and Indian navigators who discovered how to sail across the Ocean instead of coasting around it. The Arabs had been familiar with the monsoons thousands of years "before the Greek trader Hippalus took credit of their discovery to himself through his work Periplus". Some writers believe that it's the Greek sailor named Hippalus who found out the annual cycle of monsoon which was the secret of navigation in the Indian Ocean. The Romans apparently called at any one of the 19 Indian ports in which, in the words of the Periplus, "great ships sail...due to the vast quantities of pepper and malabathron". It clearly reveals the extensive trade ties between India and Egypt as Roman and Indian ships sailed to coasts all along Oman, Yemen and to the Red Sea [Horn of Africa known in ancient period as Cape Guardafui or Cape of Spices] carrying among other things sugar, pearls, precious stones, spices, unguents, and cotton clothes Muslin, all of which were in great demand. In many of these ports/ harbours on the sea coast Indians had settled for trade and that Aden and the Socotra Island had a colony of Indian merchants. Many Indian Kings especially from South India, the Pandyas sent trade missions to Rome to the Emperor Augustus around 26 BC as also during subsequent period. Indian goods were carried by sea up to the Red Sea Coast and from there to Alexandria. The Gangas of Talakad in South India had flourishing trade with the Roman Empire as this is corroborated by the recent discovery of a large number of Roman coins in the temple town of Muduktherai on the banks of Kaveri which must have been sent for Indian goods shipped to Alexandria as similar coins were discovered over there. Thus, both India and Egypt not only had direct trade ties but Egypt especially Alexandria became the Centerport for Indian goods to Europe.[10]

The Romans through the Egyptians exported to India glassware, works of art, tin and Mediterranean coral—much prized in India for its imputed magical properties and bullion. They brought back from India ivory, pearls, tortoiseshells, diamonds, onyx, agate, crystal, amethyst, opal, beryl, sapphire, ruby, garnet, bloodstone, emerald, carnelian, linen, textiles, wheat grains, handicrafts and many handmade art products. Silk from China was also brought via India. Animals from India like parrots, tigers, rhinoceroses, elephants were also brought. But it was clearly the Indian spices which were the main attraction along with costus, nard and cloves as well. The ancient Egyptians visited India frequently not only for the goods they needed but also to sell Egyptian products in the vast Indian market. It is recorded that Ptolemy II [ruled 285-246 BC] exchanged ambassadors with the Mauryan Emperors Chandragupta II [321-297 BC] and Ashoka [232 BC]. Alexandria in Egypt, ruled by Ptolemaic and Roman rulers being cosmopolitan city, was not only a major trading centre but far ahead of Rome and Athens culturally. Alexandria became the chief port of the Nile delta. The route from Alexandria to Rome was the most heavily trafficked trade route of the ancient world. Within weeks of sail brought prized goods including much sought after spices to Rome's great port at Ostia at the mouth of the Tiber. The distance was about 5000 miles from India. Thus, Alexandria was not only a place where traders from all parts of the world met, but the cosmopolitan city also attracted scholars from all over the world especially from India who interacted with their Egyptian counterparts. Apart from the trade ties between India and Egypt, the Egyptian mind was also influenced by Indian mysticism, especially the doctrine of rebirth. The ties in historical period were further intensified during the Roman period. As more and more Persians began to take interest in commercial activities, direct Indo-Egyptian trade relations in the second and third century AD declined. Although the discovery of monsoon winds in 44 AD had changed the maritime contacts between the two countries and the volume of trade had increased in first AD with every year around 120 ships travelled to India for various products, but the contacts decreased subsequently due to decline in Roman power in the aftermath of the invasions by barbarians [Franks, Visigiths Visigoths and Alamannis] shattered the prosperity and order on which trade with India depended. The Gothic invaders who dismembered the Western Roman Empire dealt a severe blow to trade with India. This decline persisted for about 1000 years but sporadic demand for Indian goods remained despite invasions and disruptions. During the period of Pliny the Elder [23-79 AD] Rome's cosmopolitan tastes had reached such a pitch, that he talks of the flavours of Egypt and India appearing in Roman kitchens.[11]

Egypt and India greatly benefited from trade with the Roman Empire, and as one writer said: "the money flowed out to foreigners". Gold and silver Roman coins reached India in great quantities as visible in the vast archaeological discoveries in South India particularly. Pliny the Elder apparently "complained that India swallowed up the colossal sum of 50 million sesterces per annum—all for the sake of pepper and other "effeminate" eastern fripperies. India and its luxuries were turning Rome into a city of wimps". India and its pepper became almost paradigmatic. To Pliny the Elder, the voyage to India was no more than a grubby quest for loot, "and so India is brought near by a lust for gain".[12] After the reign of Caracalla [211-217AD], roman coins declined in India. Soon the Roman Empire suffered one disaster after another affecting the eastern traffic. Moreover the Red Sea littoral passed under the control of the Blemmyes, a hostile African tribe, and Rome's direct trade route via Egypt was disrupted. But the Byzantine state maintained even in the sixth century a customs official at Clysma on the Gulf of Suez and a famous Greek-Egyptian monk Cosmas Indicopleustes travelled to India around 550 AD. The transformation was already visible as Syrian, Latin and Hebrew were the languages used by the merchants all along the spice routes. Socotra Island situated at the Bab-el-Mandeb near Yemen was an important link in Indo-Egyptian contacts. It appears there was a settled colony of Indian traders on the Socotra Island named as Farj Al Hind or frontier of India. The memory of this trade still survives in western India especially among the people of coastal Gujarat who worship a goddess called Sakotri Mata, named after Socotra Island. [Some also believe it is based on the Indian name Sukhtara meaning 'happy star'.] By the 10th and 11th centuries, Arab traders and Indian artisans had set up a rudimentary production supply chain, involving ivory. Arab traders along the African coast exported large quantities of elephant tusks to India, where artisans carved them into jewellery, ornaments and religious icons for export to China and the

Mediterranean. It is argued that the most lucrative item in Indo-Arab trade was the horse, which was in great demand in India. There was also a famous cloth fair near Mecca that used to be the hub for the Indian textile industry to market their products to European merchants, with Arab traders mediating.[13]

The Spread of Islam

The spread of Islam under Amr ibn al-As in major parts of Egypt brought Arabs from the heart of Arabian Peninsula to a country where idolatry, temples existed. Pharaonic culture was widespread despite the growth of Christianity, but modest trade especially Egyptian imports of Indian textiles continued. Fragments of fabric were found at Al Fustat near Cairo which functioned as a major trading centre in Egypt. Initially the direct maritime trade contacts appear to have declined since the rise of Islam between India and Egypt as the Arabs from Oman, Yemen and others like Persians began to interact with Indians on a bigger scale converting the Indian Ocean as a Muslim lake. Muslim merchants especially Arabs were now firmly established from the Red Sea, Gulf to Malacca, Malabar to Maghreb to China. The Arabs traders and mariners [Muslims] now controlled land and sea routes and used camels and ships to transport goods. The Jews now were also active with the Muslims. But Indian goods especially spices, textiles continued to reach Cairo in modest quantities for onward transmission to Europe in return for furs and amber from the Baltic's; slaves, timber and metals from the Alps and the Balkans. To one writer "pepper has perhaps been the oldest continuous link between India and Egypt and also between Asia and Europe and one that has survived, battered but intact, ever since".[14] Under these circumstances Alexandria became once again the terminus of transcontinental trade as it had become famous earlier during the Romans. Trade ties between India and Egypt were revived through the Red Sea and once again there was brisk trade. During this period the "Syrian" i.e. Byzantine merchants [Constantinople still remained the capital of the Eastern Roman empire until 1453 when the Turks took over] and the Jewish traders also began to play an important in the trade between India and Egypt. The Jews were uniquely placed as a link between the Christians and

Muslims. Many writers refer to a loose alliance of Jewish merchants known as the Rhadanites whose name appears in the Book of Routes composed around 850 by Ibn Khordabeh, Director of Posts to the Caliphs at Baghdad. The Jews were present all along the old silk route from Gaul to China. Interestingly the arrival of Muslims [Islam] at the gates of Arles and Marseilles [France] and at Saint Peter's Basilica in 846 propelled the Jews to prominence as even Charlemagne and his Frankish nobles were forced to rely on Jewish merchants for their luxuries. Due to their new role, Christian persecution of Jews virtually stopped as also forced conversions common during the Frankish Dynasty Merovingian dynasty [476-750] in Europe. It must be noted that one of the oldest surviving decrees of the Venetian Senate forbade Jews from travelling in Venetian ships.[15] The Jewish presence was noticeable due to the Fatimid Dynasty's [969-1171] connections with Maghreb areas. Like the Romans the Fatimids encouraged trade through the Red Sea by maintaining a strong navy and providing security to merchants from all over the world. According to one writer, "Cairo was then embarking on the period of its greatest commercial splendor, drawing commerce, merchants, and travellers like filings to a magnet. Alexandria regained the position it had occupied in classical antiquity as Europe's chief point of access to the exotic goods of the East".[16] In 996, a traveller to Cairo counted 160 merchants from Amalfi alone. Nahray ibn Nissim, a Tunisian Jew settled in Egypt, was dealing in products as diverse as Spanish tin and coral, Moroccan antimony, Indian spices, Armenian clothes, rhubarb from Tibet and spikenard from Nepal. The Jewish trade connections came to light from the remarkable collection of business papers, belonging to Jewish merchants, discovered in a Synagogue of Old Cairo. The documents, letters, etc. cover the period 1000 to 1250. The commercial contacts of the Genizah (Cairo) Jewish merchants under the trading guild known as the Karimis existed through their agents from China through India to Morocco and were an important link between India and Egypt. The intermediaries in most cases were Jews themselves. According to K.N. Chaudhri, "Business was done by consigning goods to friends and relatives in Fustat or Aden, which the principal remained in India. It is significant from the point of view of commercial organisation that the leading Jewish merchants of the period with business connections in distant countries did not find it necessary to travel with their own goods".[17] The major items imported from India were spices but also included were sandalwood, camphor, cloves, nutmegs, cubebs, coconuts, flaxen and cotton fabrics and ivory, pepper, lead, Kutla drug, bamboo, cane precious stones, cardamom, cinnamon, aloes, marjoram, myrrh, galangal, mastic, vermilion, parrots, saffron, mustard, cassia, garlic, musk, ginger, pearls, crystals and Sanbazaj (used for polishing stones). Wine and scents were imported from Egypt. Many Arab-Egyptian merchants settled on India's western coast like Gujarat, Konkan and on the Coromandel Coast. Jeddah now became an important link for trade between India and Egypt due to the trade being in Arab hands and also due to its proximity to Mecca—the pilgrimage centre for Muslims from all over the world. Large number of Indian scholars visited parts of the Arab world especially to Baghdad the capital of the Abbasid Empire, taking with them their works in Sanskrit on astronomy, mathematics and medicine which were translated into Arabic and Greek. This is known as the golden period in Indo-Arab cultural ties. Unfortunately this came to an abrupt end due to the savage Mongol invasion and destruction of Baghdad in 1258 AD. According to an Indian scholar the following Arab scholars helped the cause of transmitting Indian culture and knowledge to the Arab world. They are Abu Zayd al Sirafi, Sulayman al-Tajir, Al Masudi, Ibn Hauqal, al-Jahiz, al-Istakhri, al Maqidsi, Ibn Hazm, Ibn al Nadim, Ibn Abi Usaybia, Ibn al Ibari, Ibn Battuta and a host of other translators, scientists and philosophers like al Kindi, al Sarakhsi, Qustab, Luqa, al Fazari, al Khuwarizmi, Thabit b. Qurra, Thinan b. Thabit and the Caliphs and the Vazirs like al Mamoon, Yahya b. Khalid and the Barmakids. In particular Yahya bin Khalid al Barmaki (805 AD) minister under the famous Abbasid Caliph Haroon al Rashid took keen interest in Indian science, technology, philosophy and literature. He invited Indian physicians, scientists, astronomers and other scientists to Baghdad and got Indian texts in Sanskrit translated into Arabic. Al-Beruini's book Kitab al Hind highlights Indian achievements in science and other fields as also its religious tolerance. An Egyptian scholar of 15th century Al-Qalqashandi says the Indian people are bestowed with wisdom. Peace and justice can be seen in the entire country. Another Egyptian scholar is Abu Zohra who said Indians have a glorious history and civilisation. Despite the Mongol destruction of the Abbasid caliphate and the subsequent domination of the Arabs by the Ottomans, it did not substantially disrupt the links between India and the Arabs. Gradually Islam began to influence India first through Arab traders in the coastal areas and later from Sind, Persia and Central Asia.

During the Fatimid period in 10th century AD the Egyptian merchants were famous as El Karemia who traded mostly in Indian spices. Very often these merchants stayed in India for long periods and often married Indian women. They also played in important role in spreading Islam in India. These Egyptian spice merchants came to be known as Bohras (apparently from bahar-spices or bahar (outside). The Bohras still are a very important Indian trading community in Cairo, Egypt—in the business as well as a link between the two countries. According to Sahar Abdel Aziz Salem, the Fatimid zeal to spread Islam in India indicates their desire to preside over the trade of the Indian Ocean. This could strengthen the economy of the Fatimid Caliphate in Egypt while at the same time weaken that of the Abbasids (at Baghdad).[18] He also argues that many Indian traders also visited Egypt as "Indian penetration into the Red Sea might have also taken place in the Fatimid period when relations between Egypt and India were very close and friendly, since they combined both commercial and spiritual interests". It appears Mohammed bin Tughluk Shah (who was known as the Sultan of India but also of Sind, Makran, Mogadishu and Sri Lanka) sent a ship to the Egyptian Mamluk Sultan Al Naser ibn Qalaun full of precious presents and diamonds, but it could not reach Cairo as the King of Yemen looted it. This clearly reveals that Indian ships were famous in the Red Sea, Aden and along the Arabian coast. Egypt under the Fatimids flourished due to the brisk trade with India. Indian influence is seen in Egyptian mosques, especially design of the minaret, as large number of Indian ships carried Moslems for Hajj and other Holy places. Egypt under the Fatimids continued to the extent possible interaction with India in trade and other fields. Since the entire Gulf region, Arabian Peninsula and North Africa including Egypt was undergoing rapid transformation under Islamic rulers this naturally affected the cultural relations as the Indian society was also undergoing similar changes in pockets of India under

Muslim rulers both in north and South India. The Spanish Rabbi Benjamin of Tudela visited Alexandria in 1160 and found European merchants like Italians, Catalans, Frenchmen, English and Germans rubbing shoulders with merchants from all over the world. This is interesting in the background of fierce religious wars in Europe. The Fatimids encouraged trade, as they needed customs duties. Egypt also continued to be the link to the extent possible between India and Europe, and interaction with India was very lucrative especially in spice trade and other fields. During 1170-1260, the Ayyubid rulers, under whom the total volume of trade declined, as the European traders began to take active interest and increase their share, replaced the Fatimids in Egypt. Moreover, the sea route to India became vulnerable to pirates and growing incidence of taxation. Some wealthy Egyptian merchants began to buy protection from rulers in the coastal regions to protect their ships from the menace of pirates. The role of Jewish merchants/agents (who could speak many languages) increased all along the routes from Alexandria, Jeddah, Aden, Muscat, Basra, and Bushier and to the Indian Coast. This may also have partly increased the European volume of trade with the East and hence partly contributed to decline in Indo-Egyptian trade. Egypt soon came to be ruled by the Mamluks (1260-1517) and the devastation of the region from Persia to Palestine and the downfall of the Abbasids in Baghdad (1258) due to the Mongol invasion enhanced the importance of Cairo in the trade through the Red Sea area. The crusade attacks and the prominent role of Saladin in defeating the Crusaders led him to contain the growing role of Frankish merchants from gaining direct access to the Red Sea and limited their interaction to the North African and Mediterranean ports. Despite restrictions placed by the Pope on Christian traders for their purchases from Muslim countries, merchants from Genoa and Venetian did trade through Alexandria. The Egyptians conducted trade through "safe conduct passes". The Mamluk rulers assured security to merchants, property and goods etc. It appears during the 14th century Egypt and the surrounding areas went through a difficult period due to economic disruptions and consequent decline in trade mainly due to the Black Death in Egypt in 1347. Religion again came as a hindrance in Indo-Egyptian trade as in 1322, the Pope excommunicated many leading citizens of Venice for their dealings with Muslim rulers and for some time a papal ban prevailed which slowed trade with Egypt with its repercussion on trade with India. The trade simply passed into the hands of Armenian merchants from Turkey to Persia to India and the Armenian port of Lajazzo became the link for Europe reducing Egypt's importance. The Black Death in Egypt in 1347-8, [bubonic plague-Rattus rattus] which divested agriculture and adversely affected the Egyptian population, scared the foreign traders. This disease always started at the coast, and from there went up into the interior wrote Procopius. Every freighter and galley shuttling from India to Egypt and from Alexandria to Byzantium was, potentially, a "death ship".[19] According to one writer, "the exact relationship between these events and the rhythm of long distance trade through the Red Sea is not quite clear but the Cairo-Alexandria trade network however, remained open", although it did not see the brisk trade it was used to in earlier periods. It is interesting to know how an Egyptian scholar (historian) of the 15th century AD called Al-Qalqashandi appreciates India with these words. "India is a big and wide country having enormous wealth. The king lives with pomp and glory. Its ocean is full of pearls, its earth with gold and its mountains with rubies and emeralds. Its valleys have fragrance of sandalwood and camphor. The people are bestowed with wisdom. Peace and justice can be seen in the entire country". Another modern Egyptian scholar, Abu Zohra, in his book *Mohaderat Fi Muqarinat al Adyan* opines about ancient Indian religions and says: "Indians have a glorious history. They were possessed of civilisation and culture in older days. The history of their civilisation is so old that one remains unable to trace its origin".[20] Soon the crucial areas through which trade between India and Egypt was to pass came under the Ottoman Empire and this led to disruption in commercial transactions due to political troubles especially in Egypt.

But the most significant development came in the Indian Ocean with the discovery of a direct sea route from Europe to India by the Portuguese when Vasco Da Gamma with the help of an Asian pilot landed at Calicut, on 21 May 1498 in Kerala. The arrival of Europeans in South India drastically changed the entire scene concerning trade, politics and control of colonies. The Portuguese met two stunned resident Tunisian merchants who spoke Genose and Castilian. Da Gamma also met Italian merchants who had reached Calicut by land route. On March 8, 1500, Portuguese Admiral Pedro Alvares Cabral came to Calicut with 13 huge ships and a thousand-strong crew. Soon Cabral demanded the expulsion of all Muslim merchants, [Arabs, Persians, Indian Muslim merchants from Gujarat, and so on]. When the ruler Zamorin refused, Cabral seized a large and heavily laden Arab ship preparing to sail to Egypt through the Red Sea. He ordered two-day heavy bombardment of Calicut destroying most ships and the port. "The Portuguese seized or sank all Muslim shipping they lay their hands on; Muslim merchants were hung from the rigging and burned alive in view of their families ashore...Calicut's fate was just a taste of things to come. In the years that followed, similar treatment was revisited on the city and other Malabar ports.... All to the strategic end of establishing a royal monopoly over trade in the Indian Ocean". The new rulers of the Indian Ocean henceforth ordered traders of all nations to require a permit to sail waters they had freely sailed for time immemorial. "The goal was nothing less than to make the Indian Ocean a Portuguese lake. All competition would be taxed or blown out of water".[21] Soon they began to take over the spice trade in the entire Indian Ocean region. The Portuguese King Manuel crowned himself as "Lord of Guinea, and of the Conquest, the Navigation and Commerce of Ethiopia, Arabia, Persia and India". The new masters of seas now ordered Venetian merchants to buy spices at Lisbon. Soon there was drastic reduction in the supply of spices to Cairo and Alexandria—the traditional markets to which Indian traders supplied via Aden and Red Sea. Since the Turks were also at war with major parts of Europe, this led to rise in the price of spices due to shortage of supply. All this greatly undermined the traditional Indo-Egyptian trade contacts and hence impacted on the cultural and other ties as well. The Portuguese discovered that the price of a quintal [128lb] of pepper in Lisbon was a fraction of that paid in Alexandria for a like amount brought from the Indian Ocean by the traditional route in Red Sea by dhows and on the backs of camels. Even though the treasury of King Manuel was short of money, he enlisted the financial help from Lisbon's wealthy merchants who saw immense profits from direct spice trade with India. Vasco da Gamma again sailed to India in the middle of 1502 now with 25 ships, the ten largest containing 'much beautiful artillery, with plenty of munitions and weapons, all in great abundance'. Thirteen of the ships belonged to wealthy Portuguese merchants. Earlier he had come with three small vessels only. Six of the ships were sent to the Red Sea to put an end to Arab trade ships playing up to the Egyptian ports with spices. On his way to Calicut Vasco intercepted an Arab ship with cargo and hajj pilgrims returning from Mecca. The rich cargo was seized and all 700 passengers were killed in sea 'until the sea is red'. The owner of the ship was the richest Arab in Calicut, a man related to the Sultan of Egypt. Da Gamma proceeded to "conquer ...the Indian seas and shores of Asia, killing, destroying and burning the Moors of Cairo, of Arabia and of Mecca, and other inhabitants of the same India, together with their fleet, by which for over 800 years they have controlled their trade in precious stones, pearls and spices". On reaching the Indian coast he devastated Calicut upon refusal by the Zamorin to surrender. King Manuel called the destruction of Calicut as 'inestimable damage' and he was told earlier by his spies that the India spice city Calicut was 'bigger than Lisbon'. Not only many people including trader were killed but their ships were also burnt especially of the Arabs. In Calicut one rich Arab merchant Coja Mehmed Markar who traded throughout the Red Sea and much of East Africa and who lived in Cairo was taken prisoner by da Gamma's captain and almost beaten to death and killed. Coja became an enemy of the Portuguese like many other Muslim merchants who not only stayed in Egypt and traded with Calicut and other parts of India but mobilised others to persuade the Ottoman Turks to fight the Portuguese and put an end to their domination of the traditional trade routes in the Red Sea, Gulf and the Indian Ocean areas. Tired of deliberate policy of the Portuguese to obstruct Egypt's trade with India and the spice trade through the Red sea especially which had seriously undermined his finances, the Sultan of Egypt Qansuhah al-Gawri threatened to expel all Christians and destroy the holy places in Jerusalem if Portuguese ships went on interrupting trade between India and Egypt. The Egyptian emissary to Lisbon was a Christian priest from St Catherine's monastery on Mount Sinai. The Portuguese King showed his imperious spirit and issued his own threat: "let the Sultan be warned that Portugal intended to do its Christian duty by entering the Red Sea, laying waste to Mecca, destroying the tomb of the 'false prophet Muhammad' and carrying away his remains". Soon King Manuel appointed Dom Francisco de Al Meida as the Viceroy with orders to plunder, seize and destroy any ship—especially any Muslim ship—caught on high seas without a Portuguese passport [cartazes]. He ordered the mouth of the Red sea to be closed with a fort to stop any spices being sent to Europe by that route, and to "persuade all the people of India to put aside the fantasy that they can ever again trade with any but ourselves".

The Mamluk Sultan of Egypt and the Ottoman Sultan in Istanbul decided to respond to the formidable challenge posed by the Portuguese in the Red Sea and the Indian Ocean. The Turks with the help of the Venetian decided to build a fleet in the Gulf of Suez, Sinai port of Tor. There was a mutual interest in driving the Portuguese out of the spice trade of Indian Ocean and destroying the Portuguese 'floating fortresses. It is interesting to note that the Venetian "had at one stage thought of urging the Egyptians to dig a canal through the Suez peninsula as the easiest way to put ships into the Indian Ocean. They withdrew the idea, fearing that the Sultan would suspect them of wanting to open a route for their own trade." By early 1507 the Egyptians, Turks and the Venetian had completed the building of twelve huge warships. Amir Hussein was made the admiral in charge and he left Tor, Sinai, with his heavily laden warships with 1500 fighting men and their weapons, as well as the best cannons transported in cargo boats across the Mediterranean to Egypt from Turkey "because the Mamluk military caste which ruled Egypt made guns designed only for defensive use on land". It took eight months for Amir Hussein to reach Diu where Malik Ayaz, a Russian Christian converted to Islam by the Turks, was waiting to welcome Hussein's fleet. At the same time the Zamorin of Calicut who had also suffered immensely at the hands of the Portuguese sent hundred light vessels armed with cannons made by two Portuguese renegades. These ships were carrying food for the Egyptian naval armada at Diu. They would also give support when battle was joined.

The unprecedented Portuguese and later European challenge at the sea to two very ancient states, cultures and civilisations led to the formation of a unique strategic alliance between India and Egypt not only to checkmate the growing threat to their trade and commerce but to safeguard their interests. In this first known Asian Solidarity Alliance in the modern period Egyptians, Turks, Kurds and Indians came together, to contain the formidable Portuguese challenge at sea. The Muslim ruler of Gujarat, Mahmud [I] Begarha, and [1458-1511] came to establish a vast empire from Sind to Deccan. Malik Ayaz [died in1522], a Turk, who had found employment in the court of Gujarat, was made Governor of Diu who made the Gujarati coastal city a prosperous place replacing Cambay as the great transhipment centre and mart of Gujarat. Diu under the rule of Malik Ayaz had impressive fortifications. Ayaz consistently rejected Portuguese demands for a factory and trade concessions. He also controlled Sawarath, Patan, Gogha, Surat, and Rander among other areas. The Governor commanded large influence at Mahmud's court and maintained a huge military and a strong naval fleet. His ships sailed far and wide mainly trading with Gulf, Red Sea and East Africa. His navy is said to have comprised at least hundred fustas, each one with twenty-five pairs of oars, one heavy cannon, and two lighter pieces. He also had larger war vessels, and many armed merchant ships. Mahmud Begarha in alliance with Qwansauh-al-Ghauri, Mamluk Sultan of Egypt, tried to check the rising power of the Portuguese in the Indian seas. The customs revenue of Egypt had been seriously affected by Portuguese attacks on ships carrying spices from India to the Red Sea.

As seen before, the Egyptian Sultan sent a naval fleet, under the command of Amir Hussein, the Kurd, Governor of Jeddah, to drive the Portuguese out of the area. The Egyptians had heavier and powerful ships with artillery. The Indian contingent, under the command of Malik Ayaz, had thirty-four fustas. The historic naval battle between the Portuguese, Egyptians and the Indians took place near Chaul. The combined fleet defeated the Portuguese squadron commanded by Dom Lourenco de Almeida, son of the Portuguese Viceroy, Francesco de Almeida, near Chaul, South of Bombay, in 1508. The flagship in which Dom Lourenco commanded sank with the rest retreating south. The Portuguese lost at least 140 men dead and many scores were taken prisoners. Malik Ayaz was supported by the Egyptians and ships from Calicut. This victory was short-lived.

Soon Dom Lourenco's father Francisco de Almeida, the Portuguese Viceroy on learning about the defeat and death of this son began to plan his revenge attack on Diu and especially the Egyptian naval fleet. He also began contacting Malik Ayaz to change sides who remained noncommittal. The Portuguese Viceroy D. Francisco de Almeida, on 2 February 1509 reached Diu with a large naval fleet from Goa, and found the Egyptian naval fleet lined up at anchor, ordered firing mercilessly at the Egyptian ships and the "answering fire never matched this onslaught". The Portuguese ships, some carrying as many as forty guns, stood higher out of the water, so that their cannonballs hurtled and inflicted defeat on the Egyptian-Turkish fleet. The Governor of Diu Malik Ayaz according to one source "was a passive onlooker, never firing a shot against the Portuguese attack and keeping his ships well out of range". When Admiral Amir Hussein returned to Istanbul he told the Ottoman Sultan how the naval battle at Diu had been lost, and he is reported to have said: "he was betrayed at the crucial hour by the Governor of Diu, who had been born a Christian".

The Portuguese intoxicated by their naval victory went about destroying any Muslim ships, ports, harbours, burning cities and killing captains, traders, and looting and plundering anything of value in their way of death and destruction. The Portuguese had a new naval commander as Almeida successor, Afonso de Albuquerque, who became the real founder of Estado da India. He was 'fervent in his desire to kill Muslims' and had spent a lifetime of fighting in North Africa before making his first visit at fifty, to the Indian Ocean. He "dreamed of using Ethiopia as a base for destroying Mecca, and talked of bringing engineers from Madeira to work on the absurd scheme for diverting the Nile into the Red Sea and so starving Egypt into submission". Failing this his first move was to mount an attack on the powerful fortress of Aden, at the entrance of Red Sea because, "it had always been Portugal's ambition to take Aden, for then there could be a virtual blockade against any Muslim ship trying to carry spices on to Egypt". The attack was a complete failure and the Portuguese suffered heavy losses and the only satisfaction they had was in setting fire to all Arab merchant ships in the Aden harbour and in collecting reports that the Egyptians and Turks had not yet started building another naval fleet at Suez.

According to other sources Malik Ayaz continued to resist the

Portuguese demands for a fort at Diu during his lifetime. Mahmud Begarha died on November 23, 1511. The Portuguese position strategically was weak because with no base nearer than Goa or Hormouz in the Gulf, they were unable to lie off Diu for long in the face of ships from Malik Ayaz's fleet. Unable to take Diu, the Portuguese continued to raid, sack and burn Surat, Rander, Gogha, Mangrol, Somnath, Bassein and many other Gujarati ports thereby crippling trade with the Gulf and the Red Sea. Subsequently the Portuguese were granted a site for a factory at Diu by Bahadur Shah. This was mainly to stop Portuguese seizures of Gujarati ships trading with the Gulf and Red Sea including ships carrying Hajees on pilgrimage to Mecca. The Gujarati ruler in order to ward off the growing threat from the Mughal ruler Humayun gave the Portuguese permission to build a fort at Diu in return for their help against the Mughals. The Portuguese even after this concession continued to prohibit Indian trade with the Red Sea. In December 1534 and October 1535, Mahmud Begarha's successor Bahadur Shah signed a peace treaty with the Portuguese Governor Nuno da Cunha whereby the Portuguese were given the port of Bassein and its nearby lands and permission to build a fort in Diu. All Indian ships bound for Red Sea from Gujarat were to pass through Bassein and also return through this port under Portuguese control. The Portuguese, who had seen the naval power of the Gujarati rulers, nor imposed a complete ban on building of warships, nor could they use they already had. Ultimately the Portuguese killed Bahadur Shah treacherously mainly because he was very much interested in sea trade and building a powerful navy. According to one writer, "He travelled frequently by sea, and pursued an active policy of building ships for both commercial and military purposes. These ships were admired by the Portuguese themselves, and were apparently as large in number of oars as contemporary Turkish vessels Bahadur Shah had a fleet of 160 sail at his death in 1537". He had also been in continuous touch with the Ottoman Sultan "with the object of driving the Portuguese out, not only from Diu but also from India and the Red Sea". The Ottoman Sultan more than once sent ships and artillery of the Ottoman naval fleet to help the Gujarati ruler Bahadur Shah and this was quite effective. After they took over Constantinople in 1453, the Ottomans lost naval supremacy in the

Mediterranean in 1571, when they were defeated at Lepanto. The Europeans began to dominate trade in the Indian Ocean and Arab *Mudarabah* or speculative trade declined, as the former came to dominate the territories as well.

The Ottoman Sultans found they were unable to control the growing Portuguese takeover of vital trading areas in India, Gulf, Red Sea and even in the Mediterranean areas. At this stage it is necessary to briefly assess the Ottoman Empire's position which was under mounting challenge from the European powers. After they took over Constantinople in 1453 and renamed it as Istanbul, the Ottoman's were undisputed naval power in the Mediterranean. They had achieved unprecedented growth mainly due to their skill in facilitating the transport of the products from the East after taking over the traditional silk routes in Central and West Asia, such as cotton, spices, silk and agricultural produce to Europe in exchange for weapons, ships and manufactured goods. The unprecedented and truly revolutionary geographical discoveries by the Portuguese, Spaniards, Dutch, French, British and others and the direct sea route especially to India led to importation of gold and silver from the new colonies and the almost takeover of Orient trade adversely affecting the Ottomans. Soon the Ottomans were to suffer a terrible defeat in 1571 at the hands of Italians when they were defeated in a naval battle at Lepanto in East Mediterranean. This was seen as a "watershed in the history of East-West Relations." According to one writer, "Once the Ottomans were stopped at Leponto, the continued long-term autonomy of the Western Mediterranean would never again be in doubt. Leponto ensured that the growing Atlantic trade with the Americas would continue as Europeans not only became enticed by the New World treasure but found the Ottoman Empire increasingly irrelevant to their growing commercial interests in the Orient via routes around the Horn of Africa." Not only European control and hegemony over the Eastern Mediterranean was restored but with the rise of the Europeans, the Arab-Islamic lakes as the Indian Ocean, Gulf and Red Sea were known, came to be dominated first by the Portuguese, then by the Dutch, French and soon the British became undisputed masters over the area. The secret was due to the fact that the Europeans possessed large number of sophisticated ships with powerful guns than the Ottomans. This also led to the shift in focus from the Mediterranean Sea to the Indian Ocean and the Atlantic. Clearly this marked a new era in which powerful guns, cannons with ships using sophisticated technology proved to be decisive and a real strategic shift. The Ottoman advantage with cavalry was now in changed circumstances not much of an asset compared to ships owned by small states like Portugal or Venice. The Ottomans saw rapid drying of capital with the highly lucrative maritime trade carried by the Europeans with India and the East in general. In 1580 Emir Mehmet ibn Emir Es Su'udi wrote: "*The Europeans have discovered the secret of Oceanic travel. They are Lords of the new world and of the gates to India.... The people of Islam are without the latest information in the science of geography and do not understand the menace of the capture of the sea trade by the Europeans*".[22]

These momentous developments pioneered at sea by the Europeans sent the crucial spice trade shipping from Egyptian/Arab and Persian merchants as the price of spices went up due to war, scarcity of supplies and dislocation of the regular shipping between Malabar, Gulf and the Red Sea. Along with the Egyptian merchants, the Red Sea route was also busy with Persian traders from the Gulf and also the seafaring Omani Arabs. "After a few disrupted decades as the shock of the early Portuguese conquests reverberated back down the spice routes, Alexandria and Venice staged a comeback. In the 1560's, there were so many spices for sale at Alexandria that a Portuguese spy suggested that the Portuguese should abandon the Cape route altogether and ship their spices via the Levant in order to cut costs. So great was the flow of illicit spices through the Portuguese blockade that there was speculation—the Portuguese viceroy was in tacit revolt against the King".[23] The religious bigotry and excessive violence earned the Portuguese many enemies. Other Europeans followed the Portuguese in their quest for spices, colonies, slaves and wealth. But Egypt regained its place as the prime intermediary between Europe, India and the Far East as prime supplier of spice. "By unknown means and ferried by unknown hands... spices arrived ...in the souks of Cairo and Alexandria and thence to the markets of Europe like so much cosmic driftwood. Arab dhows conveyed them across the Indian Ocean to the Persian Gulf or the Red Sea. At any one of a number of ancient ports—Basra, Jeddah, Muscat or Aquaba—the spices were transferred onto one of the huge caravans that fanned out across the deserts to the markets of Arabia and on to Alexandria and the Levant".[24]

Tipu Sultan's Diplomacy

In the second half of 18th century, despite decline in its power the Mughal Emperor was still regarded as the sovereign and a large number of independent rulers in different parts of India were representatives of the Mughal Emperor. As per accepted contemporary legal ideas, every Indian ruler had to acknowledge the supremacy of the House of Timur. In South India, the Nizam of Hyderabad was the Viceroy of the Deccan of the Mughals. Other centres were the Nawab of Arcot [Carnatic], the Marathas and the Kingdom of Travancore. Despite nominal Mughal control, de facto power and influence was exercised by the English and all the above rulers were dependent on the British. Like other rulers in South India, the Maharajah of Mysore family was the tributaries of the Mughal Empire. In 1768 the Nizam had ceded the diwani of Mysore to the English. Haider Ali, an employee of the Mysore ruler due to his military skills extended the territorial jurisdiction [at the cost of Nizam and Nawab of Arcot] and became de facto ruler of Mysore between 1761-1782. He had become the most formidable political and military power of South India. In spite of his new status, Haider Ali technically remained an employee of the Mysore ruler and he never claimed himself to be a ruler of Mysore. The Nizam, the Marathas, the Nawab of Carnatic along with the Mysore Maharajah had been working to undermine Haider Ali. The Nizam viewed Haider Ali as a usurper with no legal right to his conquered lands. Both the Nizam and Nawab of Arcot and others were dependent on the British, who perceived Haider Ali as a mortal enemy and the greatest obstacle in the achievement of their ambition in India and the neighbouring Gulf region. Tipu Sultan, who succeeded his father, "forced by circumstances and the need to defend his position and patrimony decided to dethrone" the Mysore Maharajah and proclaim himself as an independent ruler. But Tipu Sultan failed to get recognition either from the Nizam or the Mughal government at Delhi due to British machinations/influence.

The British through ingenious means had extended their

influence to large parts of India subjugating numerous Indian rulers and making them vassals of the British Empire. In South India, Haider Ali and Tipu Sultan were the only major rulers who defied them and refused to become tributary to the East India Company not due to any intentional hostility towards the English but the Mysore rulers could see the British imperial ambitions based on domination and territorial expansion. Nevertheless, both Haider and Tipu expressed their desire on numerous occasions to live at peace with the British, but the latter remained hostile to both the rulers and worked hard for their overthrow. This is confirmed by the fact that Sir Eyre Coote, on hearing the news of Haider Ali's death could not help writing, "On the many beneficial effects which may be expected to arise to our general interests in India by the important news of Haider Ally's death—it opens to us the fairest prospect of securing to the Mother country the permanent and undisturbed possession of these Eastern dominions".[25]

Haider Ali was fully conscious of the British intentions and also their methods of acquiring territory. In his view "the English first try to secure a footing in other territories by out ward professions of friendship and then gradually they bring them under their full sway." He saw the British as his "inveterate enemy". This animosity continued when Tipu succeeded his father and built up a mighty military machine contrary to the expectations that after Haider's death his newly built power would cease to be a dominant factor in the south Indian politics. The British regarded Tipu as a hurdle to their imperial ambitions because he was "unquestionably the most powerful of all the native princes of Hindustan", and they feared that "his steadiness in establishing that system of government and discipline in his army, which have raised him above the other princes in India cannot fail to make him everyday, more formidable". No wonder Lord Cornwallis attacked Mysore and divested Tipu of half of his Kingdom in 1784. Cornwallis was convinced that Tipu was a "prince of very uncommon abilities and of boundless ambition, who had acquired a degree of power in extent of territory and wealth, and in forces that threatened the Company's possessions in the Carnatic and those of all his other neighbours with imminent danger". The British were keen to take over the Malabar areas [Western coast] which were rich in spices, sandalwood and pine trees as also such ports like Calicut and Cannanore in order to increase the revenues of the Company. The possession of these very lucrative areas by the company would partially compensate for the loss of colonies in North America. The British with the help of the Nizam and the Marathas as also by launching direct attack on Tipu's territories demonstrated their hostility towards Mysore. Because of his attempts to work for an alliance with the French, Ottoman Sultan, Shah of Persia, King of Afghanistan, the Sultan of Oman and other Gulf rulers, Tipu was seen as dangerous to British interests. The British saw the search for allies' abroad and pursuit of an active diplomacy coupled with the possession of a strong military by Tipu as a threat to their interests. Tipu appears to have had a clear perception of the political, economic and military advantages of closer relations with the Gulf countries. Even though, Europe and North America had become the centre for global trade, the Gulf region still remained a significant centre of political, economic activity in the 18th century and no wonder Tipu paid special attention to building ties with this area. In order to understand Tipu's diplomacy in the Gulf region one should note the imperial struggle throughout the 18th century which gave ample scope for the Gulf tribal elite's to initiate strong local resistance to contain European imperialism and economic hegemony, after it had been regarded initially as a mere annoyance which will wither away as time passes. Oman took the lead in expelling the Portuguese influence in the Gulf. This period [1791-92] also saw the emergence of the Qasimis in the area now known as the UAE.

The British defeated the Dutch and French in the area and after they had firmly established their control over India from 1690 onwards, proceeded to control trade in the Gulf region. The subsequent treaties with the subjugated Gulf rulers completed the domination of key strategic areas so very essential to retain their dominant influence in the region. These were the links in their grand imperial design. Interestingly, the British began the establishment of their control all over the Gulf region by weakening the Arab commercial and economic capacities and by subjecting them ultimately to the colonial administration of which they made India their base. In this scheme, Tipu Sultan was seen as a major stumbling block that could have undermined their grand imperial strategy. In order to achieve her goals, Britain resorted to various tactics and excuses with which to hide her true aims of which three were crucial: [1] piracy, [2] slave trade; and [3] arms trade. Even though British domination of the region started in 1688 but the real era of "Pax Britannica" in the Gulf region started with the fall of Tipu Sultan in 1799. British ascendency in the Gulf was thus total which was not only military but also economic, and their control of India played a decisive role in their success in the Gulf region. From all this, it is clear that the room to manoeuvre for Tipu Sultan was extremely limited given the British naval supremacy which enabled them to have global reach and paramountcy.

Ever since Haider Ali became the de facto ruler of Mysore in South India between 1761 and 1782 with control over a large chunk of South India, the British perceived him as a mortal enemy and relations had been strained. Under Tipu Sultan they reached a nadir primarily due to determined British efforts to isolate him and bring about his downfall. The British challenge to Haider Ali and Tipu Sultan which the former saw as a great hindrance to their interests in India and neighbouring areas was one of the most formidable an Indian ruler had to face in the second half of 18th century, and in self-defence both the Indian ruler had been compelled to take a series of bold measures. In order to understand Tipu's diplomacy in the Gulf region, and especially his ties with Oman one should note the imperial struggle throughout the 18th century which gave ample scope for the Gulf political, economic and tribal elite's to initiate strong local resistance to contain European imperialism and economic hegemony, after it had been regarded initially as a mere annoyance which will wither away as time passes. The following are some of the most significant developments in the gulf region during this period, (i) the emergence of Muscat as a major regional commercial power from 1719; (ii) the separation of Lahej and Aden and before that Hadramaut from Zaidi Yemen as of 1728. (iii) the efforts of Nadir Shah to unify Persia against foreign influence around 1747; (iv) the founding of Kuwait as a commercial centre under the Al-Sabahs about 1752; (v) the emergence of the Qasimis (now part of UAE) as a local resistance power dating from 1777; (vi) the founding of Bahrain as a commercial centre under the leadership of Al-Khalifahs of the Utab about 1783; (vii) the appearance of the Wahhabi movement on a regional basis under the leadership of Al-

Saud dating from 1792; and (viii) the emergence of the economic role of Kuwait as a mercantile port-of call, instead of Basra, about 1792 as result of the sectarian wars between the Persians and the Ottomans in Iraq. Oman took the lead in expelling the Portuguese influence in the Gulf, India and from coastal eastern Africa in their attempt to regain control of the main commercial region in the Indian Ocean. Intra European rivalry in the Gulf region gave a boost to Arab opposition to Europeans which was widespread in the entire 18th century, since Muscat entered into an alliance on one occasion with the Dutch and on another with the English to expel the Portuguese. Despite this, the Omani Sultan resisted the British demand to have a Resident, but under sustained pressure he agreed to permit the East India Company to have a Native Agency. Unfortunately, tribal factionalism of sectarian origin soon became endemic in Oman which considerably weakened opposition to European encroachment compelling groups to take help from foreigners—Persians in 1737-42 and English in 1791-8. In this sectarian strife in Oman, the English increased their influence and with the consolidation of its control over India, it began to extend its influence over the Gulf, West Asia, East Africa and the entire Indian Ocean area. This period (1791-92) also saw the emergence of the Qasimis in the area now known as the UAE. The Qasimis entered upon an unceasing struggle with the Omanis. Around this time the Wahhabi movement came out on the scene and opposed Oman. These threats also propelled the Omani Sultan to seek help from the Persians, Ottomans and later the French and the British. In view of the French preoccupation with their revolution and the ensuing chaos, the British succeeded in signing a treaty with Oman, which was the first foothold for the British colonial administration in the region which enabled them to gain control more effectively of trade throughout the Straits of Hormuz and the Gulf region. Thus, the British between 1688 and 1798 gained control of key trading areas in the Gulf and West Asian region and East Indies. The subsequent treaties with the subjugated Gulf rulers completed the domination of key strategic are as so very essential to retain their dominant influence in the region. These were the links in their grand imperial design. Interestingly, the British began the establishment of their control in all over the Gulf region by weakening the Arab commercial and economic capacities and by subjecting them ultimately to the colonial administration of which they made India their base. In this scheme, Tipu Sultan was seen as a major stumbling block who could have undermined their imperial strategy. Even though British domination of the region started in 17th century but the real era of 'Pax Britannica' in the Gulf region started with the fall of Tipu Sultan, though strictly speaking after the signing of the 1798 treaty with the Sultan of Oman. British ascendancy in the Gulf was thus total which were not only a military ascendancy but also mainly economic and organisational, institutional and their control of India played a decisive role in their success in the Gulf region.

From the above brief survey of some of the momentous developments in the Gulf region focusing on European rivalry, especially British attempts to bring it under its control, it is pertinent to note that the French had already conceded defeat to the British and were confined to few pockets in insignificant areas. Having curtailed the trade/profits of the Arabs especially those belonging the Omanis they could easily be manipulated and eventually subjugated by the British. The Ottoman Sultan due to determined attempts by the Russian Czars and mounting challenges from the Europeans had come to acknowledge British supremacy in the Gulf region in numerous ways. The Persians were busy fighting amongst themselves while it was easy for the British to foment trouble for the Afghan rulers in view of the tribal factor in Afghan politics.

The British challenge to Tipu was formidable; it prompted him to respond with equally forcible, bold and prompt measures to tackle it. Most remarkable was his attempt to seek friendship with the Sultan of Oman, Ottoman Sultan, France, Persia, Afghanistan, and other gulf countries, which were also equally, at the same time, under intense pressure and vulnerable to British power. Despite his forced involvement in British inspired wars and the huge burden of war reparations, whenever his economic and political position improved, Tipu Sultan, sent embassies abroad as he strongly believed in close cooperation with Oman and other Gulf countries in order to contain the formidable threat posed by the British to his regime. Towards this end, he began to offer numerous concessions in order to induce them to support him. To the Ruler of Oman, Tipu sent a diplomatic mission headed by Mir Abdul Rahman and Mir

Iyanullah. They were accompanied by Mirza Karim Beg Tabrizi the Persian envoy to Mysore. Like on previous such missions, Tipu Sultan sent valuable gifts to the Ruler of Muscat. This included jewels, elephants, khillats, sandalwood, ivory, pepper and cardamoms. It must be mentioned that Haider Ali had also maintained close ties with the Ruler of Muscat and also had an establishment at Muscat but this special arrangement lapsed as was customary with his death in 1782. Tipu's intense diplomatic activity with Oman which had essentially political, economic and military consideration not only showed his desire to keep up contacts with influential and powerful rulers but also to continuously seek allies in his ceaseless quest for partners to withstand the British challenge. Thus, the guiding principles of Tipu's diplomacy were to neutralise his enemies and maintain the integrity of his Kingdom and to contain British imperialism as also their expansionism. It is significant to note, that the French also maintained close ties with the Ruler of Oman but Tipu's and the Oman's respective relations with the French appear to have been complementary but independent. Nevertheless, the three-cornered friendship aroused the suspicions of the British, who became actively interested in asserting their influence at Muscat. Britain took keen interest in Oman largely in response to Tipu's and French initiatives there and to a belated appreciation of Oman's commercial strength. The British also thought Muscat would serve for refuge and supply and due to its geographic proximity could prevent harassment of British trade and communications and that the "French would maintain a free intercourse by Muscat Dingeys with Tippo" at Mangalore. In order to watch French-Tipu activities in Oman, the British used the company's Indian broker in Muscat Narottam Ram Chander Raoji, widely known as Josey, to act as informer on payment. Not only the British were concerned over preferential treatment of Tipu Sultan and the French by the Omani Ruler but they also sought to curb their influence in Oman. The Omani's acquisition of a lease for Bandar Abbas at the very time of the French mission to Shiraz could not have been a mere coincidence. It is significant to note that the British Resident at Basra Samuel Manesty, a Jew, sent highly exaggerated reports to the British of the supposedly limitless French influence in Muscat which was aimed at undermining British presence in India. In other words, he implied Muscat as having become a haven for French conspiracies. Josey added to Manesty's negative picture by reporting that a large number of Tipu's vessels arrived there annually and that some would sail with Indian products to French possessions in the Indian Ocean and African area particularly Mauritius. French commitment to Omani friendship was more a matter of the influence of its dynamic, alert and skilful representative than of a consistent government policy. Also, the French had little leverage with Oman other than the mutually disadvantageous withdrawal of trade and sometimes the ability to recover Omani vessels and cargo seized by the French corsairs. In contrast it was abundantly clear to the Omani Ruler that India was firmly in the hands of the British who could, as they had alerted, refuse Omani vessels access to Indian ports. The Ruler denied any special ties with the French and under British pressure agreed to sever all ties with them. In fact, the British were adamant (in refusal) about the presence of any Frenchmen at Muscat for any reason whatsoever. Undoubtedly, Tipu looked upon the Ruler of Muscat as an important ally and source of support against his struggle with the British, but he never abandoned France as a useful partner. He sent two envoys under Dubuc in 1798 to Paris for assistance, which appeared as a last-ditch attempt to ward off final British attack. Tipu observed: "I know not how to explain how urgent it is that your mission be instantly carried out." Tipu Sultan gave huge sum of money to Dubuc for this mission and also sent jewellery and two crores of rupees as presents to the members of the French Directory.

The British, of course, were extremely suspicious of Tipu's relations with Oman and other Muslim rulers in the Gulf region because of implications not only on their position in India but also on ties with the Mughal emperor and other Indian Muslim rulers as well. But they were simply furious over Tipu's contacts with the French whom Wellesley called "enemies of my country" and "inveterate enemies of the company"

Tipu Sultan was fully aware how the British rose to become dominant in India and elsewhere through trade, and also how they became prosperous and subsequently acquired territories due also to the weakness of the Mughal Empire and the disunity among Indian rulers. Learning from the British and other Europeans, Tipu

Sultan attached great importance to foreign trade and commerce as he viewed it to be the basis of state power and prosperity. Towards this end, he decided to establish factories in the Gulf region in which the state was the monopoly-trading agent. Realising the immense significance of Oman and the Gulf region which still remained the hub of global economic activity linking the Red Sea, Arabian Sea and the Indian Ocean, Tipu Sultan maintained Factories at Muscat, Hormuz and Jeddah. He had also advanced plans to set up factories at Aden, Bushier, Basra and other important places in the Gulf area. One of the objectives of his Embassy to the Sublime Porte was to seek exclusive trading rights in the ports of Basra, Oman and offer similar facilities at Mangalore. Undoubtedly, all of Tipu's diplomatic missions had a commercial objective. Since products from Mysore like spices, sandalwood, ivory, silk, rice, timber and cloth were in great demand, he decided to appoint Commercial Attaches and Consul-Generals abroad. Two factories were also set up in Kutch in 1789—at Mundhi and Mundra—as they imported goods from Oman and stored to be sent home and vice versa. Tipu also maintained a large staff at Muscat to look after Mysore's extensive trade interests there and in the entire Gulf region. In the first two years of Tipu's rule, he had a Vakil (or darogha) at Muscat and the Omani Ruler maintained an agent at Mangalore. Their names were respectively Mir Qasim and Ghouse Mohammed Khan. Tipu's chief broker at Muscat and Bushier was Maoji Seth and at Basra a Jew called Abdullah. Tipu Sultan maintained extremely cordial ties with the Ruler of Oman who gave special privileges like lesser customs duty to Mysore merchants which was reciprocated by Tipu Sultan. In fact by 1785-6 Tipu and the Ruler of Oman were negotiating a mutually beneficial arrangement. In response to Oman's favour to Mysore merchants, Tipu promised to remit half of all duties levied on Omani vessels trading at Mysore ports. Imports from Oman to Mysore were dates, horses, mules, and from Gulf via Muscat, silk worms, sulphur, and pearls—when the last could be had at Muscat more cheaply than at Bahrain which was the main market for pearls in the Gulf. Tipu's ambassadors to Turkey stayed in Oman for about three months, from early April to late June 1786 and a journal was kept of their dealings there. The secretary credited with having written the Persian journal was Khwaja Abdul Qadir. Keeping in view the crucial role, played by the Gulf region from all dimensions, which would enable Tipu Sultan to better understand the prevailing conditions there because of its direct bearing on his Kingdom. The delegation carried large quantities of goods produced in Mysore with them to be sold at various ports of call so that wider publicity was given to the products and hence exports boosted. Tipu Sultan encouraged Omani and Arab merchants to come and settle in Mysore and gave them special privileges as they were seen as successful businessmen. Even though no treaty resulted between Mysore and Oman but an extensive report on Muscati trade and opportunities was sent back to Mysore by Tipu's Ambassadors to Turkey. One of the crucial reasons why Mysore was prosperous was due to the state monopoly of trade. Tipu Sultan naturally placed severe restrictions on European trading companies especially the English. The British in order to circumvent Tipu's restrictions, used to send other merchants disguised as Muscati traders to make cheaper purchases from Mysore. Through his alert and vigilant intelligence Tipu Sultan learnt about British cheating and he promptly instructed that only genuine merchants who had valid passports or authorised certificate from his officials in Muscat could engage in trade at Mysore. Tipu urged foreign rulers especially the Ruler of Oman, to send him skilled people and technicians who would assist his government in the setting up of modern industries. This was possible due to his wide knowledge of the advanced countries in the West, extensive foreign trading contacts and familiarity with foreign goods. Thousands of foreign skilled workers were brought in and among them Turks, Arabs, (especially Omanis) Persians, Afghans were also present. They not only brought their technical skills but by their interaction with locals a new vision of modern world was projected. According to one writer, "No other sovereign in Indian history had given such an impetus to industrial production with foreign collaboration". Thus, he undertook the role of an international trader, manufacturer, banker and moneychanger. In most of these areas, Tipu was close to Mohammed Ali, the founder of modern Egypt. Tipu's tremendous interest in international trade and other foreign economic matters in the midst of battles, challenges from the British and other threats, reveals his far sightedness and realisation that promotion of commerce and industry was the true strength of his Kingdom. According to one writer, "If Tipu Sultan had been allowed to rule Mysore peacefully for a few more decades, there is little doubt that he would have brought about an economic revolution of the first magnitude. The seeds which he sowed did however bear fruit after his death and the state of Mysore, long before the era of planning, was in the vanguard of industrial progress and public welfare in India." It was due to Tipu's efforts that Mysore, now called Karnataka, has become India's leading silk producing state. Silk industry was developed in Mysore by obtaining silk worms from Muscat and by encouraging the plantation of mulberry trees. It was also due to Tipu's efforts that a huge quantity of sandalwood was sold in the Omani markets. Tipu Sultan gave all the incentives to grow sandalwood and saw to it that the wood and oil were exported to foreign countries especially to Oman where there was large demand. Mysore owes an immense debt of gratitude to Tipu sultan to this day, sandalwood is exported to Oman and other parts of the Gulf region in large quantities. Tipu's foreign economic diplomacy, which primarily aimed at increasing Mysore's exports through state trading even though fell short of his hopes, but was largely successful in trade with Muscat due to his pragmatic plans. This has to be considered Tipu Sultan's most significant commercial success. The British viewed Tipu Sultan as a dangerous competitor and their goal was to put an end to all his trading activities and imaginative enterprises. Tipu's factories and Agency at Muscat that was intended to improve trade between the two states was closed down after his death in1799.

The ruler of Muscat did not endear himself to the English by his friendly dealings with Tipu Sultan. After Tipu's defeat, the British ordered the Imam of Oman to stop the French and Dutch ships from trading to and from Muscat, as this was not only a threat to their own trade but in fact they were actually at war with the British during this entire period. Tipu Sultan's relations with Oman charted new and unprecedented course except for Haider Ali's limited initiative in this field. His embassies/missions to Oman and other Gulf countries not only gave him legitimacy to his rule (which was denied by his neighbouring Indian rulers and the British, but with other countries even though he could not get the help he anticipated) but had flourishing trade with them like Muscat, Aden, Persia, Afghanistan. These were undoubtedly bold and courageous initiatives, basically a response to the massive challenge from the British, taken by a shrewd and ambitious ruler who had a clear global vision. Undoubtedly, Tipu's shrewd diplomatic initiatives in the Gulf region especially his ties with Oman were bold, imaginative and he was largely successful. Unfortunately, his skilful diplomacy pushed the British redouble their efforts to neutralize Tipu's diplomatic initiatives, friendships and achievements. The British due to this worldwide contacts and modern means of transport and communication net works were able to reach out to places where Tipu Sultan intended to send his envoys, much faster and take effective and tangible steps to neutralise in advance his initiatives. Since the other Europeans including the French, had already been elbowed out by the English effectively from the Gulf region, it was far easier for them to frustrate Tipu's energetic diplomatic moves. The room to manoeuvre for Tipu Sultan was extremely limited as the British concentrated all their power, skills and resources to bring about his downfall. It must be mentioned that Tipu Sultan was ready for a compromise or reconciliation with the British but all his overtures were spurned by them and he was repeatedly rebuffed because they considered him an adversary and his ideas too dangerous and hence they decided to eliminate him.

To sum up, it must be mentioned that Tipu's historical stature is guaranteed by two great qualities that he showed through his state craft: his ability to take innumerable diplomatic initiatives that transcend the force of circumstance and his ability/willingness to take enormous risk even in the face of setbacks and formidable forces. In the ultimate analysis all of Tipu's intricate, complex international manoeuvring, risks, initiatives, friendships, and negotiations were primarily aimed at upliftment, prosperity and improving the life of the people in Mysore and providing security to them.[26]

British Rule in India: Implications on Indo-West Asia Relations

By 1799 the British had consolidated their rule all over India. From Mumbai with the aid of Indian soldiers and administrative staff, the British first went to Oman and from Oman compelled Gulf tribal leaders in present UAE to sign truce agreements and gradually controlled bulk of the Gulf region. They placed strict restrictions on them as far as dealings with other outside powers were concerned. Large segments of the Gulf Arab population who thrived on lucrative trade with India and beyond were now virtually dependent on the British dominated trade and maritime links. Apart from the destruction and havoc brought by the Portuguese, Dutch, French, the British also systematically went about destroying Arab ships, ports, and many Arab merchants were indiscriminately killed who traded with India on the pretext of combating piracy, arms smuggling and containing slave trade. The Gulf Arabs reverted to pearl fishing and the British transported their principal day-to-day requirements mostly from India. Many Indians with British protection especially the Banya trading families settled throughout in the Gulf region from Basra to Muscat including the ports of Qatar at Al Bida and Zubara. People in the Gulf region now saw such Indians as collaborators with British imperialism. The British deported undesirable people (reformers and dissident ruling family members) from the Gulf to India.

The initial history of Qatar is linked with Bahrain at least from the mid-18 century, but gradually tribal leaders in Qatar asserted their authority. The 1835 maritime truce had worked well until 1867 when Qatar was attacked by Bahraini forces allied with Abu Dhabi. In retaliation Qataris attacked Bahrain in 1868 in which over 1000 people were killed and more than 600 ships were destroyed. The British concluded a treaty in 1868 with Mohammed al Thani (1850-78) whose rule was acknowledged. Interestingly, al Thani also accepted limited Ottoman sovereignty. Earlier Al Saud presence in parts of Qatar had provided some security. Thus, Qatar was sought by Bahrain, Britain, Ottomans, and Al Saud. In these conflicting pulls and pressure the small economy of trade in Qatar—mostly pearls, textiles, dates and other items was handled by outsiders with Indians prominently present. Sheikh Jassim (1878-1913), a very shrewd but tactful leader of al Thanis initially welcomed the Ottomans. Like his father, he was also a successful merchant in pearls and dates besides being a religious leader. Thus he came to exercise political, economic and religious power. He extended his authority inside Qatar step by step focusing first on Indians and later elbowed out the Ottomans.

Sheikh Jassim's concern with the Indians grew from their competition in the pearl and date trade. He moved very cautiously against Indian merchants as they were British protected subjects. Initially he raised taxes and then gradually nationalised their trade including ships. The British supported the Indians initially and in some cases sought compensation on two occasions. By 1880's the Indians became thoroughly frustrated and left Qatar with the help of the British and this exit allowed Sheikh Jassim and his family to become significant merchants. For the next more than fifty years Qatar had no Indian trading community whereas Indians flourished throughout the Gulf region. Under Sheikh Jassim, Qatar according to one study had about 817 pearling ships and boats with 12,890 sailors and the incident of Indians showed the skills of the ruler who kept the Ottomans and as well as the British at bay. He came to understand the limits of Ottoman's power and also constraints on British power. Sheikh Jassim was perhaps willing to refrain from taking steps involving Indians, had they shared the profits with Al Thanis. The greedy and avaricious [mostly] Banya merchants invited the wrath upon themselves who behaved in arrogance with British support and threats. No wonder the Al Thanis found a trading niche from which the family not only expanded its trade but consolidated their rule. The British feared the negative fall-out from the expulsion of Indians in Qatar as this could be repeated by other Arab tribal leaders. Since their control of Persian Gulf region was crucial for their overall security and expansion of British Empire, hence their response was prompt and fairly strong. Al Thanis under Sheikh Jassim had done something no one dared in the entire Persian Gulf region. Sheikh Jassim's turbulent relations with Indians only showed his determination to consolidate Al Thani control over Qatar in the face of multiple challenges in the Persian Gulf region.

For centuries, people in the Persian Gulf, Red Sea, Arabian Sea, Indian Ocean and beyond interacted peacefully and exchanged goods and other items through merchants. This vibrant 'world system' is a term coined by historians and made familiar by Immanuel Wallerstein to designate a political-economic unit, articulated by cross-continental trade networks and larger political units extending far beyond the boundaries of individual nation states and linking them together in a larger functioning unit. The global Muslim community apart from politico-economic networks also saw the emergence of a wide network of traders and merchants stretching from Fez through Tunis, Cairo, Istanbul, Suez, Jeddah, Mecca, Aleppo, Aden, Muscat, Basrah, Bushier, Bahrain, Bandar Abbas, Hormuz, Surat, Chaul, Calicut going to South East Asia and China. This huge number of diverse networks of Muslim traders with different places, cultural backgrounds and under varied political control had adopted an innovative system of finance and banking at different periods of Islamic history which at times challenged the very fundamental notions of Islam and at times functioning and sharing some financial practices with non-Muslims. But on most occasions it was able to draw on some common elements. There was no hegemonic power or imperialist internationalism at its core as there were numerous subunits with distinctive structures and functions. The Islamic world system consisting of traders, merchants and diasporas was backed up by faith-based travellers—of preachers, scholars and Sufi saints. All this of course received direct or indirect patronage from major Islamic dynasties, innumerable princely states which made up the Islamic world system. The unique characteristic feature of this commercial maritime world Islamic system was the role of Muslims in creating a just Islamic order with emphasis on peaceful co-existence among different societies. Trade was also linked with Hajj pilgrimage and the annual event was a great unifier and brought Muslims from all known corners of the world. They were at ease in this nascent globalisation in which they not only interacted with Muslims from all backgrounds but also Armenians, Baniyas [among other Hindus], Jews, Chinese, Africans, Turks, Persians and Europeans merchants. This world Islamic economic system had its regional trade networks in the Mediterranean, the Red Sea, Persian Gulf, Indian Ocean, Eurasia, Central Asia, China and East Asia, East Africa, South and East Asia and the entire Indian Ocean area. The early Muslim Empires were Umayyads [Spain also], Fatimids, Abbasids. The subsequent major Muslim empires were Ottoman, Mughal, Safavid, Qajar, Indonesian, which prospered from the cross-cultural interactions of Muslim traders and merchants. It also made deep inroads with its networks into the Chinese Manchu Empire, small princely states of south India, Muslim communities in Caucasus, Bosnia and Sub-Saharan Africa.

The entry of Europeans into the Indian Ocean since 1498 led by the Portuguese especially into the vast network of Muslim merchants disrupted this largely peaceful and mutually beneficial trade, commerce and its multiplier benefits. The Europeans brought flags, built forts, system of permits, visas, cartazes and more importantly politics which gradually and incrementally destroyed the world Islamic system causing the downfall of Muslim Empires, dislodging Muslim elites and bringing untold sufferings to traders, merchants and common Muslims. Many non-Muslims who were working with Muslims also suffered and this led to growth in resentment against of Europeans which reflects/continues in one way or the other. All European colonialists with their crusader approach in varying degrees brought untold sufferings and cruelty on Muslims with large-scale violence, destruction, oppression, suppression and repression never seen in their history on such scale. The British endured for long to weaken and destroy the largest Muslim Empires like the Mughals [in India], Ottoman [Istanbul], Safavid and Qajar Empires [Iran] and innumerable small princely Muslim States in much of Asia and Africa. With the inevitable decline of the British, the USA has taken over this approach by supporting Israel and now directly invading and occupying Muslim states like Iraq and Afghanistan. Those Muslim states which do not submit to the Israel, USA or UK diktats or refuse to become vassals or clients are isolated by sanctions, threats of invasions and other militaristic methods misusing international organisations and other national instruments. This has greatly disrupted the peaceful atmosphere needed for reviving the vigorous interaction which existed among peoples of Asia leading to trade, prosperity and vibrant cultural links and mutual respect and tolerance.

The First World War: Its Impact

After the First World War, Turkey emerged as a modern nation under the leadership of Mustafa Kamal Pasha. Having abolished the Ottoman monarchy and the Caliphate on 5 March 1924, Ataturk made Turkey a secular republic, and was determined to make a clean break with the past. Establishing democratic structures along with cultural modernisation made Turkey a model nation state. Its impact was felt in Ira'n, Egypt, India and elsewhere. Even though Mahatma

Gandhi and the Indian National Congress Party had supported the Indian Khilafat Movement, but soon it lost its very *raison d'être* when it became obvious that the struggle was futile in the face of a determined leader like Ataturk. Jawaharlal Nehru soon began to appreciate the developments in Turkey especially the policy of secularism in a predominantly Muslim country. Earlier he had admired the brave struggle of the Turks against western imperialism. The Turkish struggle for independence and its early success made a deep and lasting impact on the Indian freedom movement. Besides Mahatma Gandhi and Jawaharlal Nehru, Maulana Abul Kalam Azad was also familiar with developments in Turkey. He had widely spoken, at numerous fora and written (as a journalist) extensively in his newspapers on the extra-ordinary happenings in Ottoman Turkey both during and after the First World War.[27]

The Second World War was a turning point for Turkey. Due to the territorial demands of the USSR on Turkey especially the strategically important Turkish Straits [Bosphorus and the Dardanelles] and other issues, the Turkish leaders decided to reorient their foreign policy in favour of the West in general and the US in particular. Turkish leaders accepted US offer of economic and military aid under the Truman Doctrine. Soon Turkey joined NATO and took active part in the Korean War on behalf of the West. Later it joined the Baghdad Pact in 1955 and came to establish close ties with Pakistan and Iran. The US encouraged closer ties between the three Muslim countries especially with the military establishment. Turkey also became the first Muslim country to recognize and have ties with Israel much to the embarrassment of the Islamic [especially Arab states] world. Whereas Turkey identified itself wholeheartedly with the West and US in particular in the cold war, India pursued nonaligned policy in its foreign policy with a tilt towards the USSR and struck up a close proximity to Greece and Cyprus.

Despite the obvious ideological and foreign policy divergences, Indo-Turkish relations grew albeit slowly. As early as on 14 December 1951 India and Turkey signed Treaty of Friendship which came into force on 9 August 1952 after the exchange of the instruments of ratification which took place on 25 July 1952, in accordance with Article 9. The treaty has nine articles. Article one says "there shall be perpetual peace and friendship" between the two countries. It also says both "shall at all times strive to maintain and strengthen such peace and friendship and to promote and deepen the cordial relations between the peoples" of Turkey and India. As per article three both agreed to strengthen and develop cultural ties between their respective countries and to assist each other as far as possible in industrial and agricultural progress. On behalf of the President of India, Ambassador C.S. Jha signed the document and from the Turkish side for the President of Turkey Fuad Koprulu, Deputy of Istanbul, Minister of Foreign Affairs signed. Maulana Azad visited Turkey when he was India's Education minister and signed several agreements in the fields of education, culture and scientific cooperation. He signed the cultural relations agreement with Turkey on 29 June 1951. The agreement has 12 articles. The opening sentences of the cultural agreement are quite interesting. It speaks like this: "Conscious of many centuries of cultural relations between Turkey and India, and inspired by a common desire [to] develop closer cultural relations in the future in the spirit of the UNESCO, and desirous of promoting and developing in every possible way and on a sound basis such relations and understanding between the two states, especially in the realm of science and education, [both] have decided to conclude a cultural agreement".[28]

Even though India's Prime Minister Jawaharlal Nehru had serious reservations over Turkey's pro-west foreign policy and its support to Pakistan on the Kashmir and other issues but he was, attracted towards Turkish policy and commitment to secularism. It is this crucial reason more than anything else which prompted him to visit Turkey in 1960 although it was ill timed because the democratically elected Turkish Prime Minister Adnan Menderes was overthrown by the Turkish military in a *coup*. Jawaharlal Nehru was keen to meet the leader of the opposition Ismet Inonu—a close associate of Mustafa Kamal Ataturk. The new Turkish military rulers were not keen in arranging a meeting for Nehru. It was possible for Nehru to meet Inonu only at the reception hosted by the Indian embassy in Ankara. Interestingly Inonu is reported to have told Nehru not to trust the Chinese, as it had become common knowledge about Nehru's friendship with Chinese leaders despite very disturbing developments concerning Tibet and their stand on the border issue. Later when the Chinese attacked India in 1962 Ismet Inonu succeeded in sending arms to India despite serious Pakistani objections. Despite this gesture subsequently India was dismayed over Turkish support to Pakistan during the 1965 Indo-Pak war and the close ties established between the military generals in both the countries.[29]

Turkey's close alliance with the west and its membership in such military alliances like NATO and CENTO was cause for deep concern in India. Nehru criticised the western backed military alliance systems—Middle East Command, Middle East Defense Organization, SEATO, and Baghdad Pact. About the Baghdad Pact he said it "has in fact created in West Asia far greater tension and conflict than ever before. It has certainly put one country against another among countries that were friendly to one another".[30] He was particularly opposed to US bilateral military assistance to Pakistan, Iran, Turkey and John Foster Dullesian strategy of collective security through military pacts. Nehru proposed the concept of collective peace and enlisted the support of other non-aligned countries. Together with China he proposed the Panchsheel or Five principles of peaceful coexistence. No wonder the bilateral military cooperation pacts with the US and support to Turkey and Pakistan and domination of Turkish political system by the military and other factors led to a drift in Indo-Turkish relations. But it must be stressed that there were no fundamental bilateral problems between India and Turkey. In addition to these issues Cyprus was added to the list. Soon after the island's independence from Britain in 1960 the divide between the two communities inhabiting the Island nation—Greek and Turkish Cypriots widened over a number of constitutional, ethnic and other issues. India began to support the Greek Cypriot leader Archbishop Makarios for a variety of reasons including his non-aligned foreign policy. Makarios was a popular leader in the Non-aligned movement.

West Asia: Perceptions of Nascent Nation

Jawaharlal Nehru was the first major Asian leader who identified the implications of European imperialism and set about to work for Asian identity, development and cooperation. He was conscious of the emerging challenges as well as the opportunities available to work towards a new vision, greater role for Asian countries to maintain security, stability and peacefully resolve emerging conflict situations primarily created by European colonialism. He was also a leading proponent of the concept of 'Collective Asian Security' for maintaining world order. It is in this context one should see Nehru's initiative to organise the first Asian Relations Conference in Delhi at Indian Council of World Affairs, Sapru House in March 1947 in which during the inaugural speech, he fervently pleaded for Asian unity, cooperation, solidarity and identity. Nehru said: "We stand at the end of an era and on the threshold of a new period of history... we can look back on our long past, and look forward to the future that is taking shape before our eyes...the time has come for us, peoples of Asia, to meet together, to hold together and to advance together. It was not only a vague desire, but a compulsion..." With considerable clarity, he pinpointed the strategic role of Asia in global politics in, what he called, the 'atomic age': "In this atomic age Asia will have to function effectively...Indeed, there can be no peace unless Asia plays her part. There is today conflict in many countries, and all of us in Asia are full of our own problems. Nevertheless, the emergence of Asia in world affairs could be a powerful influence for world peace". Nehru, therefore, pleaded for a 'close union of countries bordering on the Indian Ocean, both for defence and trade purposes', a system of defence, stretching from the West to Southeast Asia in which 'India because of her intrinsic importance and her strategic position was to play a significant role'. He desired that 'the coordination of various countries in Middle East, India and the Southeast Asia is not only possible, but undoubtedly certain in the future.' He indicated that the question of 'Asiatic Federation' was necessary, both for defence and trade purposes. The gathering of such large number of Asian leaders in Delhi and the conference call for Asian unity "announced the arrival of Asia on the world stage". Later Nehru declared "...the world is something bigger than Europe... Asia counts in World Affairs. Tomorrow it will count much more than today." Solidarity with fellow Asian and African countries was a conviction and this was evident when Nehru said: "We are of Asia and the peoples of Asia are nearer and closer to us than others. India is so situated that she is the pivot of Western, Southern, and Southeast Asia. In the past, its culture flowed to all these countries and they came to it in many ways. Those contacts are being renewed and the future is bound to see a closer union between India and Southeast Asia on one side, and Afghanistan, Iran and the Arab World on the other."[31]

It is in this backdrop one should see Nehru's opposition to western backed military alliance systems—Middle East Command, Middle East Defense Organization, Baghdad Pact, Central Treaty Organization, South East Asian Treaty Organization, NATO as also bilateral military alliances. He was particularly opposed to US military assistance to Pakistan, Iran, Turkey and former US Secretary of State John Foster Dulles's strategy of Collective Security through military pacts. He proposed the concept of collective peace and enlisted the support of Egypt's new leader Nasser and others. Together with China he proposed the Panchsheel or five principles of peaceful coexistence. The Afro-Asian conference held at Bandung, Indonesia in 1955 was a reaffirmation of the concept of area of peace articulated by Nehru. His approach to secure peace through regional cooperation, Panchsheel, non-aligned policy received a rude shock when the US intervened in Iran in 1952-53 to overthrow Dr. Mohammed Mossadeq over the issue of oil nationalisation. He was also particularly shocked at the violent turn of events when Israel attacked Egypt and subsequently Anglo-French forces intervened in Egypt in 1956 with the clear purpose of overthrowing the Nasser regime. So far he had reluctantly supported Nasser and tried to balance between Egypt and Britain but with the invasion of Egypt, he publicly condemned the aggressors and assured Nasser of his full support and cooperation. In a letter to the US Secretary of State on 31, October 1956 Nehru wrote: "I cannot imagine a worse case of aggression. If this aggression continues and succeeds all faith in international commitments and the UN will fade away and the old specter of colonialism will haunt us again... The whole future of the relations between Europe and Asia hangs in the balance. There can be no peace; howsoever it might be imposed if it means conquest by force of arms". Nehru publicly branded Israeli action as a case of "clear, naked aggression". Regarding the Anglo-French intervention, he remarked: "After fairly considerable experience in foreign affairs, I cannot think of a grosser case of naked aggression than what England and France are attempting to do..." He further said: "In the middle of the 20th century, we are going back to the predatory method of the 18th and 19th centuries. But there are self-respecting, independent nations in Asia and Africa which are not going to tolerate this kind of incursion by the colonial powers." Towards Britain he remained "not unfriendly and expressed his views more in sorrow than in anger", but he did not conceal the strength of his feelings and his deep regret that Britain, with her record of liberal policies, should now have become again the symbol of colonialism. "Unless these wrong courses are halted the future appears to me to be dark indeed..." Furthermore, Nehru told the Indian Parliament on 16 November 1956: "During all the controversies since the nationalization of the Suez Canal Company, Egypt has conducted herself with a large measure of propriety and forbearance. Without the least justification, Egypt was attacked not only by Israel but also by the UK and France. Whether there was any previous consultation among the aggressor countries, I do not know. But it is obvious that their plans fitted in and the Anglo-French attack helped Israeli aggression and was helped by it." Although Nasser emerged victorious diplomatically from the Suez Crisis, US attempts to push the Eisenhower Doctrine rekindled the Western attempts to dominate the area. In the aftermath there were two fiercely competing security systems working in the region—an Arab security system led by Egypt and supported by some Arab states and from outside by USSR, China and India. The other was the Western backed security system supported by Turkey, Iraq, Iran, Pakistan, US and Britain. This was indirectly supported by Israel, Saudi Arabia, Jordan and others. The formation of UAR, bringing Egypt and Syria together in February 1958, overthrow of the monarchy of Iraq in July 1958 and Egyptian intervention in Yemen to support the republican regime led to a virtual alliance between US and Israel. This and the King's or Islamic alliance between US allies in the Gulf region led to defeat of Egypt, Syria and Jordan in the 1967 war. Since then the conservative countries led by Saudi Arabia dominated (all US allies) the region. US interests came to be identified as support to Israel and Arab allies, safeguarding its oil and other commercial interests and also to contain Soviet and Communist influence in the Gulf region.[32]

West Asia and the Oil Politics

The Gulf coastal area in which the GCC states are located has since times immemorial been a meeting place for people not only from the neighbourhood but also for people from as far away as China, Malaya, Java and others. Due to its strategic location at the crossroads of extremely ancient trade routes, as also very near to several great river-based civilisations, Arab people of the Gulf region have been interacting with traders, sea farers, and others. Around 3400-3000 BC the great Dilmun civilisation in what was then known as Uwal, the modern day Bahrain and in the present Eastern Saudi Arabia. Due to its proximity to the Mesopotamian, Sumerian and Magan centres of civilisations, the people from the Harappan civilisation, Sind, Gujarat, Nile based Pharaonic civilisation also came to the Gulf for trade. The Magan civilisation which flourished in Oman was the link between Egypt and India like it was between India and the Dilmun and Mesopotamian civilisations. It is commonly believed that Gulf Arabs had extensive trade relations not only with the immediate neighbourhood but with far off lands like china as well. It must also be mentioned that the Gulf was located very near to the famous Silk Route through which bulk of the Asian supplies reached different centres. There is considerable historical evidence from places in the Gulf like Thaj, Al Hinna, Ayn Jawan, Hatta, Qatif, Dahra, Failaka, Tell Abraq (UAE), Mazyad near Jabal Hafeet, Tarub in Eastern Saudi Arabia, Ed-Dur on the coast of Umm Al Qaiwan, Mleiha in Sharjah, Qalat of Bahrain to suggest that traders came to such places from all over Asia. With the rise of the Sassanians (in Persia) the Gulf became a "Sassanian lake" and cities on the Persian Coast from Tiz, Suru, Huzu, Qays, Najiram, and Rishahr became famous trading centres. But the most well known were Siraf and Hormuz and at all the places Arabs were present in considerable numbers. Hormuz welcomed merchants of different religions and from all regions of the world. And the city was called the Citadel of Security. Sassanid monarchs were defeated by the Arabs who spread Islam. In fact, the last Sassanid monarch even sent emissaries to the Chinese emperor to plead for military help but all in vain. After the rise of Islam, Arab merchants made their presence felt all along the Persian coast. Soon Arabia became entranced by the magnificence of goods from China. The Chinese city of Canton (Zaitun as Ibn Battuta wrote which he visited) was well known to the Gulf Arabs. Since Chinese products such as silk were famous and unequalled "the lure of China war irresistible" to the Arabs even though the round voyage to China took a year and a half which was very risky. Even to this day in Arabic porcelain is called 'Chinese'. Even the Red Sea came to be known for the Arabs, Sea of China', because it was from there in the earliest times that ships began their voyages with cargoes of ivory, incense and gold to barter for luxuries in that country. The Emperor of China was known to Arabs as Sahib al Sin. Even prophet Mohammed advised Muslims to venture out to China for education. According to Captain Buzurg ibn Shahriyar (Persian), the author of the Wonder of India around 1150 AD, Persian and Arab merchants in the East were already numerous enough to launch a seaborne raid on Canton, presumably to avenge some mistreatment. Due to upheavals in China around 880 AD more than 1 lakh foreign traders and their families were massacred. Wealthy Jewish merchants from Sohar, Uwal, Hormuz, Uqair, Satun, Julfar, Dibba, Basra, al Zarqa (Qatib) Muscat brought silk, porcelains, precious stones from China. But by far the most robust or vigorous interaction was between the Gulf Arabs and Indians especially from all along the West Coast. Not only basic necessities like rice, textiles, went but Indian traders settled all along the coast from Basra to Muscat. Ceylon was well known to the Arabs as Sirandib—the Isle of Rubies. Malay and Sumatra and the Malacca Straits were familiar to Arabs. Although due to the Mongol invasion of Iran and much of the Arab world (Mashreq) especially the destruction of Baghdad in 1258 (also Basra) affected the Gulf Arabs also but they continued their maritime contacts with Asia. It was only with the arrival of the Europeans starting with the Portuguese who reached Calicut in 1498 that the supremacy of the Gulf Arabs disappeared soon after except for Omani influence in East Africa. The Europeans due to bigger ships mounted with heavy guns evicted the Arabs from many posts and cities all over Asia, even though it was the Arabs who showed the way to all major trading centres in Asia, to the Europeans. It is only with the discovery of oil that Arabs came to prominence.[33]

The 1973 Arab-Israeli Conflict in which Egypt and Syria

launched a surprise attack on Israel on 6 October came as a rude shock to the US. Coupled with this was the oil embargo by OAPEC members on US and its allies who supported Israel. Soon Kissinger threatened the Arabs of a US military occupation of the oil rich Gulf region if they tried to strangulate western economies. At the same time he embarked on the shuttle diplomacy and brought about temporary peace between Israel, Egypt and Syria. Meanwhile, British withdrawal from East of Suez led to independence to UAE, Bahrain, Qatar and a new ruler in Oman. Earlier Kuwait had been given independence in 1961 which was challenged by Iraq. This was eventually resolved by Arab League Peace Keeping Force and Arab mediation. Similarly South Yemen also became free from Britain in the wake of the 1967 AIC. After its withdrawal, Britain was looking forward to the "recession of the wave of anti-colonialism in the hope that disillusioned Asian statesmen would then be willing to cooperate with the West". Not only the Gulf Arab rulers/families were beholden to the British, now after independence they were more than willing to cooperate with the West. The defeat and division of Pakistan in 1971 made the US focus its attention on the Shah of Iran, House of Saud and other pro western regimes. Egypt's President Sadat took the initial peace attempts to its logical end by visiting Israel in 1977 and concluding the Camp David Peace Accords in 1978 and a bilateral peace treaty with Israel in 1979.

Around this time the Iranian revolution broke out in early 1979 with Khomeini mobilising the people on the basis of Islam. This was a major blow to US influence. The House of Saud was shaken by the Mecca Mosque take over in November 1979. In Saddam Hussein the US found an ally to invade Islamic Iran and gradually supported by the GCC states which was formed in 1981. The US dual containment policy led to the Iran-Iraq war for 8 years from September 1980. In the midst of this war Israel bombed the Iraqi nuclear reactor at Osirak near Baghdad. The US tried to win over Saddam Hussein to its side but the Iraqi ruler had his own independent ideas. Although the Iran-Iraq war came to an end in July 1988 but Saddam's concerns multiplied due to fall in oil prices in view of over production by UAE, Kuwait, Saudi Arabia and others. Iraqi domestic position had become precarious and with no funds coming from GCC or elsewhere, Saddam invaded Kuwait in August

1990. For the US, Saddam Hussein's blunder came as a big gift. The US administration mobilised over 30 countries for a grand coalition of countries to expel Iraq from Kuwait. UN economic sanctions were imposed on Iraq and coalition forces led by US launched an attack on Iraq and expelled the Iraqi forces. Kuwait was liberated by the end of February 1991. It must be mentioned here that the US undermined all peaceful efforts by Arab League, OIC, UN and others to get Iraq out peacefully from Kuwait. From the very outset the US was determined to destroy Iraq's military which would lead to the overthrow of Saddam Hussein. The Indian government partly shared the fear of the West, in particular the US, that Saddam Hussein would control thirty percent of the world's oil reserves, if he were not pushed out of Kuwait. No wonder India allowed (initially) the refuelling of US military planes and went along with the sole superpower (US) at the UN.[34]

Around this time it was clear that the cold war was coming to an end with the disintegration and collapse of the USSR. Earlier after suffering heavy losses Moscow had decided to withdraw from Afghanistan. Although Iraq was a close ally of Moscow, the new Russia leaders had no inclination to come to the rescue of Iraq as they needed western support to tide over their own economic problems. Despite the Iraqi expulsion from Kuwait, defeat at the hands of US and acceptance of UNSC Resolutions on WMD's, and its border with Kuwait, the UN sanctions on Iraq were maintained. The civil war in South involving the Shias and the Kurds in northern Iraq provided the US-UK combine to impose no fly zones on much of the Iraqi territory. Under the pretext of protecting the Kurds and Shias, both the countries resorted to daily (almost) bombing of Iraqi facilities both military and civilian which had already been devastated in the 1991 war.

West Asia's old trouble spot Palestine, under Israeli occupation since 1967 AIC had seen the largest Arab state Egypt sign a Peace treaty with Israel in 1979. Soon after, in 1982 Israel invaded Lebanon to evict PLO and in the process committed atrocities against civilians and Palestinians in particular. The Palestinian Intifada broke out in later 1986 in occupied territories which led to escalating violence from both sides. Hezbollah, Hamas, Islamic Jehad and many other Palestinian groups resorted to violence against Israel in response to

Israeli repression and state terrorism. Saddam had linked his withdrawal from Kuwait to Israeli withdrawal from Arab lands. This had proved to be popular at the mass level. In order to neutralize this and the Intifada, the US organized the Madrid peace conference in October 1991 and soon after saw the Oslo Peace process inaugurated in September 1993, between Israel and the Palestinians, under which at the end (in 1998) the Palestinians were to have an independent state of their own after Israeli withdrawal under UNSCR 242. In 1994 Jordan became the second Arab country to sign a peace treaty with Israel. Soon after many Arab countries like Qatar, Oman, Tunisia, Morocco and Mauritania came to have lower level contacts and offices with Israel. But the Arab Israeli Peace Process suffered due to assassination of Israeli PM Yitzhak Rabin and the emergence of Likud under Netanyahu and Ariel Sharon who undermined the Oslo peace accords. US President Clinton tried to salvage the situation at the Camp David Summit in July 2000 but failed. The result was the second Intifada and more violence. By early 2001 West Asia and the Gulf region had come to see violence on a large scale not only due to the Intifada but also as a fallout from Afghanistan's Taliban and other groups opposed to US, Israel and its Arab allies. Even countries like Saudi Arabia had come to witness greater violence within its territory. All this led to the 9/11 events in the US, which linked global violence/terrorism to the region. The new Bush administration propounded a new National Security Strategy (of the US) whose main feature is preemptive strikes and offensive counter—proliferation strategies. Under this the US wants to restore nuclear weapons to the centre stage of national security policy. All these led to the undermining of multilateralism especially the UNO. Soon after 9/11, the Doctrine of the War on Terror was proclaimed by President Bush. This unlimited war on terror is based on the twin doctrines of hegemony and preemption. The US attacked Afghanistan and overthrew the Taliban government. Then the US Nuclear Policy Review identified seven countries against which nuclear weapons may be used in the US national interest in certain cases. These are Asian countries—China, Iran, Syria, Iraq and North Korea. Russia a Eurasian power is the sixth. The doctrine of the war on terror is primarily focused in Asia—from West Asia—Gulf region to East Asia which is seen as the 'theatre of war'. After Afghanistan, Iraq became the next target of the US. It was invaded in March 2003 and Saddam toppled on the pretext of WMD's, human rights violations and support to terrorism. All of it was in violation of UN and International law. The US invasion and occupation of Iraq and Afghanistan has given new boost to Islamic groups who are resorting to violence. Shia-Sunni-Kurdish sectarianism has led to civil war in Iraq with fear of its disintegration. Now the US is threatening Syria via Lebanon and Iran on the nuclear issue. Regime change which was applied in Afghanistan and Iraq is being threatened in Iran and Syria. This had led to greater violence in Iraq as both Syria and Iran support the Iraqi resistance which was fighting US occupation. Religious groups from Hamas, Hezbollah, Islamic Jehad, Al Qaeda and many more have emerged which preach violence to counter US-Israeli hegemony.[35]

But after 1973 India's economic, political contacts widened with the oil rich Arab Gulf States. This partly alleviated India's balance of payment situation caused due to increase in oil prices. The 70's and 80's saw India's ties growing with Gulf states as India began to import its oil requirements from them, growing remittances from Indian workers, exports and investments became important. All these issues brought India and the GCC States closer. The outcome of the 1973 war convinced Sadat that in the prevailing international situation a limited success in the war was the maximum that Arabs could achieve and he visualized that only through diplomacy the AIC could be solved. He calculated that the US alone could compel Israel to vacate Arab lands hence his famous saying that 99 percent of the cards in the AIC are with the US. This led to peace treaty with Israel in March 1979 ending thirty years of armed confrontation with Israel. India's response to the Camp David accords War "uncritical but guarded". In fact, New Delhi did not openly endorse or condemn the accords. One reason cited for the incoherent Indian response was the Egyptian factor. Although India wanted to sheer clear out of any intra-Arab disputes but New Delhi still valued friendship with Cairo and all efforts were directed towards preventing Egypt's suspension from NAM at Havana NAM Summit. Earlier the emergence of Janata party in 1977 raised the question of a review in India's Arab policy. This was mainly due to A.B. Vajpayee of the Jan Sangh becoming the Minister of External

Affairs, who had been a vocal critic of India's support to the "Arabs and who advocated close ties with Israel. It was during this period that Israeli leader Moshe Dayan paid a secret visit to India in August 1977. Unfortunately for Israel Dayan achieved nothing concrete as Prime Minister Morarji Desai refused to establish diplomatic ties with Israel unless the latter withdrew from all Arab lands. He told Dayan that if he establishes ties, his government would collapse. To the surprise of the Israelis A.B. Vajpayee reiterated India's traditional policy towards Arabs when he said: "there is no change in India's stand. Israel must vacate all occupied Arab territories and the legitimate rights of the Palestinian people must be restored".[36] Since then up to 1992 successive Indian governments highlighted the absence of ties with Israel as an indication of support to the Arabs. The outbreak of war between two major NAM members Iran and Iraq (in September 1980) was a cause for deep concern to India. Of particular significance to India was the fact that both were New Delhi's major suppliers of crude oil supplying about 75 per cent of Indian oil imports. In addition many Indians were working in several projects sending remittances. Indian policy makers feared major powers involvement in yet another conflict in the Gulf area where developments related to security and instability had a direct bearing on India's security. India as Chairman of NAM did try hard to find a solution of the Iran-Iraq war but without success. Non-involvement in internal or intra-regional disputes has been an integral part of India's Arab policy and it applied to Iran-Iraq as well, though in fact both sought India's support against the adversary which India found hard to provide. On surface, India was strictly neutral but friendly ties with Iraq gave a certain tilt towards Baghdad. India's inability to mediate in the war exposed the inadequacy of Indian diplomacy in the region. Much to the dismay of India, towards the end of the Gulf war, great power naval presence substantially increased in the Gulf area and in seas surrounding India which assumed large dimensions in the wake of the 1990-91 Iraq-Kuwait crisis. The Soviet withdrawal from Afghanistan and the disintegration of USSR together with the end of the cold war and the emergence of Pax Americana in the Arab world initiated a gradual but necessary change in India's policy towards the Arab world while at the same time continuing its basic policy. It can be said that it is now much more realistic as well as practical in terms of its objectives. In the wake of the 1990-91, the Kuwait Crisis and Madrid Peace Conference which was held in October 1991, India decided to establish diplomatic ties with Israel on 29 January 1992 under the Congress government led by P.V. Narashima Rao.[37] Things changed dramatically after 1991 when both decided to sit down and negotiate their problems. With this new development India was encouraged to break the ice with Israel, the Jewish state was no more a pariah as before. There were also major changes as far as PLO was concerned. After Arafat appeared before the UN in 1974 and PLO was recognised by Arab states at Rabat, the PLO went on a peace offensive under Egyptian influence after it moved to Tunis in 1982-3 when Israel invaded Lebanon. In 1988 Arafat accepted UNSCR 242 and renounced violence and recognised Israel. After the 1991 Madrid Conference and the Oslo Peace Accords of September 1993 many expected Israel to withdraw from Arab lands leading to final peace between Israel and its neighbours, and formation of a Palestinian state. But the assassination of Israeli PM Rabin in November 4, 1995 and the emergence of Netanyahu and Sharon led to the collapse of peace with Israel. Many have accused Arafat of rejecting Israeli peace offers in Camp David (July 2000) talks with Clinton and Barak. Although Arafat was willing to concede 77 per cent of historic Palestine and wanted Israel to withdraw from the 23 per cent of Palestine, i.e. Gaza, West Bank and East Jerusalem, Israel offered Gaza and parts of West Bank, but refused to remove the Jewish settlements, rejected the right to return of the Palestinian refugees and reiterated its stand that Jerusalem will remain the eternal and undivided capital of Israel. Moreover it continued building its apartheid security wall in West Bank and said its control over water resources in West Bank will remain absolute. Meanwhile, Sharon reoccupied Palestinian lands in March 2002, carried out indiscriminate arrests, killings, curfew, house demolitions, humiliating check points and so on.

The result has been that deprivation, destruction and death rained on the Palestinians. Palestinian suicide bombings against Israelis and the Jewish state's excessive use of force continued. Arafat was seen as an obstacle to peace and Israel painted him in the darkest colours since the Al Aqsa intifada in September 2000. The result was US

President Bush and his neo-con dominated team refused to meet and deal with Arafat whom he described as an obstacle to peace. If Arafat had accepted US-Israeli proposals at Camp David he would have become the hero eligible for another Nobel Prize. But Arafat avoided violent end to his life by rejecting the proposals and remained largely popular among the Palestinians. Soon Sharon projected Arafat as a terrorist. Under the circumstances the US and UK were telling others that the road to peace in Palestine runs through Baghdad. Iraqi WMD's and the toppling of Saddam regime became priority for Bush. The result was US invasion of Iraq in March 2003. Israel had bombed Iraqi nuclear reactor in May 1981 and since then Israeli policy had been to destroy Baathist Iraq which was perceived as a threat to Israeli security. Soon after the US invasion and occupation of Iraq the Quartet—the US, EU, UN and Russia—announced the Road Map for Peace between Israel and Palestine calling for a "Viable and independent Palestine". Sharon raised 14 objections to the plan and the US insisted on political reforms in the Palestinian Authority. Arafat appointed Mahmoud Abbas and subsequently Ahmed Qoreai as PM but Israel continued its policy of relentless killings of Palestinians in the Gaza and West Bank, demolition of houses, confiscation of land and construction of Jewish settlements on Palestinian land. Hamas and Islamic Jehad and young Palestinians took to violence in the aftermath of such an Israeli attitude. The death of Arafat in November 2004 and the election of Mahmoud Abbas as PA President on 9 January 2005, together with heavy resistance in Iraq to US occupation, growing anti-Americanism sweeping the Arab-Muslim world, made the US put pressure on Sharon to implement the Road Map for peace. The Sharam el Sheikh summit in Egypt involving Mahmoud Abbas, Sharon, Mubarak and King Abdullah of Jordan has Palestinian state and no full withdrawal from West Bank are negative developments. What we may come to see in future is partial peace and less harsh treatment of Palestinians by Israel.[38] After the Iraqi elections in January 30, 2005 for the 275 member National Assembly, the sectarian divide in Iraq will further widen in line with US policy of divide and rule with religious groups and parties gaining ground thereby undermining secularism which was the basis of Iraqi political system under Baathist rule. Shias will dominate Iraq and the Kurds would try to achieve maximum autonomy. The US has found political sectarianism very useful to control Iraq. The Sunnis will continue to be killed and suppressed by the US in future just like the British who killed and suppressed Shias (using Indian soldiers) during and after the World War I. The US forces will remain in Iraq to provide security to the Iraqi governments which will be manipulated and the 10 or 12 military bases being prepared will form a permanent feature of US military presence in Iraq. From Iraq the US will implement its regional strategy towards Iran, Syria, Saudi Arabia and others. This will only make Iraq the magnet and training ground for Islamists from all over the world. It might become a more dangerous place than Afghanistan and Somalia. Since Iraqi oil is going to last at least for 50 years and with growing US demand for oil, Iraqi oil is indispensable for the US. So far the US used to get its job done in the Arab world through Israel, now both Israel and the US will work in tandem to rearrange the whole Arab world according to their strategic needs. As Lord Curzon said whichever states dominates the Arab world it will be in a position to influence India is coming true. Pax Americana and Israeli domination of the region should be a wakeup call for India to devise new policies to prevent fragmentation, violence, wars, instability and terrorism which is spreading fast in the Arab world and whose impact will be surely felt in India as well.[39]

Cultural Diplomacy as a Key Factor

Maulana Abul Kalam Azad played a key role in bring India and Egypt closer and also made Indo-Arab ties a cornerstone of India's West Asia policy. He had visited Al Azhar and established closer ties with prominent Arabs leaders. On account of his experiences, he advocated closer ties with the Arab world. He viewed Egypt as the centre of Arab learning and as the cultural capital of the Arabs. Addressing the conference for cultural cooperation between India and Asian countries at New Delhi on 29 August 1949, Maulana Azad who was India's first Education Minister said: "Political alliances are based on a spirit of bargaining while cultural contacts deepen mutual understanding." Both Nehru and Nasser came to have similar views on global issues. Nehru sympathized with Arab nationalism represented by Nasser as the urge of the Arab people. In supporting Nasser's Arab nationalism, Nehru cemented the ties between India and Egypt. Both signed a treaty of friendship and cooperation on April 5, 1955. It must be stressed here that Nehru urged Nasser and other Arabs not to rule out the negotiations as a means of settling the Palestine issue. He also took care not to involve India too deeply in the dispute with Israel and at no time did India endorse the illogical claims of some Arab leaders. After Gamal Abdel Nasser came to power in Egypt (1952) Nehru was keen to have extensive cultural ties with Egypt to give substance to the close political relations. He attached great importance to his friendship with Egypt as he viewed Cairo as the key to the success of India's policy in the Arab world. He also saw this friendship as an example of India's stand as a secular country. He emphasised that both India and Egypt are the inheritors of two glorious and ancient civilisations. India sent several eminent Indians who were academics as ambassadors including A.A.A. Fayzee who worked very hard to strengthen Indo-Arab cultural ties. A Cultural Agreement was concluded in 1958 between Egypt and India and a Chair of Indian Studies in Cairo University was established. Indian Archaeology and history is also taught. Soon the flow of artists, writers, scholars, journalists, exchange of books, periodicals, films, music and dance groups, art shows, exhibitions and other types of cultural exchanges became common between India and all the Arab countries with whom India signed cultural exchange programmes. For this purpose Maulana Azad established the Indian Council for Cultural Relations. In January 1992, ICCR established the Indian Cultural Centre at Cairo, Egypt and named it after Maulana Abul Kalam Azad. MACIC is the only cultural centre run by the ICCR in the entire Arab world. This clearly signifies the importance of Egypt in India's cultural diplomacy in the contemporary period, as also continuation of the age-old links between the two ancient civilisations. MACIC has become the hub or nerve centre of Indian cultural activities in Cairo, Egypt and perhaps in the region.

Throughout the Arab world Indians like Rabindranath Tagore, Mahatma Gandhi, Jawaharlal Nehru, Maulana Azad are well known. Indian music and dance groups are very popular, especially ballet troupes, folk dance groups. Indian Hindi films are very much liked by Arabs and often bag awards at film festivals. Many films personalities have visited the Arab world and have got warm welcome throughout the area. Cairo University has established the Center for Asian Studies and likewise the Zagazig University has an Institute for Asian Studies where many Egyptian and Arab Scholars study on India. Arabs like Dr. Taha Hussein, Neguib Mahfuz, Yusuf Idris, Tawfik al Hakim and other Arab writers have become well known in India. Many seminars and conferences in India have attracted several Arab scholars. Several books have been published on Indo Arab ties further enriching the cultural ties. The ICCR has invited several eminent Arab personalities to deliver the annual Maulana Azad Memorial lectures some of which have been published. Diplomatic and commercial ties between India and the Arabs are good but it is the cultural ties which will prove to be more enduring. Over the last 50 years there has been an exponential increase in the number of scholars, exhibitions, film shows and other cultural contacts between India and the Arab world. After the establishment of diplomatic ties with Israel, Indo-Arab ties at the political level since 1992 had seen some strains, but the steady growth in Indo Arab cultural ties both directly and under the ICCR has sustained the relationship. Indian scholars, with Arabic knowledge have played a key role in strengthening India's cultural diplomacy with the Arab World.[40]

Notes

1. V. Gordon Childe, *The Most Ancient East,* 208, cited in Sudhansu Kumar Ray, *Prehistoric India and Ancient Egypt* (New Delhi: Cambridge Book and Stationary Store, 1956), 39.
2. Shereen Ratnagar, *Encounters: The Westerly Trade of the Harappan Civilization* (London: OUP, 1980).
3. Jack Turner, *The History of a Temptation* (New York: Vintage Books, 2005), 204.
4. Margaret A. Murray, *The Splendour that was Egypt* (New Delhi: Cambridge Book and Stationary Store, 1956), xxi.
5. S. Maqbul Ahmad, *Indo-Arab Relations: An Account of India's Relations with the Arab World from Ancient upto Modern Times* (New Delhi: ICCR, 1969); Turner, *The History*, 238-239.

6. Ray, *Prehistoric India*, 7-12; Shereen Ratnagar, *Understanding Harappa Civilization in the Greater Indus Valley*, (New Delhi: Tulika Books, 2001).
7. Mohammed Hassan El-Zayyat, *India and Egypt: Modern Relations between two Ancient Nations* (New Delhi: ICCR, 1984), 12; Turner, *The History*, 147.
8. See also Abdullah Al-Madani, "Arabian Gulf during the British Era: The Impact of India," in *History, Culture and Society in India and West Asia*, ed. N.N. Vohra (New Delhi: Shipra, 2003), 109; Turner, *The History*, 62.
9. Saryu Doshi, "Influences and Interactions," in *India and Egypt: Influences and Interactions*, eds. Saryu Doshi and Mostafa El-Abbadi (New Delhi: Marg Publications, 1993), xiii; Sir George Watt, *The Commercial Products of India* (London: J. Murray 1908); Turner *The History*, 63-64.
10. El-Zayyat, *India and Egypt*, 14; S.B. Miles, *The Countries and Tribes of the Persian Gulf* (London: Cass, 1996), 491-92.
11. Ray, *Prehistoric India*, 38; Turner, *The History*, 238-39.
12. S. Maqbul Ahmad, *India and the Neighboring Territories,* Leiden: 1960; Turner, *The History*, 82.
13. S.M. El Mansouri, *Art and Culture of India and Egypt* (Calcutta: K.L. Mukhopadhyay, 1959), 46, Nayan Chanda, "The Early Globalizers," *India and Global Affairs Journal,* October-December 2008, 58-65.
14. M. Saleem Khan, *Early Muslim Perception of India and Hinduism* (New Delhi: South Asian Publishers, 1997); Turner, *The History*, 66.
15. N.A. Faruqi, *Early Muslim Historiography: A Study of Early Transmitters of Arab History from the Rise of Islam to the end of Umayyad Period, 612-750*, (New Delhi: Idarah-i Adabiyat-i Delli, 1979); Turner, *The History*, 96-97.
16. M.K. Dhavalikar, "Early Contacts," in Doshi and El-Abbadi, *India and Egypt*, 50; see also S. Maqbul Ahmad, *Indo-Arab Relations* (Bombay: Popular Prakashan, 1969); Turner, *The History*, 104.
17. K.N. Chaudhuri, *Trade and Civilization in the Indian Ocean: An Economic History from the Rise of Islam to 1750* (New Delhi: Munshiram Manoharlal Publishers, 1985), 59.
18. *India and Egypt*, eds. Doshi and El-Abbadi, xiv; see also Sahar Abdel Aziz Salem, "Commerce and one Faith," in *India and Egypt*, eds. Doshi and El-Abbadi, 96.
19. M. Saleem Khan, *Early Muslim*, 102; Tara Chand, *Influences of Islam on Indian Culture* (Allahabad: The Indian Press, 1965); Turner, *The History*, 180-1.
20. Andre Wink, *Al-Hind, The Making of the Indo-Islamic World*, vol. I (New Delhi: OUP, 1999).

21. K.N. Chaudhuri, *Trade and Civilization in the Indian Ocean*, 59-60; Turner, *The History*, 20.
22. V.D. Hanson, *Carnage and Culture* (New York: Anchor Books, 2002), 265-269; Quoted from Lewis Bernard, "Some Reflections on the decline of the Ottoman Empire," *Studies Islamica*, 9 (1959): 118; A.K. Pasha, *India and West Asia: Continuity and Change*, (New Delhi: Gyan Sagar, 1999), 7-15; Ibid., 67; see also Mawlana Syed Sulaiman Nadvi, *Indo-Arab relations: an English rendering of Arab o' Hind ke ta'lluqat,* trans. M. Salahuddin (Hyderabad : The Institute of Indo-Middle East Cultural Studies, 1962); Turner, *The History*, 22, 42, 45-47.
23. *National Herald*, New Delhi, September 28, 1992.
24. Riyaz Punjabi and A. K. Pasha, eds., *India and the Islamic World* (New Delhi: Radiant Publishers 1998), 97; M.S. Agwani, "India and the Arab World," in *Indian Foreign Policy: The Nehru Years*, ed. B.R. Nanda (New Delhi: Vikas Publishing House, 1976), 72-3.
25. A.K. Pasha, "Indo-Egyptian Cultural Relations: Retrospect and Prospects," in *Modern Egypt: Culture, Religion and Politics*, ed. Bari Zohurul (New Delhi: Shipra Publications, 2003), 199; see also Saryu Doshi and El-Abbadi, eds., *India and Egypt: Influences and Interactions*, (New Delhi: Garg Publications, ICCR, 1993).
26. A.K. Pasha, "Tipu and the Ottoman Empire," in *Tipu Sultan: A Great Martyr*, ed. B. Sheik Ali (Bangalore: Prasaranga, Bangalore University, 1993) 219-232; Mohibbul Hasan, *History of Tipu Sultan* (New Delhi: Aakar Books, 2005), 128-138.
27. A.K. Pasha, "Tipu Sultan's Relations with the Ottoman Empire," *Détente*, New Delhi, vol. X, nos. 4 and 5, January-April, 1992, 6-11; I.H. Qureshi, "The purpose of Tipu Sultan's Embassy to Constantinople," *Journal of India History*, vol. 24 (1945), 77-85.
28. Quoted from Lewis Bernard, "Some reflections on the decline of the Ottoman Empire," *Studies Islamica*, no. 9 (1959), 118; see also K.N. Chaudhuri, *Trade and Civilization in the Indian Ocean: An Economic History from the Rise of Islam to 1750* (Cambridge: Cambridge University Press, 1985); K.N. Chaudhuri, *The Trading World of Asia and the English East India Company 1600-1760*, (Cambridge: Cambridge University Press, 1978); Patricia Risso, *Oman and Muscat: An early Modern History* (London: Croom Helm, 1986).
29. Virendra Verma, "Tipu Sultan's embassies to Constantinople and Kabul," *Journal of Historical Research*, vol. XVI, no. 1, August 15, 1973, 51-56; Mohibbul Hasan, *Waqai-i-Manzil-i-Rum: Tipu Sultan's Mission to Constantinople* (New Delhi: Aakar Books, 2005), x-xiii, 1-4, 61-63; A.K. Pasha, ed., *Perspectives on India and the Gulf States* (New Delhi: Detente Publications, 1999), 1-23, 210-211; Azmi Özcan, *Pan-Islamism:*

Indian Muslims, the Ottomans and Britain, 1877-1924 (Leiden: EJ Brill, 1997), 11-12.

30. Iqbal Hussein, trans., "The Diplomatic Vision of Tipu Sultan: Briefs for embassies to Turkey and France, 1785-86," in *State and Diplomacy under Tipu Sultan Documents and Essays*, ed. Irfan Habib (New Delhi: Tulika Books, 2001), 19-65; see also Khaldoun Hasan al-Naqueeb, *State and society in the Gulf and Arab Peninsula: A different perspective* (London: Routledge, 1990), 31-42; A. K. Pasha, ed., *India and West Asia: Continuity and Change* (New Delhi: Gyan Sagar, 1999), 1-15; I. Hussein Qureshi, "Tipu Sultan's Embassy to Constantinople, 1787," in *Resistance and Modernization under Haidar Ali and Tipu Sultan*, ed. Irfan Habib (New Delhi Tulika Books, 1999), 69-78.
31. A. K. Pasha, "Indo-Egyptian Cultural Relations: Retrospect and Prospects," in *Modern Egypt: Culture, Religion and Politics*, ed. Zohurul Bari (New Delhi: Shipra Publications, 2003), 229; see also Roy, ed., *Tipu Sultan and his Age: A Collection of Seminar Papers* (Kolkata: The Asiatic Society, 2002); A. K. Pasha, "Tipu Sultan Diplomacy in the Gulf Region," Gulf Studies Programme, *Working Paper* No. 10, CWAAS, SIS, JNU, New Delhi, February 1997.
32. A. K. Pasha, "Indo-Egyptian Cultural Relations," 9; see also K.M. Panikkar, *Asia and Western Domination* (London: Unwin and Allen, 1953); K.M. Panikkar, *Malabar and the Dutch* (Bombay: D.B. Taraporevala Sons & Co., 1931); M. Reda Bhacker, *Trade and Empire in Muscat and Zanzibar: Roots of British Domination* (London: Routledge, 1992), 34-5.
33. B. Sheik Ali, *Tipu Sultan* (New Delhi: NBT, 1972); B. Sheik Ali, *Tipu Sultan : A Study in Diplomacy and Confrontation* (Mysore: Rao & Raghavan, 1982); see also A. K. Pasha, ed., *India & Oman*, 1-21; A. K. Pasha, " South India and the Gulf: Trade and Diplomacy during the late 18th century," in *History, Culture and Society in India & West Asia*, ed. N.N. Vohra (New Delhi: Shipra 2003), 237-249. See also Akhtarul Wasey, "Turkey and Evolution of Indian Culture," *Islam and Modern Age*, vol. XXXIII, no. 4, November, 2002, 87-94; R.L. Shukla, *Britain, India and the Turkish Empire, 1853-1882* (New Delhi: People's Publishing House, 1973); B.R. Nanda, *Gandhi: Pan Islamism, Imperialism and Nationalism in India* (New Delhi: Oxford University Press, 2002); Najma Heptullah, *Indo-West Asian Relations: The Nehru Era* (New Delhi: Allied Publishers, 1991); A. K. Pasha, "Nehru and the Crises in West Asia," *Detente*, vol. IX, no. 1, May-June 1990, 4-9; Prithvi Ram Mudiam, *India and the Middle East* (London: British Academic Press 1994); Bin Zia Saad, *Turkish Freedom Movement and the Role of Al Hillal of Maulana Azad , 1912-14* (M Phil diss., CWAAS, SIS, JNU, New Delhi 2005).
34. See also Roy, ed., *Tipu Sultan and his Age*; Pasha, "Tipu Sultan Diplomacy in the Gulf Region"; Pasha, "Tipu Sultan's Relations"; see also Ulrike

Freitag, William G. Clarence-Smith, eds., *Hadhrami Traders, Scholars and Statesmen in the Indian Ocean, 1750's-1960's* (Leiden: EJ Brill, 1997); V.D. Hanson, *Carnage and Culture* (New York: Anchor Books, 2002), 265-269 ; Richard Hall, *Empires of the Monsoon: A History of the Indian Ocean and its Invaders* (London: Harper Collins,1998), 195-224; Nanda, *Gandhi;* Hanson , *Carnage*, 267-269; Allen Calvin, *Sayyids, Shets and Sultans: Politics and Trade in Masqat under the Al Bu Sa'id, 1785-1914* (Ph.D. Thesis, University of Washington, 1978); Pamela Nightingale, *Trade and Empire in Western India 1784-1806* (Cambridge: CUP, 1970); Denys Lombard and Jean Aubin, eds., *Asian Merchants and Businessmen in the Indian Ocean and the China Sea* (New Delhi: OUP, 2000); John Keay, *The Spice Route: A History* (London: John Murray, 2005); Richard Wellesley Wellesley (Marquess) and Martin Robert Montgomery, *The Despatches, Minutes and Correspondence of the Marquess Wellesley K.G. during his administration in India (1836)*, vol.1, 307-8, cited in Keay, 55; Denys Forrest, *Tiger of Mysore: The Life and Death of Tipu Sultan* (London: Chatto & Windus, 1970), 244; Sultan Muhammad Al-Qasimi, *The Myth of Arab Piracy in the Gulf* (London: Routledge, 1988), 22-28; Pasha, "*Tipu Sultan and Saddam Hussein: Regime Change - History Repeats Itself*," (paper presented in a National Seminar on *Contemporary Oman and Emerging Indo-Omani Relations,* 25-26 October 2005, organised by Gulf Studies Programme, Centre for West Asia and African Studies, School of International Studies, Jawaharlal Nehru University, New Delhi); see the text of Treaty of Friendship and Culture Agreement in A. K. Pasha, *India and Turkey: Past and Emerging Relations* (New Delhi: Academic Excellence, 2006), 159-161; see also Mushirul Hasan and Margrit Pernau, eds., *Regionalizing Pan Islamism; Documents on the Khilafat Movement* (New Delhi: Manohar, 2005); Sanjay Subrahmanyam, *Explorations in Connected History: Mughals and Franks* (New Delhi: Oxford University Press, 2005); Pasha, "India and West Asia," 240-269; Pasha, "India's Cultural Diplomacy ," 295-310.

35. See also Nadvi, *Indo-Arab Relations*; for details see R. C. Majumdar et al., *An Advanced History of India* (New Delhi: Macmillan, 1978), 346; M.N. Pearson, *Merchants and Rulers in Gujarat: The Response to the Portuguese in the 16th Century* (New Delhi: Munshiram Manoharlal Publisher, 1976), 67-85; Saryu Doshi, ed., *India and Egypt*; James Rennell, *Memoirs: Marches of the British Armies in India during the Campaign of 1790 and 1791* (London: 1792), cited in Mohibbul Hasan, *History of Tipu Sultan* (Calcutta: World Press, 1971), 392-3; B.S. Gidwani, *Sword Of Tipu Sultan : A historical novel about the life and legend of Tipu Sultan Of India* (New Delhi: Allied Publishers Private Limited, 1989), 239-40; Roger M. Savory, "The History of the Persian Gulf 600-1800," in *The Persian Gulf States - A General Survey*, eds., Cottrell Alvin et al., (Baltimore, MD: Johns Hopkins

University Press, 1980), 38-39; Vikram Sampath, *Splendours of Royal Mysore: The Untold Story of the Wodeyars* (New Delhi: Rupa and Co, 2008); Sultan Muhammad Al-Qasimi, *The Myth of Arab Piracy*, 26-28; Praxy Fernandes, *Storm over Seringapatam; the incredible story of Hyder Ali & Tippu Sultan* (Bombay: Thackers 1969), 163, 211; A.D. Gupta, *Malabar in Asian Trade 1740-1800* (Cambridge: Cambridge University Press, 1967); A. Lewis, "Maritime Skills in the Indian Ocean, 1500-1968," *Journal of the Economic and Social History of the Orient*, vol. 6, 1973; see also B.J. Hamilton, "The Role of Monopoly in the Overseas Expansion and Colonial Trade of Europe before 1800," *American Economic Review*, vol. 38, 1948; A. Das Gupta, *Indian Merchants and the Decline of Surat 1700-1750* (Wiesbaden: Steiner, 1979); A.M. Abu-Hakima, *History of Eastern Arabia 1750-1800: The Rise and Development of Bahrain and Kuwait* (Beirut: Khayats, 1965).

36. Edward Simpson and Kai Kresse, eds., *Struggling with History: Islam and Cosmopolitanism in the Western Indian Ocean,* (New Delhi: Hurst and Co. Foundation Books, 2007); see also Denys Forrest, *Tiger of Mysore*, 117; Sanjay Subrahmanyam, *Explorations in Connected History*; Muzaffar Alam and Sanjay Subrahmanyam, eds., *Indo-Persian Travels in the Age of Discoveries, 1400-1800* (New Delhi: CUP, 2007); see also Panikkar, *Asia and Western Domination,* ; Panikkar, *Malabar and the Dutch*; Bhacker, *Trade and Empire*, 34-5; Marie-Francoise Boussac and Jean-Francois Salles, *A Gate Way from the Eastern Mediterranean to India: The Red Sea in Antiquity* (New Delhi: Manohar, 2005) ; Marie-Francoise Boussac and Jean-Francois Salles, *Athens, Aden, Arikamedu: Essays on the interrelations between India, Arabia and the Eastern Mediterranean* (New Delhi: Manohar, 2005); Himanshu Prabha Ray, *Archaeology of Sea Faring: The Indian Ocean in the Ancient Period* (New Delhi: ICHR, 1999); Ali, *History of Tipu Sultan*; Ali, *Tipu Sultan : A Study in Diplomacy*; see also A. K. Pasha, ed., *India and Oman: History, State, Economy and Foreign Policy* (New Delhi: Gyan Sagar, 1999), 1-21; see also Pasha "South India and the Gulf ," 237-249. See also Akhtarul Wasey, "Turkey and Evolution," 87-94; see also R.L. Shukla, *Britain, India and the Turkish Empire, 1853-1882* (New Delhi: People's Publishing House, 19730.

37. Uma Iyenger , ed., *The Oxford India Nehru* (New Delhi: Oxford University Press, 2007) 471, 511; A. K. Pasha, "Gulf-Asia Historical Relations: An Overview," *World Focus*, vol. XXX, no.5, May 2009, 183-196; R.R. Sharma, ed., *India and Emerging Asia* (New Delhi: Sage Publications, 2005), 12-79; See also Mahavir Singh, ed., *Building a New Asia* (New Delhi: Shipra, 2005); Hari Sharan Chhabra, *Nehru and Resurgent Africa* (New Delhi: Africa Publications, 1989); A. K. Pasha, "Asian Security: Flash Points in the Gulf Region," *World Focus*, vol. 26, nos. 10-12, October-December, 2005, 25-33; A. K. Pasha, "India and

West Asia," *World Focus*, vol. 25, October-December 2004, 41-46; Agwani, "India and the Arab World," in *Indian Foreign Policy : The Nehru Years*, ed. B.R. Nanda (New Delhi : Vikas Publishing House, 1976), 72-73; Jawaharlal Nehru, *India's Foreign Policy. Selected Speeches, September 1946 – April 1961* (New Delhi: Publications Division, Government of India, 1961), 2-3.

38. Prithvi Ram Mudiam, *India and the Middle East*, 56; K.R Singh, "India and WANA," in *India's Foreign Policy: Studies in Continuity and Change*, ed. Bimal Prasad, New Delhi: Vikas, 1978, 247-59; A. K. Pasha, *Arab-Israeli Peace Process: An Indian Perspective* (New Delhi: Manas Publications, 2000); J.N. Dixit says: "There was even an extraordinary unrealistic assessment from our mission in Baghdad that Saddam Hussein should be treated with kid gloves because he was not likely to be defeated by the combined forces of the international community under the UN umbrella led by the US," J.N. Dixit, *India's Foreign Policy, 1947-2003* (New Delhi: Picus Books, 2003), 213; *The Hindu*, April 14, 2008; Speech of Jawaharlal Nehru on May 3 1955 in *India and the Gulf*, ed. I. P. Khosla (New Delhi: Konarak Publishers, 2009), 294.

39. A. K. Pasha, "India and West Asia: Continuity and Change," in *India's Foreign Policy in a Changing World: Essays in Honour of Professor Bimal Prasad*, ed. Nalini Kant Jha (New Delhi: South Asian Publishers, 2000), 240-69; *The Hindu*, December 6, 2005; Marc Lynch, "Beyond the Arab Street: Iraq and the Arab Public Sphere," *Politics and Society*, vol.31, no.1, March 2003, 55-91; Naveed S. Sheikh, *The New Politics of Islam: Pan–Islamic Foreign Policy in a World of States* (London: Routledge Curzon, 2003), 60, 8.

40. A. K. Pasha, "India's Cultural Diplomacy in West Asia," in *Udayana: New Horizons in History, Classics and Inter-Cultural Studies*, eds. A.K. Sinha and A.K. Singh (Delhi: Anamika Publishers, 2007), 295-310.

Contributors

Mustapha Kamel Al Sayyid teaches at the Cairo University and at the American University, Cairo.

As'ad Ghanem is Lecturer at the School of Political Science, University of Haifa.

Mohanad Mustafa is Lecturer at the College for Academic Studies at Or-Yahuda, Israel.

Gulshan Dietl is Professor at the School of International Studies, Jawaharlal Nehru University, New Delhi.

Michael C. Hudson is Director of the Middle East Institute, Singapore.

Itzchak Weismann is Professor of Islamic Studies and Head of the Jewish-Arab Center at the University of Haifa.

Sima Baidya is Assistant Professor under the Gulf Studies Programme in the Centre for West Asian Studies, School of International Studies, Jawaharlal Nehru University, New Delhi.

Kingshuk Chatterjee is Assistant Professor at the Department of History, University of Calcutta.

Sujata Ashwarya Cheema is Assistant Professor at the Centre for West Asian Studies, Jamia Millia Islamia University.

Navras Jaat Aafreedi is Assistant Professor at the Department of Social Sciences, School of Humanities and Social Sciences, Gautam Buddha University, Greater Noida.

A.K. Pasha is Professor and the Director of the Gulf Studies Programme at the Centre for West Asian Studies, Jawaharlal Nehru University, New Delhi.

Index